SHOULD A DOCTOR TELL?

Medical Law and Ethics

Series Editor
Sheila McLean, Director of the Institute of Law and Ethics in Medicine, School of Law, University of Glasgow

The 21st century seems likely to witness some of the most major developments in medicine and healthcare ever seen. At the same time, the debate about the extent to which science and/or medicine should lead the moral agenda continues, as do questions about the appropriate role for law.

This series brings together some of the best contemporary academic commentators to tackle these dilemmas in a challenging, informed and inquiring manner. The scope of the series is purposely wide, including contributions from a variety of disciplines such as law, philosophy and social sciences.

Other titles in the series

The Generosity of the Dead
A Sociology of Organ Procurement in France
Graciela Nowenstein
ISBN 978-0-7546-7432-0

Clinical Ethics Consultation
Theories and Methods, Implementation, Evaluation
Edited by Jan Schildmann, John-Stewart Gordon and Jochen Vollmann
ISBN 978-1-4094-0511-5

Ethical Issues of Human Genetic Databases
A Challenge to Classical Health Research Ethics?
Bernice Elger
ISBN 978-0-7546-7492-4

Issues in Human Rights Protection of Intellectually Disabled Persons
Andreas Dimopoulos
ISBN 978-0-7546-7760-4

The Legal, Medical and Cultural Regulation of the Body
Transformation and Transgression
Edited by Stephen W. Smith and Ronan Deazley
ISBN 978-0-7546-7736-9

Should A Doctor Tell?
The Evolution of Medical Confidentiality in Britain

ANGUS H. FERGUSON
University of Glasgow, UK

ASHGATE

Published by
Ashgate Publishing Limited
Wey Court East
Union Road
Farnham
Surrey, GU9 7PT
England

Ashgate Publishing Company
110 Cherry Street
Suite 3-1
Burlington, VT 05401-3818
USA

www.ashgate.com

British Library Cataloguing in Publication Data
A catalogue record for this book is available from the British Library

The Library of Congress has cataloged the printed edition as follows:
Ferguson, Angus H.
Should a doctor tell? : the evolution of medical confidentiality in Britain / by Angus H. Ferguson.
pages cm.—(Medical law and ethics)
Includes bibliographical references and index.
ISBN 978-0-7546-7960-8 (hardback)—ISBN 978-0-7546-9910-1 (ebook)—ISBN 978-1-4724-0246-2 (epub) 1. Confidential communications—Physicians—Great Britain. I. Title.

KD7519.P48F47 2013
344.4104'12—dc23

ISBN 9780754679608 (hbk)
ISBN 9780754699101 (ebk – PDF)
ISBN 9781472402462 (ebk – ePUB)

MIX
Paper from responsible sources
FSC® C013985
FSC www.fsc.org

Printed in the United Kingdom by Henry Ling Limited, at the Dorset Press, Dorchester, DT1 1HD

Contents

Acknowledgements

Writing an interdisciplinary book based largely on primary source data is no simple task. It is a pleasure to have the opportunity to acknowledge the input and assistance that I have received throughout the process of writing this one. Some of the material used here is drawn from previous studies undertaken at the Centre for the History of Medicine at the University of Glasgow and generously funded by the Economic and Social Research Council. I owe a debt of gratitude to the staff and students in the Centre, and in Economic and Social History, for promoting a positive research and teaching environment in which the ideas for this book developed and came to fruition. In particular, guidance from Marguerite Dupree and Anne Crowther, who gave generously of their time and expertise during the early stages of my work on the history of medical ethics. Together with Malcolm Nicolson and Lawrence Weaver they have continued to contribute to the development of my career over the past few years and I am grateful for this ongoing interest and input. David Sutton was always a source of great conversation and fresh perspective over regular coffees and lunch breaks.

I thank the staff at the University of Glasgow Library for their practical support in sourcing and importing research materials for a project that crossed subject areas and academic disciplines as well as centuries. I spent many fruitful hours examining original eighteenth and nineteenth century texts in the excellent facilities of the Special Collections department – although the panoramic view across the city was always a tempting distraction. Much of the primary source material on which this text draws comes from the National Archives, Kew and the archive of the British Medical Association, Tavistock House. I have made many research trips to both, seeing many changes over the past decade, but I have always greatly enjoyed time spent at each. The efficiency of the National Archives is remarkable, both in its online facilities and in the process of ordering documents on site – the latter with a time-lag just sufficient to encourage a reinvigorating mug of coffee between submitting an order for documents and their arrival in your designated box in the reading room. The British Medical Association has been exceptionally helpful in permitting access to archival material and providing workspace. In particular I thank Lee Sands, their Information Officer, who provided expert assistance in identifying relevant source material as well as making the necessary arrangements for my, often prolonged, visits to Tavistock House. I am also indebted to the General Medical Council for their willingness to provide access to relevant material in both London and Edinburgh. Although, for reasons discussed in Chapter 1, less primary source material from the General Medical Council has been included in this book, it is utilised more in other publications (Ferguson, 2013) and in my ongoing work on confidentiality.

I wish to thank Alison Kirk at Ashgate and Sheila McLean, who had the vision to recognise the merits of publishing a historically-focused book within a contemporary series of Medical Law and Ethics. As might be expected for a book that takes a fresh approach, and breaks new ground for research, there have been setbacks and delays in the development of the manuscript and Alison has shown considerable patience and grace throughout. I am deeply indebted to Sheila McLean, the series editor, who has always been a generous source of advice and support for my research on medical confidentiality. I am grateful to the editorial and publishing team at Ashgate: Sarah Charters, Sarah Horsley and Anne Nolan for so efficiently facilitating the transformation of the original draft manuscript into the final published book; and to Alison Shakespeare, Steve Drew and John Roost at 4Word for proof reading the text.

To my family – each of whom has played a significant role in supporting me during the development of this book – a big thank you for many things, including the accommodation and homely welcome on my many research trips.

In 2012, I took up post as Lord Kelvin Adam Smith Fellow in the College of Social Sciences at the University of Glasgow. This fellowship has not only enabled me to finish the research and complete the writing of this book, but also provides an opportunity to focus on developing further work on medical confidentiality over the next few years. I am very grateful for this, and look forward to building on the foundations laid in the following chapters, in order to advance research on this important issue and maximise its impact on future thinking and policy.

A.H. Ferguson 2013

List of Abbreviations

ARM	Annual Representatives Meeting (BMA)
BMA	British Medical Association
BMJ	*British Medical Journal*
CEC	Central Ethical Committee
GMC	General Medical Council
GP	General Practitioner
LCO	Lord Chancellor's Office
MH	Ministry of Health
NA	National Archives
NHS	National Health Service
PSC	Professional Secrecy Committee (BMA)
RB	Representative Body (of the BMA)
RCP	Royal College of Physicians
RCS	Royal College of Surgeons
VD	Venereal Disease
WO	War Office

Preface

It might be assumed that a book with the title *Should A Doctor Tell?* provides a normative analysis of where the boundaries of medical confidentiality ought to be drawn. Equally, as a historical study, it could readily be anticipated to be a straightforward contribution to descriptive ethics, providing a narrative of developments in past practice (Sugarman and Salmasy 2012). In fact, for the reasons outlined below, while this book has relevance to both approaches to medical ethics, it should not be considered as simply falling directly within either. Rather, it seeks to break new ground and provide a fresh perspective on medical confidentiality within the field of medical law and ethics.

Medical confidentiality is integral to facilitating the transfer of information between patient and doctor that is necessary for efficient diagnosis and effective treatment. With a long pedigree, explicitly recognised in codes of medical ethics since at least the Hippocratic Oath, medical confidentiality appears to be in the DNA of Western medical practice. Research on patients' views often reveals an ingrained belief in the sanctity of patient-doctor communications. To many, it is a surprise to learn that the general rule of medical confidentiality is subject to a number of exceptions and that patient information can legitimately be shared with an array of people, in a variety of contexts, for a range of reasons.

Ethical guidance given to doctors recognises that they should respect the confidential nature of information disclosed to them by patients (BMA 2013, GMC 2009). Similarly it recognises that, at times, doctors ought to breach medical confidentiality in the interest of the patient, an identifiable third party or the public – for example to facilitate the legal justice system or public health objectives, or protect individuals from harm. In such broad terms medical confidentiality can be seen as a general, but qualified, obligation not to disclose patient information. However, once it is accepted that medical confidentiality is not absolute, questions arise as to where its boundaries should lie. Textbooks of medical law, codes of medical ethics, and professional regulations and guidance all attempt to detail these boundaries by citing relevant statutes, common law precedents and obiter dicta; sometimes referring to the ethical principles involved. However, as most recognise (see for example, BMA 2013), the protean nature of medical confidentiality makes it unrealistic to set down comprehensive, prescriptive rules detailing exactly when it should be kept or breached. Rather, the right course of action is often acknowledged to be dependant upon the specific circumstances and details of each case.

Given that, in each case there are different interest groups with contrasting agendas, priorities and perspectives on the issues involved, it is unsurprising that the boundaries of medical confidentiality have been a recurring subject of negotiation, debate and, at times, confrontation. While most works on the subject seek to strip away these elements in order to present the boundaries of medical confidentiality in the clearest possible terms, this book rather draws attention to them. There are several reasons for this. Firstly, in addition to the influence of ethical theory, moral principles, and statute and common law, the boundaries of medical confidentiality have been, and are, shaped by social and cultural factors and contingent events. By factoring these in, detailed historical analysis can provide a more comprehensive understanding of the choices and decisions that have led us to where we are now. As highlighted at points in the text, it can also reveal that where we are now might not be – in some cases definitely is not – where we thought we were. Long established precedents, cited in the textbooks from which successive generations have learnt their understanding of medical law and ethics, turn out to be less secure foundations than previously appreciated.

The book therefore combines legal and medical history to examine the evolution of the relationship between law and medicine. It incorporates a descriptive approach to medical ethics, drawing on the historical methodologies outlined by Amundsen and Lederer (Sugarman and Sulmasy 2001 and 2012). However it also has normative significance. While its protean nature makes medical confidentiality ill-suited to straightforward normative analysis, a better understanding of the issues that have been raised and discussed, and the impact of past decisions, can inform what we believe the law ought to be, and assist those involved in the decision making process.

The confrontations over notification of abortion and the denial of medical privilege to VD doctors summoned to give evidence in divorce cases, represented clashes between medical law and medical ethics. In each instance, regardless of the law, doctors believed they ought not to disclose the relevant information. Analysis of these examples gives deeper insight into the development of normative thought on confidentiality, and the reasons why, at critical junctures, doctors felt compelled to challenge or capitulate to demands for disclosure. While many have questioned whether the absence of medical martyrs indicates a lack of genuine belief in the moral importance of medical confidentiality, historical examination reveals both that such test cases were closer to becoming a reality than hitherto realised, and the reasons why the doctors involved acted as they did.

The evidence presented also suggests that the common law denial of medical privilege has been built on highly questionable foundations and, at key points, was defended using citations of a precedent that had been surreptitiously doctored to manufacture a false continuity of judicial opinion. It also highlights how a misunderstanding of a precedent from the early 1920s has led to the inaccurate belief that a judicial demand for medical evidence in court can override medical confidentiality, even when the latter is incorporated into statute law. The analysis therefore suggests that the whole question of medical privilege is due fresh consideration.

On an issue like medical confidentiality, historical work is necessary to improve understanding of how the boundaries of confidentiality in medicine have evolved and been shaped by a variety of forces, interests and influences. The result is not only a better understanding of how we got here, but also of where 'here' actually is. As a topic of ongoing interest and debate, where the correct course of action is often contingent on the specifics of the case, a more informed understanding of past action can make a significant contribution to normative, as well as descriptive, ethics.

For my parents, Jim and Betsy,
celebrating their golden wedding anniversary

Chapter 1
An Introduction to the History of Medical Confidentiality

Medical Confidentiality

Medical confidentiality is a cornerstone of medical practice. It promotes trust in the doctor–patient relationship, helping to redress the imbalance between the expert medical knowledge, and associated power, of the doctor compared to the relative medical ignorance and vulnerability of the patient. The understanding that doctors must respect confidentiality gives patients greater confidence to be open and honest, revealing personal and sensitive information in order to facilitate efficient and effective diagnosis and treatment. Confidentiality can therefore be regarded as an integral element of what Pellegrino (2003) terms the 'internal morality of medicine' – the ethical principles distilled from the primary healing purpose of the doctor–patient relationship. Seen solely in these terms, the importance of medical confidentiality appears ahistorical, its function being as relevant today as at the time of its recognition within the terms of the Hippocratic Oath.

While it is important to identify and analyse the basic ethical principles that underpin medical practice, equally it is vital to recognise that medical consultations are neither uniform in character and purpose, nor do they exist in a vacuum. Rather, they take a variety of formats and are subject to influence from external forces connected to the socio-political, cultural and legal context in which they exist. This book examines medical confidentiality in Britain, analysing how its boundaries have been defined and contested amidst significant changes in society, law and medicine over the past two-and-a-half centuries.

In Britain, confidentiality has long been recognised as an essential component of ethical medicine, and the professional duty to respect patients' confidences has been explicitly acknowledged in many sources. It is highlighted in codes of medical ethics, regulations and professional advice issued by the British Medical Association (BMA) and the General Medical Council (GMC); textbooks of medical deontology and medical law; as well as in specific statutory instruments, judicial opinion and obiter dicta. However, in Britain, medical confidentiality is a qualified, rather than an absolute, principle. Statute and common law, public policy, regulatory guidance and professional ethics all recognise instances when confidentiality must be breached. While the importance of medical confidentiality is widely acknowledged, it has not been incorporated as a general rule in UK statute law.

This book traces and examines the evolution of the boundaries of medical confidentiality in Britain since the earliest modern common law precedent in the late eighteenth century. Rather than simply listing, and quoting lines from, the accumulation of precedents and policy on the issue, developments are analysed in order to distil the factors that have influenced and underpinned key decisions. Consideration is given to the extent to which oft-cited precedents arose out of detailed examination of competing principles or were influenced more by pragmatic concerns. Similarly, the background to professional guidance is examined to determine the factors affecting the advice given and the policy direction advocated. The analysis adds further weight to the long-recognised importance of confidentiality as a concept at the heart of medical practice, professional autonomy and doctors' identity. It also reveals, in greater detail than ever before, the numerous ways in which the boundaries of confidentiality have been debated and shaped by practical concerns and contingent events.

Essentialism and Presentism

Historical work on ethical issues must guard against two potential pitfalls: essentialism and presentism (Amundsen 2001, Baker and McCullough 2009, 4–5). As already noted, the function of confidentiality in facilitating the primary healing purpose of the doctor–patient relationship can encourage an abstract, purely theoretical, analysis – the 'tendency to see ideas as free-floating in time and space' (Amundsen 2001, 134) – characteristic of essentialism. Similarly, medical confidentiality is a feature of the broader debate regarding the boundaries of privacy in the modern information age. Research on the history of medical confidentiality is therefore vulnerable to a charge of presentism – the attempt to project current concerns back into history and manufacture a long pedigree for the issue based on twenty-first century understandings and agendas.

Confidentiality is a prime candidate for recognition as the issue with the longest pedigree in contemporary medical ethics. It is also a topic that has generated regular and recurring debate. As illustrated in the examples given below, and discussed in detail in later chapters, analysis of these debates reveals evidence of genuine, as opposed to assumed, continuity. It also catalogues significant changes, both to the boundaries of confidentiality and to the way in which the issue has been considered and understood. Such changes have been brought about by developments within medicine in addition to external forces acting upon it.

Continuity

There are two obvious examples of continuity in the history of medical confidentiality in Britain. The first is the long-standing recognition that doctors owe an obligation of confidentiality to their patients. This professional duty has been consistently acknowledged in judicial opinions, statutory instruments, codes of ethics and numerous other sources throughout the period under investigation. At least rhetorically, the importance of confidentiality in engendering trust in the doctor–patient relationship, and thereby facilitating the diagnostic process, has been generally recognised. This stands in contrast to the recurring tendency of some doctors to reject unwanted encroachment into areas traditionally considered confidential by citing the Hippocratic Oath as evidence of their long-standing ethical obligations as a profession – despite the fact that no official body existed to generally enforce the terms of the oath in Britain.

While doctors' obligation of confidentiality to their patients has been consistently accepted, the implications of breaching it have not always been so clear cut. Did inappropriate disclosure constitute a breach of contract? Was it sufficient grounds, without an additional allegation of libel or slander, for the patient to take action against the doctor in court? Should the doctor be struck off the medical register or simply admonished with a verbal or written warning by the GMC? Was breach of confidentiality no more than an indiscretion – reflecting poorly on the doctor's character and potentially damaging to his/her professional reputation with patients? The obligation was broadly and consistently recognised, but the specific consequences of failing in the duty were not always clear.

The second element of continuity revealed in the detailed analysis that follows, is that the boundaries of confidentiality have been a subject of regularly recurring debate. Two related factors have contributed to this. Confidentiality has been justified using a variety of arguments, including professional duty and professional autonomy, patient autonomy, the right of individuals to privacy, and the positive consequences for individual and public health that a guarantee of confidential diagnosis and treatment promotes. Similarly, exceptions to medical confidentiality encourage consideration of dual loyalty professional duties, the need to protect competing rights, and the positive consequences to public welfare or justice that a particular breach of patient confidentiality will entail. In addition, there is a wide variety of formats of medical consultation, which take place in a range of circumstances. When the array of uses to which patient information can be put – both within and beyond the diagnostic and therapeutic process – is factored in, it is clear that establishing comprehensive, definitive and consistent rules, capable of universal application, is an unrealistic goal. The attempts to pass a private member's bill providing statutory recognition for even a limited form of medical privilege, discussed in Chapter 7, demonstrate the difficulty of defining detailed rules on confidentiality, and defending them in the face of interdisciplinary scrutiny from a variety of interest groups with competing agendas. Unsurprisingly, this resulted in the rekindling of debate on seemingly resolved issues, and unfinished business from old disagreements was carried over into discussions of new challenges and concerns.

Change

Broadly speaking, the challenges that provoked debate and redefinition of medical confidentiality can be grouped into three categories: external, internal and administrative. While confidentiality is considered integral to the patient–doctor relationship, even the terms of the Hippocratic Oath implied that there may be times when information should be disclosed 'abroad'. Over time, exceptions to the rule of confidentiality came to be defined in more detailed terms. An early example of this was the common law denial of medical privilege to doctors, meaning a physician or surgeon had to give evidence in court when summoned to appear as a witness. As the analysis in many chapters of this book reveal, privilege was an issue of recurring controversy as doctors stressed the importance of confidentiality and their duty to the patient in the face of judicial emphasis on a doctor's duty to assist the law and the ends of justice.

Doctors' obligations under common law were matched by increasing demands for information under statute law in the nineteenth century. Legislation on contagious and infectious diseases required doctors to notify cases in order to protect public health. Cases of criminal abortion were to be notified to the police. New medical roles reflected an evolving position and function for medicine in a changing socio-political context. Growing concern over public health required local medical officers whose primary task was the protection and promotion of the collective welfare of the community, rather than the diagnosis and therapy of individual patients. As economic competition pressured governments into consideration of the health and welfare of the workforce, doctors were tasked with assessing and certifying claims for sickness benefit under National Insurance. Doctors involved in insurance and welfare schemes were under pressure to combine a therapeutic relationship with patients with surveillance and assessment roles undertaken on behalf of the employer and state. Similar dual loyalty demands were part and parcel for doctors working in military and prison environments and increasingly became a feature of many doctors' lives in the twentieth century.

However, challenges to the traditional confidentiality of the doctor–patient relationship did not only come from external forces. The increasingly scientific and technological basis of diagnosis and therapy entailed greater specialisation in medical training and practice, contributing to the transition from individual practice in a competitive private market to integrated general and specialist provision of healthcare – latterly as part of a nationalised health service (NHS). The patient–doctor relationship was subsumed within the complex bureaucracy of a public service leviathan, drawing on the focused expertise and combined input of a variety of healthcare professionals and workers, requiring patient information to be shared across healthcare teams.

The effective running of the NHS system required each patient to have a set of medical records, with a corresponding need for administrators. The rise of the information state in an era defined by total war and total welfare (Higgs 2004) added a new dimension to the debate over medical confidentiality. The centralised state accumulated growing amounts of personal data on citizens, including health information on publicly treated patients. The advent of computers made it easier to store, link and share large amounts of data for a variety of purposes including administrative efficiency, institutional or service audit, and research. While this had many potential benefits, it also brought concerns about the threat that systems posed to individual privacy.

Consequently, by the latter twentieth century, debates about the boundaries of medical confidentiality increasingly turned to the language of autonomy and rights. Human rights legislation recognised individuals' right to a private life and the Data Protection Acts provided stricter regulation of how personal information was stored, used and shared. Challenging the paternalistic approach that had often been characteristic of medical practice and research in the past, the emergent discipline of bioethics (Johnson 1998; Boyd 2003) emphasised the importance of patient autonomy and the right of the patient to decide the uses to which personal information was put.

Ideal Types

Over the last century in particular, the demand for patient information has grown as the utility beyond its immediate diagnostic and therapeutic value has increased. In the early twenty-first century it is sought after for research, statistical surveys, and the auditing and improvement of public services. While changes within medicine and in the socio-legal context in which it operates have undoubtedly affected how medical confidentiality has been viewed, the evolution of its boundaries should not be regarded as a simple sequence of definitive changes. Certainly, understandings of medical confidentiality in the eighteenth century were based on concepts of gentlemanly honour. Over the course of the nineteenth and early twentieth centuries, debates increasingly acknowledged the dual loyalty demands facing doctors in relation to legal obligations, public health measures and changing forms of medical employment. By the second half of the twentieth century, medical specialisation and the advent of healthcare teams within the NHS required the traditional model of confidentiality based on the doctor–patient relationship to be extended to cover members of an interdisciplinary healthcare team. At the outset of the twenty-first century, the growth in use of computers and information technology, the rise of the information state and the growing utility of medical information beyond its immediate therapeutic value contribute to a discussion framed in terms of the human right to privacy, patient autonomy and data protection.

However, while each aspect is characteristic of a particular period, they are not mutually exclusive. Current guidance (BMA 2012, GMC 2009) still refers to the importance of confidentiality as a basis of trust in the doctor–patient relationship, even though that relationship has changed dramatically over the past two centuries. The importance of patient consent to disclosure was highlighted in debates long before bioethics stressed consent as an element of patient autonomy; and there are still doctors who would view breach of patient confidentiality as a deeply dishonourable act, in addition to any disciplinary or legal consequences that might follow.

Interest Groups and Issues

Medical consultations take place in a variety of settings and information obtained during the practice of medicine can be of utility to a range of interest groups. The traditional patient–doctor relationship revolved around diagnosis and therapy, and confidentiality was a core element of the process. By the later nineteenth century, new roles, such as medical officer of health, were established. Their primary purpose was not a direct therapeutic relationship with individual patients, but rather the protection of collective well-being – at times seen to be dependent on breaches of individual confidentiality to notify cases of contagious or infectious disease as required by statute law. The development of health insurance, initially in private schemes and subsequently under centralised National Insurance, created hybrid, or dual loyalty, roles and obligations for doctors. A panel doctor had both a therapeutic responsibility to the patient and a surveillance responsibility, to the organisers and other members of the scheme, to minimise abuse of the system. In certain settings, for example the military or prison medical service, in addition to the therapeutic relationship with the patient, the doctor had an obligation to share information with a commanding officer or prison governors.

Doctors were also used to provide examinations and reports in a variety of settings ranging from occupational physicians assessing an individual's fitness for work, to the assessment of physical injury or incapacity in connection with accident litigation. While such information was often requested from the patient's own medical records or doctor, an independent assessment might be sought from a doctor with no therapeutic relationship with the patient. A similar non-therapeutic relationship often applied in settings involving medical research.

While medical information was primarily gathered within the context of the patient–doctor relationship, it was increasingly shared with, or processed and used by, others – ranging from a growing spectrum of healthcare workers and administrative staff to lay officials and legal teams. The interest in, and utility of, medical information must therefore be considered from a variety of perspectives and in a range of contexts. The analysis in subsequent chapters aims to do this, and it is worth highlighting at the outset some of the relevant interest groups involved.

The Law

Legal attitudes have been influential in shaping the boundaries of medical confidentiality over the past two centuries. One of the earliest exceptions to the general rule of confidentiality arose out of judicial insistence that a doctor must give evidence, including details of information gained during consultations with patients, when called to testify as a witness in court. This common law denial of medical privilege, established in the late eighteenth century, has been consistently adhered to since, despite regular attempts to argue in favour of change.

However, consideration of the legal perspective is not limited to records of individual case rulings. In addition to examining in detail the precedents that have influenced policy and practice on medical confidentiality, consideration is also given to relevant obiter dicta and views expressed less formally, or publicly, by senior judges and law officers of the Crown within correspondence and memoranda. Legal attitudes are also revealed through opinions expressed at meetings of medico-legal societies, in articles published in legal journals, in legal advice given to doctors and medical organisations, and in official reports.

The Government

Through statute law and policy initiatives since the mid-nineteenth century government activity has impacted on medical regulation, education, employment patterns and objectives. Both directly and indirectly these have affected the boundaries of confidentiality in the doctor–patient relationship, from legislation requiring notification of infectious disease to the use of ministerial discretion to limit disclosure of some medical records. The analysis considers relevant developments in statute law and public health policies, the advent of National Insurance, the establishment of the Ministry of Health (MH) and the impact of the National Health Service (NHS). Attention is given to committees set up to enquire into specific issues, such as the extent of Crown privilege in the 1950s and 1960s, as well as the correspondence and memoranda generated within government departments at times of heated debate, for instance the controversy over confidentiality at VD clinics in the early 1920s.

The Medical Profession

Use of the phrase the medical profession can give the misleading impression that doctors share a single identity with a consensus opinion. At the outset of the period under analysis, doctors operated very much as individuals in a private marketplace in which physicians, surgeons and apothecaries, though ostensibly undertaking separate specialised tasks, were often rivals in competition with each other and with a variety of informal, untrained and quack healers. Changes to medical knowledge, training and regulation over the course of the nineteenth and twentieth centuries helped to produce a more uniform professional identity, but the broad distinction between general practitioners (GPs) and hospital consultants contained a growing spectrum of practitioners with increasingly focused and specialised knowledge. The analysis in subsequent chapters cannot claim to represent the full range of medical opinion on questions of confidentiality. Rather, the emphasis is on examining the advice proffered within textbooks of medical jurisprudence, deontology and ethics and by influential medical bodies, in particular the BMA.

Unlike the Royal College of Physicians (RCP) or Royal College of Surgeons (RCS), which are both included at points, the BMA represented a broad cross-section of doctors in both primary and secondary care (Bartrip 1996). The BMA Central Ethical Committee (CEC), became a focal point for enquiries relating to pressing ethical issues, including confidentiality, and the advice it offered was often – though not always – directly adopted by the BMA Council and Annual Representatives Meetings (ARM) which determined the direction of BMA policy on the issue. The analysis draws on examination of the minutes of meetings of relevant committees, including the CEC and Council, as well as the correspondence and memoranda generated by members' recurring interest in defining and defending the boundaries medical confidentiality as an integral element of professional identity and a measure of professional autonomy.

The Regulatory Body

Established as part of the Medical Act of 1858, the GMC was intended to act as disciplinary body and regulator of the medical profession. The names of qualified doctors were included on a central medical register, entitling them to certain privileges. However, the GMC had power to strike from the register the names of doctors found guilty of serious professional misconduct, thereby severely limiting their ability to practice. While in theory the GMC could have been influential in the evolution of debates over medical confidentiality, in practice it was largely absent as a proactive force until its post-Merrison renaissance in the late 1970s. While the analysis includes a few references to GMC input, for instance its preparation of a memorandum for the Russian ambassador in 1899, as discussed in more detail in Chapter 3, the GMC really only became active in providing advice and guidance on confidentiality towards the end of the period under investigation (see for example Ferguson 2013).

Format and Structure

The boundaries of medical confidentiality are constantly being negotiated. Significant areas of debate in twenty-first century medicine include concerns about the use of identifiable patient information in research or the linkage of Electronic Health Records with other personal data and the implications of advances in genetics/genomics. Modern textbooks of medical law and ethics typically pay little attention to historical aspects of the subject. Citations of the relevant lines from the Hippocratic Oath tend to be followed by short excerpts from statements in selected court cases. This book aims to provide greater historical insight into the evolution of medical confidentiality in Britain, taking account of a range of perspectives on the issue and giving consideration to the broader context, as well as the specific details, of debates and developments. Beyond this introduction, the analysis is split into eight chapters, each focused on an important development, a particular perspective, a specific issue, or a period of change.

Chapter 2

Since the late eighteenth century the law has been the most authoritative voice in determining where and when doctors must tell. Chapter 2 examines the case which underpins the common law position on medical privilege: the Duchess of Kingston's Trial for bigamy in 1776. As noted throughout this book, the case has been widely cited in writings on the topic. The precedent impacted the law in the United States and the countries of the British Empire, and though it has, over time, been amended in many of these places, it remains largely unchanged in Britain. While lines from Lord Mansfield's ruling in the case are still cited in modern British texts, little attention has been paid to the details of the trial or the relevance of medical confidentiality to the case. Detailed historical analysis raises questions about the security of the foundations on which the common law denial of medical privilege have been built. It suggests that the appeal made by the King's surgeon, Caesar Hawkins, that the evidence he was required to give was protected by medical confidentiality, was both inaccurate and motivated more by personal status and financial interests than medical ethics. Chapter 2 details the background to the case and the spectacle and theatre of the trial, before examining the subsequent impact of the precedent.

Chapter 3

Chapter 3 examines the period between the Duchess of Kingston case and the courtroom battles of the early 1920s. This was a period of significant change for medicine, in terms of education, practice and regulation. The rise of public health as a significant public policy agenda required new civic medical roles, such as medical officers of health, while statute legislation placed more community-focused obligations on doctors to notify cases of infectious or contagious diseases. Collective welfare measures – whether organised through friendly societies or National Insurance – often pressurised doctors to fulfil surveillance as well as therapeutic roles. Doctors in the army found themselves facing similar demands from the military chain of command. The growth of competing obligations for doctors, combined with mixed signals from the courts, at times produced confusion – as illustrated by the conflict over notification of abortion. The legal views sought by the RCP in 1896 underpinned the guidance on the issue in Robert Saundby's early textbook of medical ethics. However, by 1914, the judiciary took umbrage with the medical profession's position – despite the fact that the judge who gave voice to criticism in 1914 had himself been the source of the legal advice received by doctors in 1896. The ensuing confrontation between legal and medical authority took place in private meetings and correspondence – absent public knowledge or scrutiny. While the demands of war diverted attention in the short term, intense debate was quick to recommence in the early interwar years.

Chapters 4, 5 and 6

These chapters examine medical, legal and public policy perspectives on the early interwar debates over medical confidentiality and privilege. The case most often cited as relevant precedent from the interwar years of the twentieth century was a petition for divorce: *Garner v Garner* [1920]. Heard at a time of controversy over confidentiality in relation to venereal disease (VD) treatment, the case is generally accepted as having clarified the position that VD doctors had no more right to claim privilege in civil divorce hearings than any other doctor in any other court. Yet, closer examination suggests that the doctor's protest in *Garner* was based on an unrealistic interpretation of government regulations on the confidentiality of VD treatment as preventing disclosure in any situation, even when the patient had given full consent. As analysis of *Garner* and its aftermath shows, the decision did little to clarify the position for doctors, patients or the Ministry of Health. It also exposes the inaccuracy of citations of *Garner* as evidence of a court's authority to demand disclosure even in cases where the doctor's obligation of confidentiality is backed by statute law.

While recognising the importance of the courtroom as a key battleground for competing ideas about medical confidentiality, Chapters 4, 5 and 6 also seek to present a more complete understanding of the forces that shape the boundaries of medical confidentiality. To this end, consideration is given to the formulation of policy and guidance on the issue within the Ministry of Health, the BMA and the Lord Chancellor's office (LCO). As well as examining public statements and internal correspondence, analysis is undertaken of the discussions, sometimes confrontations, which shaped policy and practice. These took place away from the public eye and are revealing both of the evolution of thought within, and of the process of negotiation between, important interest groups.

The early 1920s was a period of intense debate for a number of reasons. VD diagnosis and treatment was publicly funded and run through a national system of clinics that guaranteed confidentiality to patients. However, the utility of VD as evidence in the large number of civil divorce proceedings following the First World War, meant that judges overrode the guarantee of confidentiality contained in the Ministry of Health's VD regulations and demanded medical testimony from VD doctors in court. In the absence of medical privilege – the position established in the Duchess of Kingston trial 150 years earlier – doctors were forced to comply. Both the Ministry of Health and BMA petitioned legal authority on the merits of statutory protection for medical confidentiality, but they also contemplated direct challenges to judicial demands for medical evidence under common law. Independently, each considered using a medical 'martyr', who, when called as a witness, would refuse to breach confidentiality and go to prison for contempt of court in an attempt to garner support for a change in the common law. Examination of these discussions gives context to the precedent of *Garner*. It also highlights cases that have been overlooked in the existing literature, yet are found to hold important insights into the development of legal, medical, and political thought on where the boundaries of medical confidentiality should lie. *Needham v Needham* [1921] is a prime case in point.

Chapter 7

The debates on confidentiality in the early 1920s did not definitively resolve the issue. Having previously examined the attempts to challenge the common law, Chapter 7 examines two subsequent attempts to gain statutory recognition for medical privilege through private member bills introduced in the House of Commons by Ernest Gordon Graham-Little in 1927 and 1936. While both failed, they served to underline the significant challenges facing any attempt to change the law, including the difficulty of defining the nature and extent of the privilege sought. However, the issue had not been definitively resolved on the comparative merits of the principles involved; rather the outcome was affected more by the ease of defaulting to the status quo when faced with equally imperfect alternatives. Those in favour of a change in the law faced an uphill struggle to define and justify the case for a limited form of medical privilege. Those opposed to medical privilege had the considerably easier task of defending the status quo by pointing to weaknesses and inconsistences in any argument for change. Over the course of the second half of the twentieth century, changes in the law, in medical practice and in the broader socio–political context entailed that the boundaries of medical confidentiality continued to be contested.

Chapter 8

Having considered attempts to extend the boundaries of medical confidentiality through recognition of medical privilege in common or statute law, Chapter 8 notes that Crown privilege consistently excluded military, and some civilian, medical records from disclosure in court. However, by the 1950s, the boundaries of Crown privilege were under increasing pressure. The drive to limit the extent of the privilege resulted in a number of committees and reports, and provides insight into both the principles and practical concerns underpinning the debate. Earlier attempts to gain medical privilege for VD doctors had struggled to define and justify any limitations that would apply. Similarly, the defenders of Crown privilege recognised the difficulties associated with justifying each exception in increasingly specific terms. They therefore sought to maintain the status quo whereby certain classes of documents were exempted from disclosure regardless of their particular contents.

Chapter 9

The final chapter gives an overview of developments in the latter part of the twentieth century. While long-standing issues, such as VD and medical privilege, continued as features of discussions on confidentiality, they were joined by new challenges. Increased specialisation in medicine and the incorporation of different workers into healthcare institutions and teams within the NHS entailed that, even considered solely in terms of the diagnostic and therapeutic process, an extended model of confidentiality was required that went beyond the traditional boundary of the doctor–patient relationship. The implications of technological developments, notably computers, for the storage, sharing and linkage of information had significant repercussions for medical administration, research and audit. In this context, concerns over medical confidentiality were one aspect of a broader debate about the security, and uses, of personal data in the modern information age.

Chapter 2
The Duchess of Kingston Precedent

'A precedent embalms a principle' stated Lord Stowell while Advocate General, words later echoed by Benjamin Disraeli in a speech in the House of Commons in 1848 (Cohen 1960). Medical law plays a significant role in guiding medical practice. However, both the law and medicine operate within a context of, and to an extent reflect and shape the opinions of, a perpetually changing society. For these reasons, common law precedent is important in the ongoing interpretation of the law. Single cases can have a lasting influence on individuals, professions and society as a whole, by means of clarifying penumbral issues within the legal framework and embalming core principles for future practice.

The trial of the Duchess of Kingston for the crime of bigamy in 1776 has certainly been regarded as defining the principle that doctors have no privilege to refrain from giving information gained under professional confidence in court. As illustrated throughout this book, the denial of medical privilege has been enforced, and the Duchess of Kingston's case cited as precedent in many textbooks of medical law since the late eighteenth century – often quoting lines from the opinion expressed by Lord Mansfield during the trial. However, as later chapters demonstrate, while the precedent has been regularly cited in the two-and-a-half centuries since the trial took place, little attention has been paid to the details of the case. This chapter examines the circumstances of the trial and the appeal for medical privilege within it. The analysis suggests that, far from providing a solid foundation for the common law denial of medical privilege, the oft-cited precedent had little to do with medical confidentiality at all.

The Duchess

Many have been drawn to write accounts of the more scandalous aspects of the infamous Duchess's life (Brown 1927, Elwood 1960, Leslie 1974, Gervat 2003). This is unsurprising given the wealth of such material the Duchess provided. John Bernard Burke (1849) provided the following assessment of the Duchess:

> With talents of no mean order, with personal attractions that charmed every eye, and with accomplishments, captivating, even after the influence of beauty had ceased to exert itself, the celebrated lady, the heroine of the extraordinary episode in real life we are about to recount, lived a memorable example of the inefficacy of wealth or grandeur to secure happiness.

Among the litany of tales was her appearance at a Masquerade, dressed as the character of Iphigenia – her costume leaving her, in Burke's words 'almost in the unadorned simplicity of primitive nature'. Or her brief career in politics, when, shortly after Bonnie Prince Charlie had captured Carlisle during the Jacobite uprising of 1745, and amidst a room full of inebriated dinner guests at Leicester House, the Prince of Wales expressed his disapproval of the new government by dictating a letter giving instructions to appoint the young Elizabeth Chudleigh as Secretary for War. However, her many biographers have bypassed her significant, if unintended, contribution to defining the boundaries of medical confidentiality. Even when the case was cited in early writings on the history of medical confidentiality, it was done so *en passant*, with little discussion of the original details of the case (Maehle 2003, Morrice 2002a, Morrice 2002b). Yet, as later studies have demonstrated (Ferguson 2006, Mendelson 2012) the story is no less scandalous than the other areas of Elizabeth Chudleigh's life. Detailed analysis of the trial reveals that the precedent that became the foundation of the common law on medical privilege arose from little more than an attempt by a surgeon to secure his private interests and personal status as a gentleman in eighteenth-century high society.

Background to the Trial

Elizabeth Chudleigh's indictment stated that she had married a second husband, Evelyn Pierrepoint, Duke of Kingston, while her first husband, Augustus John Hervey, who had recently become Earl of Bristol, was still living. Standing accused of being twice married, she was rumoured to have originally been engaged to a third person, the Duke of Hamilton, a betrothal which never came to fruition as a result of the interference of her aunt, Mrs. Hanmer. Obviously intent that her niece should discontinue the relationship with Hamilton, she intercepted and destroyed the correspondence which he sent to Elizabeth while on his Grand Tour. Consequently, Elizabeth believed he had lost interest in her and their engagement (Lee Osborn 1915).

Under pressure from this same aunt, Elizabeth secretly married Hervey, by the light of a single candle, in a small church in Lainston in 1744. The reasons for such secrecy appear to have been related to the fact that Hervey, as the younger son of a younger son, had no resources except his meagre pay from the Navy; while Elizabeth would lose her position as maid of honour to the Princess of Wales if she were known to be married (Brown 1927, Lee Osborn 1915). Following the ceremony, the couple spent the next three days together at Mrs Hanmer's house before Hervey returned to his ship. His wife, maintaining her name as Elizabeth Chudleigh and her status of maid, returned to her service in Leicester House.

Hervey was abroad for approximately two years. In that time there was little, if any, correspondence between the newlyweds. On his return to London, Hervey had to threaten to publish the fact of their marriage in order to gain an audience with his wife. However, in the following November, Elizabeth was delivered of their only child, a boy who died when only a few months old. Over the next twenty years, with a series of deaths making it increasingly likely that Hervey would become the Earl of Bristol, Elizabeth swayed between denying that the wedding had ever taken place, leaving her free to seek marriage and title elsewhere, and reinstating evidence of their marriage, when it looked likely this would entail her becoming the Countess of Bristol.

In 1769, using the couple's mutual friend, the surgeon Caesar Hawkins, as a messenger, Hervey indicated to his wife that he wanted a divorce. In response, Elizabeth instigated a suit, heard in an ecclesiastical court, against Hervey for jactitation of marriage: an injunction against Hervey making, what she argued were, false claims about them being married.[1] Although the case was decided in her favour, Hervey's weak defence led many to suspect that the whole suit was a collusive venture by the couple, both of whom wanted to remarry. Only Elizabeth did so, becoming the Duchess of Kingston shortly afterwards.

After five years of marriage, the Duke of Kingston died, leaving the Dowager Duchess the bulk of his property and wealth in his will. This was not well received by the Duke's nephews, Evelyn and Charles Medows. As heirs to the estate, both had much to gain through discrediting the claim of the Duchess, now living in Rome, by establishing her prior marriage to Hervey, the new Earl of Bristol. It was as a result of their efforts that on Monday 15 April 1776, Elizabeth, Duchess Dowager of Kingston, stood trial in Westminster Hall accused of the crime of bigamy.

The Spectacle and Theatre of the Trial

The trial of a Duchess by the House of Lords, in a specially constructed court in Westminster Hall, naturally received much publicity. *The Gentleman's Magazine* showed a continued interest in all things connected with the case. In its January edition it reported that the date of the trial had been fixed for 15 April. The following month it noted the appointment of the Lord High Steward to the trial by the King. In March, it reported a motion considered by the House of Peers on whether they could legally proceed with the trial, the decision being made in the affirmative (*The Gentleman's Magazine* 1776). This crescendo of publicity in anticipation of the hearing meant that by the time the full account of the trial was printed in the magazine, it came with a postscript stating: 'The importance of the above trial, and our desire to gratify our readers with the substance of it at once, has obliged us to postpone the Account of American Affairs'. The fact that it took priority over American affairs at the time of the War of Independence is a measure of the impact that the Duchess's trial had on popular awareness. Similarly, the *Annual Register*

1 Jactitation of marriage: A false assertion that one is married to someone to whom one is not in fact married (Martin 2002).

for 1776 devoted six pages to a detailed account of the trial (*The Annual Register* 1788). Samuel Foote's play: *A trip to Calais* (1778), added to public interest in the Duchess in the lead up to her trial, with an overt character assassination of her through the fictional Lady Kitty Crocodile. The Duchess attempted to suppress publication of the play by offering Foote financial incentives, though when these were rejected, her friend Lord Mountstuart approached the Lord Chamberlain to forbid its production – prompting a colourful exchange of letters with Foote (Gentleman's Magazine 1809, 35–40).

The trial itself was resplendent in ceremony, replete with all the etiquette and theatrical display of courtesy which the trial of a Duchess by her peers in full parliament demanded. The contemporary writer Hannah More provided the following description:

> Garrick would have me take his ticket to go to the trial of the Duchess of Kingston; a sight which, for beauty and magnificence, exceeded any thing which those who were never present at a coronation or a trial by peers can have the least notion of. Mrs Garrick and I were in full dress by seven … You will imagine the bustle of five thousand people getting into one hall! (Hole 1996)

After a description of the grand entrance of the Peers into the court at Westminster, Bathurst's (1776) account of the trial relates how the Duchess was called and brought, making three reverences on her approach before falling to her knees at the Bar. On being permitted to rise, the Duchess curtsied to the Lord High Steward and to the House of Peers, the compliment being returned her by his Grace, and the Lords. Granted permission to address the court, the Duchess recounted her voluntary return from Rome, at serious risk to her life, in order to submit to the law. She requested that the court would understand that her poor health and oppressed spirits affected her ability to recollect certain facts, but 'it can only be with the loss of life, that I can be deprived of the knowledge of the respect that is due to this high and awful tribunal'. Such dramatic and overstated deference make it simple to see where Foote found inspiration. In court, the Duchess sought to win the support of those who stood in judgement of her by portraying herself not only as courteous and cooperative, but also as an ill and oppressed lady.[2] These traits reflected the manipulation and self-interest, concealed behind a façade of grief for her dead husband, in Foote's (1778) caricature of the Duchess as Kitty Crocodile.

Theatrics aside, there could be no doubt of the seriousness of the charge. In court it was stated that bigamy was:

> A crime so destructive of the peace and happiness of private families, and so injurious in its consequences to the welfare and good order of society, that by statute law of this Kingdom it was for many years (in your sex) punishable with

2 This performance was later matched, with greater success, by Linda Kitson in the infamous case of *Kitson v Playfair* in 1896 (see Chapter 3).

> death; the lenity, however, of later times has substituted a milder punishment in its stead. (Bathurst 1776)

It is worth noting not only the severity of the charge, but also the description of the ill-effects of the crime. It was destructive to private families and it had injurious consequences for society. Consequently, it was at times necessary for the law to intrude into individual's private lives in order to protect the welfare of society. In legal proceedings of this nature, such intrusion was inevitable, but it became increasingly evident as witnesses were called to testify, that there was doubt over its nature and extent. That the social welfare could be adversely affected by an individual's behaviour emphasised the potential for conflict between a patient's interests in maintaining secrecy, a doctor's interests in maintaining honour and the wider interests of society. As discussed in detail in later chapters of this book, balancing individual interests with those of society became an increasingly common element of debates over medical confidentiality over the course of the next two centuries.

The first witness called was Ann Craddock, servant to Elizabeth Chudleigh's aunt, the interfering Mrs. Hanmer, and wife to Hervey's servant.[3] She was very forthcoming with her evidence, testifying that she had witnessed the marriage between the accused and Hervey and saw them in bed together afterwards. Craddock stated that while she never actually saw a child from the marriage, she did observe that Elizabeth appeared to be with child. Subsequently, the accused told her that a boy had been born in Chelsea but before she was taken to see him, Elizabeth informed her that he had died. Anne Craddock's evidence was straightforward, she made no protest when asked to give evidence and was perfectly willing to divulge information received in conversation with the accused. This was not a pattern repeated with subsequent witnesses.

Next to be called to give evidence, and central to our interest in the case, was the surgeon, Caesar Hawkins. Hawkins had served as Serjeant-Surgeon to King George II and, at the time of the trial, held the same post to the subsequently 'mad' King George III (Hibbert 1998). He had known Elizabeth and Hervey for around thirty years, having initially attended them in a professional capacity, an acquaintance that later developed into friendship. Counsel, on asking if Hawkins knew from the parties of any marriage between them, received the reply: 'I do not know how far any thing, that has come before me in a confidential trust in my profession, should be disclosed, consistent with my professional honour' (Bathurst 1776). The question and answer were repeated. With Hawkins's reluctance to answer, the point was referred to the Peers to decide, and there followed a lengthy statement on the matter by Lord Mansfield.

Mansfield (William Murray) was Lord Chief Justice, renowned for his emphasis on making prompt decisions. Noting the pronounced laxity in the practices for the

3 This marriage took place in 1752, after the marriage of Chudleigh and Hervey, and is noted here as it shows Craddock had links with both families.

reporting of precedent in the eighteenth century, James Oldham (1992) suggests that this goes some way to explaining the 'rarity of cases in which Mansfield was prevented by prior authority from reaching a desired result'. However, Mansfield's authoritative approach did not meet with universal approval. Oldham notes that critics saw his 'chancellorlike' behaviour as inappropriate for a common law judge. Nonetheless, Mansfield carried a great deal of influence in the shaping of the law in the second half of the eighteenth century.[4] In what seems to have been a typically quick and definitive response, Mansfield gave the following statement. Given the influence it has had in determining the law on medical privilege for the last 250 years, it is worth quoting Mansfield's comments at length.

> I suppose Mr. Hawkins means to demur to the question upon the ground, that it came to his knowledge some way, from his being employed as a surgeon for one or both of the parties; and I take it for granted, if Mr. Hawkins, understands that it is your Lordships opinion, that he has no privilege on that account to excuse himself from giving the answer, that then, under the authority of your Lordships judgement, he will submit to answer it : Therefore, to save your Lordships the trouble of an adjournement, if no Lord differs in opinion, but thinks that a surgeon has no privilege to avoid giving evidence in a court of justice, but is bound by the law of the land to do it; (if any of your Lordships think he has such a privilege, it will be a matter to be debated elsewhere, but) if all your Lordships acquiesce, Mr. Hawkins will understand, that it is your judgement and opinion, that a surgeon has no privilege, where it is a material question, in a civil or criminal cause, to know whether parties were married, or whether a child was born, to say, that his introduction to the parties was in the course of his profession, and that in that way he came to knowledge of it. I take it for granted, that if Mr. Hawkins understands that, it is a satisfaction to him, and a clear justification to all the world. If a surgeon was voluntarily to reveal these secrets, to be sure he would be guilty of a breach of honour, and of great indiscretion; but, to give that information in a court of justice, which by the law of the land he is bound to do, will never be imputed to him as any indiscretion whatever. (Bathurst 1776)

The rest of the House, without discussion, agreed. Seemingly placated by this response, Hawkins answered the question by stating he had understood, from the conversation between the two parties, that there was a marriage but that he had nothing of proof, 'I mean nothing as legal proof, but *conversation*'. The importance of the stress on the word *conversation*, as it appears in the original text, must not be overlooked. At this stage of his evidence, Hawkins was not revealing information he had gained in the course of his work as a medical man.

---

4 An account of his life can be found both in the *Dictionary of National Biography* and in *The International Magazine of Literature, Art and Science*, 1850, 1(3).

Certainly, his reluctance to divulge information stemmed from a concept of gentlemanly honour which was relevant to his success as an elite surgeon, but the information had not been gained in a professional capacity. His introduction to the accused and Hervey had been on a professional level, when he was called to be present at the birth of their child. Though present, Hawkins did not deliver the child himself and at the trial he stated he could not remember who had delivered it. However, professional attendance aside, his knowledge of any formal marriage between them was gained through conversation. Much of the medical world of the eighteenth century equated ethical practice with courtesy, manners and etiquette – a hierarchical world in which successful practitioners strove for the status of gentlemen (Fissel 1993). Hawkins's request not to break the confidence of the two parties was based on the ethic of a gentleman's honour. As already noted, Hervey and Elizabeth Chudleigh had used Hawkins as their mutual envoy for correspondence in the lead up to the earlier ecclesiastical trial. During his evidence in the criminal trial, Hawkins recounted how Hervey had wished to convey the regard and respect which he had for Elizabeth and to assure her that he would 'appear and act on the line of a man of honour and of a gentleman; that he wished (he said) she would understand that his soliciting me to carry the message should be received by her as a mark of that disposition' (Bathurst 1776).

Hawkins had therefore been entrusted not only with delivering the pertinent information from one party to the next, but with being a symbol of gentlemanly honour. Put in this context, it is clear that during the trial he was keen not to betray the trust which had been put in him and, what is more, he was trying to accentuate the status of honourable and trustworthy gentleman bestowed upon him by Hervey. While Hawkins may have been drawing on a perceived long-standing duty of medical practitioners to maintain patient confidences, his actions, when seen within the specific context of this trial, show Hawkins to be making his request in a manner that would appeal to the code of honour of the upper echelons of society represented in the courtroom.

It is of little surprise that a trial of this nature, at this time, became centrally focused on the issue of honour. The honour of the peerage was itself being brought into question with such a scandalous trial for a crime involving three of its members. Similarly, it should come as no surprise that a medical man was so prominent in the proceedings. By the nature of their profession, medical men were party to private and sensitive information about patients and their families. Recognising this, the contemporary medical ethicist John Gregory (1772) wrote: 'Hence appears how much the characters of individuals, and the credit of families may sometimes depend on the discretion, secrecy, and honour of a physician.' In light of these words, it is worthy of particular note that it was a surgeon, not the socially superior physician, who was embroiled in the wrangle for recognition within the role of honourable gentleman, on the high profile stage of this prominent trial in such a powerful court.

Hawkins was the first of the witnesses to question the need to disclose information, but he was by no means the last. The Honourable Sophia Charlotte

Fettiplace requested to be excused from giving evidence on the grounds that she had no knowledge of the issue other than what arose from her former connection as friend and confidante of the Duchess. The Lord High Steward responded with a categorical statement that she must disclose what she knew for the purposes of justice. Still, the issue was not resolved.

The next witness was Viscount Barrington. While the various reports of the trial list Barrington simply as a friend of the Duchess, William Wildman Barrington served as Member of Parliament for Berwick-upon-Tweed and later Plymouth. He held a number of state offices throughout his career, including Chancellor of the Exchequer, and at the time of the trial he was serving his second term as Secretary for War – the position to which Elizabeth, fleetingly, had been promoted during the postprandial antics of a royal dinner party decades earlier. Barrington's opening remarks made clear his reluctance to follow the court's line of thought and divulge all information: 'if any thing has been confided to my Honour, or confidentially told me, I do hold, with humble submission to your Lordships, that as a man of honour, as a man regardful of the laws of society, I cannot reveal it.'

When reminded of the court's reaction to Hawkins's request, Barrington acknowledged the response but stated: 'I think every man must act from his own feelings, and I feel, that any Private Conversation intrusted to me, is not to be reported again.' This is a very important statement. Barrington asserted that it would contravene his honour to reveal what he had learnt in conversation with the Duchess, yet that is precisely the method by which Hawkins had apprehended that there was a marriage, information he had been forced to divulge. While Hawkins's request to maintain confidences had been summarily refused, Barrington's petition, at least initially, fell on more sympathetic ears. In the discussion in open court, Lord Camden stated: 'As to casuistical points, how far he should conceal or suppress that, which the justice of his country calls upon him to reveal, that I must leave to the witness's own conscience.' Camden may have imposed the weight of the situation on Barrington's conscience, but this was clearly more lenient in contrast to the Lord High Steward's categorical response to Sophia Charlotte Fettiplace. The Duke of Richmond went further: 'For one I think it would be improper in the noble Lord to betray any private conversations. I submit to your Lordships, that every matter of fact, not of conversation, which can be requested, the noble Lord is bound to disclose.'

After an adjournment to discuss the matter, the Peers returned and the Lord High Steward informed Barrington that he was bound by law to answer all questions put to him. With the matter now decided, both counsel for the prosecution and defence stated that they had no questions for Barrington. Thus, even when the court had taken the opportunity to adjourn and consider the matter – more than was deemed necessary when Hawkins made his request – the opposing counsels appeared reluctant to compromise Barrington's honour. Lord Radnor, however, did take the opportunity to ask Barrington direct questions relating to his conversations with the Duchess which made mention of her marriage to Hervey. Having taken further advice from counsel, Barrington gave a tentative but positive response, making the evasive qualification that he was not lawyer or civilian enough to judge whether it was a legal marriage.

The first witness for the defence was Berkley, attorney to Hervey. He immediately declared his interest in the cause, stating that his knowledge of the business arose from his professional position in relation to Hervey. Consequently, he posed a similar question as Hawkins and Barrington had done before him; did his professional position, as attorney to one of the parties in the cause, exempt him from answering questions from counsel? In his own words, would the disclosing of information gained in the lawyer–client relationship be 'consistent with honour to myself and the duty I owe to him?' As with Hawkins, it was Mansfield who attempted to clarify the legal position by stating that the privilege of attorneys extended only to information received from clients in order to gain legal advice relevant to their defence. The questions being put to Berkley did not request the divulging of secrets of the client, but rather sought collateral facts and 'it has often been determined, that as to fact an attorney or counsel has no privilege to withhold his evidence'. It is noteworthy that Mansfield treated this as a firmly established point of law, and he concluded his remarks by stating his supposition that Berkley only raised the question in order to emphasise that there was no indiscretion in his giving evidence. Questions proceeded and Berkley, having now had his honourable intentions publicly confirmed by the court, cooperated in answering them.

Professional Reputation and Personal Honour

Professional reputation and personal honour were prominent themes throughout the trial, and it is worth pausing to consider the court's reaction to the various petitions for exemption from testifying. In Hawkins's case, his request was thrown out with no discussion beyond the statement by Mansfield. When Berkley was called, he sought clarification on his position relative to the established privilege granted to members of the legal profession. The reply of Mansfield recognised the existence of a qualified legal privilege and his assertion that Berkley was only looking for justification of his giving evidence provides a demonstration of witnesses' desire to maintain honour and reputation while satisfying the court's requirements. This point holds true for Hawkins. In a competitive market, a medical man in the eighteenth century relied on reputation, perceived status and etiquette in order to gain wealthy patients and the accompanying fees. By appealing for privilege on the basis of his professional status, Hawkins was attempting to safeguard his reputation as an honourable and trustworthy gentleman. Such overt moral characteristics were central to the success of his practice and, consequently, his livelihood.

Kiernan (1988), in his examination of the code of honour among the upper classes, provides two alternative sources for a sense of honour: innate virtue or conformity to stereotyped rules of conduct. In practice, he states: 'an individual's honour … had little to do with any ethical convictions; its meaning was much closer to 'prestige' … [used] to impress his underlings as well as his peers.' There is little doubt that a large element of the motive of each witness who challenged the court on the question of honour can be attributed to a desire to be recognised for observing social mores in a distinguished court at the focal point of public attention. Yet, perhaps a slightly different light should be cast over Hawkins's motivations.

Roy Porter's (1985a) analysis of the career of the eighteenth-century surgeon William Hunter argued that mainstream histories of medicine which compartmentalised physicians, surgeons and apothecaries into a three-tiered hierarchy in which only the physician could achieve the status of gentleman, were overly rigid. Rather, while hierarchy did exist, the power which the patient had to choose from the wide variety of formal and informal healers available left opportunity enough for enterprising individuals to gain social advancement and wealthy clients, without practising physic. Porter draws on Jewson's classic paper on eighteenth-century medical life (1974) in which he states that the ethical propriety of medical men was a central criterion for their selection. While the ambitious physician was required to establish his credentials as a gentleman, he had to distinguish himself further from the rest of the marketplace crowd. As Jewson notes, 'physicians were encouraged therefore to bring themselves before the public eye by every devious method of self advertisement their prolific ingenuity could devise'.

In light of Porter and Jewson, Hawkins's performance in court might be viewed, not as a demonstration of status to equals and underlings, but as a defence of his elite position within the profession, with all its financial trappings. By using his enforced appearance in court as a means to advertise his ethical propriety to a packed courtroom attended by Royalty, filled with Peers, and on, through conversation and publication, to the wider public, Hawkins sought to retain the confidence of his clients and perhaps even gain further custom (Pelham 1845). As noted earlier, the regular and extensive coverage in *The Gentleman's Magazine* indicates the interest shown in the Duchess's trial. This would have brought Hawkins's performance in the witness box to the attention of many clients, actual and potential, among the upper class. At its peak this publication had an estimated circulation of over 10,000 copies and considerably more readers. In Porter's words, it can 'thus safely be assumed to mirror the sober opinions of the enlightened reading elite, the catholic taste of anyone with the rank, education, or presumption to consider himself genteel' (Porter 1985b). Certainly, the proceedings did Hawkins's career no harm; he became a Baronet in 1778.

While all witnesses were eventually compelled to answer all questions put to them, there were obvious differences in the method and manner of treatment they received from the court. Whereas Hawkins's request was summarily rejected, Barrington's was given more detailed consideration. Indeed, the court was adjourned while the matter was debated, and there was certainly some evidence of agreement with his position. The conversation between a Viscount and a Duchess was more worthy of consideration for a privilege of confidentiality than that between a medical man and his clients. Or perhaps the court was more willing to accommodate the principle of private duty as asserted by a Viscount in his platonic dealings with a Duchess, when compared with a similar plea from a medical man whose desire for honour was more obviously entangled with his commercial interests, thereby compromising the purity of his appeal to moral principles.

The Outcome

The Duchess was unanimously found guilty of the crime of bigamy. The decision itself was a spectacle as 119 members of the House of Peers, starting with the youngest, the Duke of Argyll, stood in turn, placed his right hand on his chest and declared 'Guilty, upon my honour' (Howell 1816). It is no small irony that the only claim for privilege which was successful in its petition to the court was the guilty Duchess's request for the privilege of the peerage, exempting her from being burnt on the hand – the usual corporal punishment for bigamists. After her trial the Duchess (technically no longer a Duchess but rather the wife of the Earl of Bristol), hearing that the Duke's nephews were about to proceed against her, left England, being conveyed across the Channel to Calais in an open boat by the captain of her yacht as a *ne exeat regno* was issued against her. She was, however, left in possession of her fortune.

The most enduring legacy, of a Duchess who courted controversy throughout her life, was the legal implications of her trial for bigamy, including its impact on the determination of medical privilege. At a basic level the case illustrates salient points, including the potential for medicine to become embroiled in debates in which the balance of private life and public interest are challenged and defined. Professional and personal interests, observed in the actions of both Hawkins and Berkley, were also prominent in the trial, and it is clear that confidentiality was firmly grounded in the concept of honour. Attention has also been drawn to differences in the method and manner of the court's treatment of the petitions from Hawkins, Barrington, and Berkley, observing in particular the leniency of the approach to Barrington and the confirmation of legal privilege with Berkley. Yet, the response of the court to each request for exemption from testifying must be seen as only half the story. As Frevert (1995) notes in an examination of honour in duelling, 'securing victory over their opponents was not the main concern of eighteenth-century duellists … It was not the outcome of the duel which determined whether or not the duellists were men of honour, but the fact that the duel was staged at all.'

By challenging such an authoritative court on a point of law, witnesses sought to highlight, and ensure any disclosure was not perceived to contravene, their sense of honour. The courtroom duels were fought for prestige, personal and professional interest, all of which could be maintained in the act of the challenge as much as in the outcome itself. Unlikely as it may seem, this precedent has influenced, and in many ways bound, the whole of an evolving medical profession on the issue of medical confidentiality ever since. It has been cited in textbooks of medical law through to the twenty first century, though none have analysed its roots within the private agendas and personal interests of this sensational case.

An Enduring Precedent

The English legal system has a firm historical foundation in common law and judicial precedent. Even with the increase in statute law from the nineteenth century, much of which confirmed prior practice, judicial precedent still influenced the interpretation of penumbral issues. As Chief Justice Lord Kenyon put it in 1792, the discretion of the court 'will be best exercised by not deviating from the rules laid down by our predecessors; for the practice of the Court forms the law of the Court' (*Wilson v Rastall* [1792] 99 T.E.R. 1286). Manchester (1980) points out that one of the crucial elements in a judge's awareness and knowledge of the common law was gained through accurate published reporting of cases. While this was not widespread in the eighteenth century, the perceived importance of the Duchess's case led the House of Peers to order an official report to be made. In fact, in addition to Bathurst's account of the trial published in 1776, the case was fully reported by both Hargrave (1781) in his collection of State trials and in a similar published work by Howell (1816). Clearly then, in addition to populist reporting, the legal mind was given ample opportunity to read any one of at least three detailed accounts of the trial, with reports continuing to be published during the twentieth century (Melville 1927 and 1996 reprint).

Evidence of judicial awareness of the precedent can be found in several later cases in which questions of confidentiality and privilege were raised. The ruling against Caesar Hawkins was cited by Justice Buller in *Wilson v Rastall*, ([1792] 100 E.R, 1287). The case related to the bribing of voters in an election and it was clearly stated that privilege extended only to members of the legal profession when they were acting in that specific capacity in preparation for legal proceedings. *Wilson v Rastall* was, in turn, further cited in *Rex v Gibbons*, ([1823] 1 Car & P 97). In the latter case, a surgeon, called to give evidence about a confession made to him by a woman accused of murdering her bastard child, objected on grounds of professional privilege. The judge dismissed the appeal, drawing attention to the Duchess of Kingston precedent as having clarified the legal duty imposed on medical practitioners to disclose information in court. *Rex v Gibbons*, was later cited by Lord Chief Justice Best in *Broad v Pitt* ([1828] 3 C & P 518). During this case, the defendant's ex-attorney was called as a witness. He was asked about a conversation which he had had with the defendant, when the latter had executed a deed which the witness had prepared for him as his professional adviser. The witness contended that the conversation was confidential, but was ruled against on grounds that the communication was not made for the purposes of bringing or defending a legal action. Amidst what became a famous statement on the secrecy attached to confessions to a clergyman, Best clearly indicated that there was no privilege for a medical man and cited the Duchess's case as evidence.

Rex v Gibbons and *Broad v Pitt* were subsequently cited as evidence of the absence of medical privilege in textbooks on the law of evidence (see Phipson 1942, the same point was made without citing any cases in Phipson 1921).

Influence in Scotland

The House of Lords was the highest court of appeal in Britain, except with regard to criminal cases in Scotland. As the Duchess was tried for the crime of bigamy, the precedent was not necessarily binding on the Scottish criminal courts.[5] It is therefore important to examine the impact of the Duchess's trial in Scotland (see Ferguson 2011). In addition to the published reports, written treatises were a further source of the principles of law as established in particular decisions. Interestingly, a number of nineteenth-century Scottish jurists categorically stated that surgeons and physicians had no privilege in a court of law, but cited no cases in relation to this point (for example: Burnett 1811, Hume 1819, Tait 1834). One exception was William Gillespie Dickson (1855), whose treatise cited the Duchess of Kingston as its earliest precedent.

Another case to which Dickson pays particular attention is that of *AB v CD* ([1851] 14 D. 177). Heard in the Scottish Court of Session, the case established that secrecy was an essential element of the contract between a medical man and his employers. The case involved an elder of the kirk session in an undisclosed parish in Scotland, whose wife gave birth to a child only six months after their marriage. In a misunderstanding of his position, the medical man called on to give his opinion on the age of the child, indicated to the minister of the parish that the child was not premature. The elder was dismissed from the kirk session and brought an action against the doctor for breach of confidentiality. The doctor's lawyers attempted to counter this on the grounds that secrecy could not be taken to be an essential element of the contract between a medical man and his clients as there were instances in which the medical man could be forced to divulge patient information. Their justification for this position was the fact that a medical man could not claim privilege in court, and they cited the Duchess of Kingston precedent as evidence. Although the court did not accept the defence's argument with regard to there being *no* secrecy involved in the doctor–patient relationship, Lord Fullerton did make clear that the medical profession did not have any form of privilege to decline giving evidence in a court of law.

While *AB v CD* [1851] is the earliest case cited in many works relating to medical confidentiality in Scotland, the issue of medical *privilege* was not raised for discussion, so Fullerton's comments were no more than obiter dicta. In fact,

5 While the present focus is on the Duchess's impact in Britain, the precedent denying medical privilege influenced legal thinking in jurisdictions around the world. Detailed analysis of this, comparing Britain with the countries of her former Empire, is the focus of my current research.

while the Duchess's trial was cited in further Scottish cases, it appears that the specific question of medical privilege was never the issue of immediate focus.[6] Thus, even Wilkinson (1986), was forced to state that while there is no reported Scottish decision on the point, 'it is settled practice that he (a medical practitioner) may also be compelled to speak to communications passing between him and his patient'. The case cited with this is, once again, *AB v CD* [1851]. With Wilkinson's work cited, in connection with the absence of medical privilege in the witness box, by the online edition of the *Stair Memorial Encyclopedia*, it is quite clear that the Duchess's impact in Scotland was not inconsiderable.[7]

Medical Jurisprudence

The discipline of medical jurisprudence, encompassing both forensic medicine and medical police, gained impetus as a necessary element of taught medical education during the course of the nineteenth century (Todd Thomson 1831, 9). The legal examination of medical men in the witness box was often a severe testing ground, not just for the individuals involved but also for the reputation of the professions they represented. One contemporary commentator went so far as to question whether there was 'any object of dread, paramount in the eye of the medical practitioner, to the *witness-box*?' (Smith 1825, 5). In response, courses of medical jurisprudence began to be incorporated into medical teaching. In conjunction with the rise in taught courses, there was a burst of literature on the subject in the early nineteenth century. In their textbook of medical jurisprudence, one of the earliest in Britain, Paris and Fonblanque (1823) cite the trial of the Duchess of Kingston in a section dealing with medical confidentiality. The advice given follows the line of thought taken by Mansfield, and they quote his statement in full. Paris and Fonblanque's work was cited by many other writers and commentators in the field, thereby bringing the attention of students and practitioners of law and medicine to the Duchess's case, ensuring its continued influence in the growing field of medical jurisprudence (see, for example, Lyall 1826, Todd Thompson 1831, Traill 1840). The case was also cited by William Mawdesley Best in his *Treatise on the Principles of Evidence* (Best 1849, 283).

6 See for example: *AB v CD* 7 Fraser (Court of Session) 72; *Watson v McEwan*, 12 SLT 248 & 599 & 13 SLT 340 & 7 Fraser (Court of Session) 109.

7 *The Stair Memorial Encyclopedia* is a comprehensive collection of Scots law. Discussion of medical privilege is found in the section on Medical Law: sub-section 4 Issues Involving Medical Treatment; sub-section 4 Medical Confidentiality and Privacy; (d) Lawful Disclosure of Information: Exceptions to the General Principles of Confidentiality; section 313 No Privilege of Medical Confidentiality.

Opposing views

However, not all commentators shared the same view. John Gordon Smith recognised that breach of confidentiality, when absolutely required in court, was firmly established by legal precedent. In a footnote relating to the courts at Westminster he stated: 'perhaps it may not be impertinent to call the particular attention of the reader to the nature of the courts that sit there. In the Appendix, will be found illustrations as to what has been ruled on this point: in one instance in the *House of Peers*, which on the occasion in question, sat in Westminster Hall.' This seems to be a reference to the Duchess of Kingston Trial. However, in his book he presented an alternative viewpoint, based not on the previous practice of the courts or national law, but rather on theories of general right (Smith 1825).

Dissent from Mansfield's precedent was not only to be found in textbooks, but also in obiter dicta. In the Scottish case of *McDonald v McDonalds* ([1881] 8 R 357), in which an insurance company tried to claim privilege with regard to a medical report it was asked to produce in evidence, it was stated that 'although it has been decided by the English Courts that a medical man who acquires information from his patient … cannot refuse in a Court of Justice to disclose the information they possess, yet these decisions have been regretted by later English Judges, and none have been pronounced hitherto by the Scottish Courts'.

The reference to judicial regret may have related to the comments of Buller J in the case of *Wilson v Rastall* ([1792] 100 E.R. 1283). Citing the example of Caesar Hawkins in the Duchess's case he suggested, 'there are cases to which it is much to be lamented that the law of privilege is not extended; those in which medical persons are obliged to disclose the information which they acquire by attending in their professional characters' ([1792] 100 E.R. 1287). Even such a high legal authority as Lord Chancellor Brougham, in his decision in *Greenough v Gaskell*, ([1833] 1 MY&K 98), raised questions over the wisdom of the current state of the law. In his discussion of the legal privilege enjoyed by lawyers, he observed: 'it may not be very easy to discover why a like privilege has been refused to others, and especially to medical advisers', a line often left out of citations of the precedent, as noted in Chapter 6.

While not all commentators or judges agreed with the precedent established during the Duchess of Kingston's trial, in the absence of a test case the law remained unchanged. When, at the outset of the twentieth century, John Glaister, Professor of Medical Jurisprudence and Toxicology at the University of Glasgow, came to write his influential textbook of *Medical Jurisprudence and Toxicology*, he indicated that the absence of any privilege for medical witnesses was the established law of the land. This, he stated, had been first laid down by Lord Mansfield in the Duchess of Kingston's trial from which he quoted at some length (Glaister 1910).

A further indication of the fundamental importance of the Duchess precedent is the fact that it resurfaced in various sources whenever the question of medical confidentiality was brought to widespread attention. In 1896, at the time of the infamous *Kitson v Playfair* case (discussed in Chapter 3), the *British Medical Journal (BMJ)* for that year contained two articles which cited the Duchess of Kingston as the benchmark precedent (*BMJ* 4 and 18 April 1896). When, in 1899, the Russian ambassador sought advice on Britain's policy on medical confidentiality, the Home Office referred the request to the GMC (NA HO45 9988 X72989). The resultant memo, indicating that the absence of any privilege of confidentiality had been established at the Duchess's trial, was published in the *BMJ* (11 March 1899). Around the same time, the precedent formed the basis of an article on 'Professional Confidences of Medical Men' in *Justice of the Peace* (21 April 1900, 245–6). In the early 1920s, when there were a number of high profile legal cases in which medical privilege was claimed, the Duchess's case was cited as precedent in all manner of sources, ranging from medical journals, legal journals, newspapers such as *The Times* and the *Evening Standard* to the minutes of the BMA's CEC.[8] These citations brought the Duchess's trial to the attention of medical and legal professionals as well as the wider public, and their importance should not be overlooked. For instance, the articles from the *Law Journal* and the *Solicitors Journal* were picked up with some interest by the newly established Ministry of Health, and were included in their file on medical confidentiality in the early 1920s. Similarly, William Brend's article in the *BMJ* in early 1922, was cited during a special meeting of the BMA Council, held to discuss the question of medical confidentiality, and became required reading for members of the BMA's Professional Secrecy Committee (PSC) before its first meeting in March of that year.[9]

This trend continued throughout the second half of the twentieth century when references to the Duchess could be found in case reports, medical and legal articles, textbooks and specialist monographs on medical confidentiality (for example: Bernfeld 1967 and 1972; Gurry 1984, 352; McHale 1993, 13; McHale and Fox 1997, 481; Kennedy and Grubb 1994, 639). The Duchess of Kingston precedent is undoubtedly understood to be the basis of the common law denial of medical privilege in court. As subsequent chapters of this book detail, there have been numerous attempts to challenge and change the common law and give greater protection to confidential medical information in legal proceedings. It is noteworthy that while Mansfield's statement and the Duchess precedent were nearly always mentioned, no one appears to have examined in any detail its basis or the circumstances of the original case. Had they done so, they would have discovered that the modern law has been built upon questionable foundations.

---

8 The following is by no means an exhaustive list of citations of the Duchess precedent in the early interwar years: *Garner v Garner* [1920] 36 T.L.R 196 ; *Needham v Needham*, Daily Chronicle, 10 June 1921; *BMJ* 24 April 1920, 14 January 1922, 9 October and 13 November 1926; *Lancet* 1 April 1922; *Law Journal* 18 June 1921; *Solicitors Journal* 24 January 1920; *The Times* 15 January 1920; *Evening Standard* 26 January 1922; BMA, CEC minutes 9 November 1920 and 15 December 1921.

9 *BMJ* 14 January 1922, 64–66.

Chapter 3
The Long Nineteenth Century

> Medicine does not operate outside the law; and the law in the industrial period has been subject to sharp changes in response to economic and political demands. Eastern and Western states have put medical knowledge to many purposes, and have been able to implement this knowledge in a way which was impossible even to the most centralised bureaucracies of the ancient world. The rise of the medical expert, encouraged by modernising states, solved many technical problems and raised many ethical ones. (Crowther 1998)

While little changed over the course of the nineteenth century with regard to medical privilege in court, other developments put new strain on the confidentiality of the doctor–patient relationship. The economic, social and demographic changes associated with the industrial revolution produced new concerns about public health in rapidly expanding towns and cities. Combined with economic and military competition among European nations, this provoked the state into taking a more active interest in the health and welfare of the population as the century progressed. New medical roles, such as municipal medical officers of health, came with an explicit emphasis on prioritising community welfare over individual privacy. Legislation requiring notification of contagious or infectious diseases, or criminal abortions, was symptomatic of a growing emphasis on the collective within aspects of the public policy and legislative agenda. This added a new dimension to the dual loyalty demands on doctors, putting pressure on the traditional model of confidentiality in the patient–doctor relationship. However, such external changes were mirrored by changes within medicine over the same period. Changes in the structure, practice and regulation of medicine contributed to greater unity in professional identity. Whereas Caesar Hawkins had sought to defend his individual reputation and status in 1776, by the turn of the twentieth century challenges to confidentiality were met by a more united professional defence. While elite doctors might still value gentlemanly honour, the profession was developing modern codes of ethical practice in response to its evolving role in a changing society.

Professional Identity and Ethics

As McCullough (2009) notes, the emphasis in most writings on medical conduct in the eighteenth century was on practitioners' behaviour towards each other. For the elite of the profession, the ideal of conduct was based on the code of personal honour and gentlemanly manners displayed by Hawkins in the Duchess of

Kingston trial. In the absence of standardised understandings of disease causation, progression or treatment, theories of diagnosis and therapy were often specific to each doctor. In a fiercely competitive marketplace, economic self-interest could be advanced by the degradation of rivals in addition to personal promotion. While correct attire and gentlemanly manners advertised a doctor's credentials to the market, pamphlets and broadsheets were used to attack the competence of competitors as well as highlight a doctor's own successes. As the eighteenth century progressed, patients found it increasingly challenging to distinguish whom to trust amidst the 'myriad concepts of medicine, health, and disease and treatments … It became increasingly difficult to infer with confidence from good manners to good character. Manners could be purchased from manners coaches and put on, just as one put on a proper suit' (McCullough 2009, 405). Public confidence in the moral and intellectual authority of doctors was undermined, and medicine's reputation was tarnished as a result.

In response, a number of writers sought to reform medical practice, advocating a new ethical approach to medicine from the late eighteenth century. Baker (2009) notes six reformers who sought to shift the primary focus of medical practice away from narrow economic self-interest, towards building new foundations in sympathy and science. Elaborate theories of disease causation and techniques of diagnosis and therapy were not to be devised simply to impress lay patrons, but should be developed using a scientific approach that sought to apply, test and improve on the theory and techniques practitioners had learnt in their training. This growing emphasis on a scientific approach to cases was to be combined with a strong sense of sympathy as the underpinning driving force of good medicine. Five of the reformers Baker discusses were connected to the medical school at Edinburgh University.[1] The importance of sympathy in the medical ethics they envisaged stemmed from the common sense thought of Scottish Enlightenment philosophy. In the writings of John Gregory, sympathy was the core virtue of good medical practice – the visceral response provoked by seeing a fellow human being in pain or distress that motivated a doctor to care for and competently assist those in need (see McCullough 1998, 2009, Haakonssen 1997).

Over the course of the nineteenth century, medical practice came to reflect increasingly standardised understandings of pathological anatomy, with associated developments in diagnostic instruments and techniques. By the later decades of the century, the scientific basis of medical knowledge extended to germ theory, and the laboratory joined the clinic as a site of medical investigation and diagnosis. Large numbers of students received their education and sense of professional values from the same, relatively small number of medical school teachers. As Waddington notes, 'as a result of these changes in the structure of medical education medical students underwent a new and more intensive process of professional socialisation that both fostered a sense of professional community and asserted the primacy of professional rather than lay values' (Waddington 1990). While Waddington noted

1 John Gregory, Samuel Bard, Thomas Percival, Benjamin Rush and Michael Ryan.

the positive effects of an increasingly standardised knowledge base and education in producing a common professional identity and associated set of values, much of his writing attempted to deconstruct the professionalisation of medicine during the nineteenth century (1975, 1977, 1984).

In assessing the prolonged drive for statute legislation to regulate medical practice, Waddington emphasised the economic benefit which would accrue to registered practitioners in a marketplace where state regulation gave them a monopoly on practice. Viewed in this way, the 1858 Medical Act was not motivated by practitioners' desire to protect the interests and well-being of the public. Rather, self-interest drove reforms of medical practice. The regulation of medicine through fixed standards of professional entry qualifications and disciplinary hearings for misconduct were essentially the guise which passed off selfishness as altruism.

Sociological analyses of nineteenth-century medical reforms often interpreted them as no more than a facade behind which qualified practitioners could protect their self-interest and monopolise the overcrowded marketplace. Similarly, they dismissed the writings of Gregory and Percival as medical etiquette rather than medical ethics. However, such interpretations met with severe criticism from medical historians (Baker 1995, Baker and McCullough 2009). Chester Burns (1995), while not denying the primacy of intra-professional relationships in Thomas Percival's *Medical Ethics* (1803), notes that Percival additionally drew out the doctor's social obligations not only in public health but also his duty to the law, including medical testimony in court. This point was also evident in the writings of Michael Ryan (1831), who saw the need for medical practitioners to understand the moral and legal responsibility which community expectations could place on them through the embodiment of collective opinion in statute law. Judicial decision could override traditions the profession promoted among its members and, as Anne Crowther (1995) notes, in the absence of a widely accepted modern day code of ethics the medical profession often looked to the law for guidance.

Courses on English law highlighted the importance of judicial interpretation of statute law, without which it was often 'impossible, even for lawyers, to form any opinion of their meaning and effect (Amos 1829). Yet, as the example of Glaister's writings on abortion illustrate, discussed later in this chapter, judicial interpretation was not always consistent. Practitioners could turn to their textbooks of medical jurisprudence seeking ethical guidance, but what they found there often obscured rather than clarified correct practice. As Baker and McCullough (2009) summarise, recent scholarship has tended to recognise Gregory and Percival as the founding fathers of modern medical ethics; their writings reflecting philosophically-informed understandings of the role of medical professionals in their relationship with patients, colleagues and society. Both writers noted that doctors were given access to the private homes and lives of patients, often seeing them at their most vulnerable. In these circumstances, patients might act in uncharacteristic ways or disclose private thoughts. Therefore discretion and secrecy were important elements of the ethics they prescribed for the medical profession (Gregory 1772, Percival 1803).

The British Medical Association

Important off-shoots of the battle between GPs and consultants over the terms of the 1858 Medical Act were the development of medical journals and societies specifically designed as forums for the views of the majority of medical practitioners who worked in general practice. Having been set up as the Provincial Medical and Surgical Association, the British Medical Association (BMA), as it came to be known from the mid-1850s onwards, became an immensely powerful organisation, representing a large section of the medical profession. Its subcommittees, such as the CEC, were set up to look at specific issues of controversy, including medical confidentiality. Perhaps the most effective mouthpiece of the GP's position in the run-up to the Medical Act of 1858 was Thomas Wakely's medical journal *The Lancet*. Wakely, both as a medical practitioner and as an MP, was a highly outspoken advocate of medical reform, focusing in particular on the need for greater recognition of GPs, as well as reform in the education and regulation of practice as a whole. In Porter's words, Wakely 'battled to raise medicine into a respected profession, with structured, regulated entry and lofty ethical ideals – called restrictive practices by their foes' (Porter 1997). The need for GPs, the majority of the profession, to have an effective voice in the ongoing debates on the development of medicine, led to the growth of, and a growing influence for, medical journals and associations.

The General Medical Council

The 1858 Medical Act established the General Council for Medical Education and Registration with the remit of establishing and maintaining a register of all qualified medical practitioners. A single register containing the names of all those qualified to practise medicine was a significant step towards the establishment of a unified profession, giving registered practitioners long-sought recognition. Section 29 of the 1858 Act provided the GMC, as the regulatory body came to be known, with the power to hold disciplinary inquiries into the professional conduct of practitioners and to remove from the register the names of those who were judged to have been guilty of infamous conduct in a professional respect. It therefore lends itself as a prime candidate for examination as a body that set and maintained guidelines of professional practice in medicine, including the issue of medical confidentiality. Unfortunately, as Russell Smith's (1993) examination of the GMC shows, the matter is somewhat more complex. After initial teething problems the GMC set up an adversarial, quasi-legal, system of hearings to consider allegations of professional misconduct. The members of the GMC who heard and decided cases were all medically trained, though they had recourse to legal opinion. As such, the body could have represented a significant prescriptive force in the regulation of the evolving medical profession. In the event, it faced many problems in getting beyond the role of a reactionary system of discipline in individual cases.

Although its decisions were published in the medical press after 1864 – prior to that, decisions had only been made known to GMC members – the GMC did not give reasons for, or explanations of, its decisions in disciplinary cases. Partly because of this, the committee did not adhere to the doctrine of precedent, meaning that each new case was decided in isolation. Coupled with the facts that decisions were given extempore and decision-makers changed frequently, it was not easy to discern consistent rules on complex issues. Clearly the ad hoc reporting of ad hoc decisions, minus their explanatory basis, was not a satisfactory way to inform practitioners of how to avoid allegations of professional misconduct. The GMC did issue declarations of acceptable standards of professional conduct, which it arrived at by distilling what it perceived as the relevant ethical principles from a series of disciplinary decisions in cases of a similar nature. While this sounds good in theory, the aforementioned process entailed problems for its implementation in practice. As Smith indicates, 'there was often a considerable lapse of time between the initial hearing of disciplinary cases relating to a particular matter and the appearance of the GMC's Warning Notice with respect to any given issue'.

Of the 13 issues of conduct which Smith considers, the most pronounced gap belongs to 'breach of confidence'. The first formal inquiry and erasure from the medical register for breaching confidentiality came before the GMC on 5 July 1869. The GMC issued its first published guidelines on the question on 24 November 1970, over 101 years later. While the GMC became an important source of guidance, following a review and reformulation of its role in the 1970s, prior to that it served predominantly as a reactionary disciplinary body. However, as discussed later in this chapter, it did provide some unpublished guidance on medical confidentiality.

Growing State Activity in Health and Medicine

An important factor in the development of debates over medical confidentiality in Britain was the increasing role of the state in medical affairs during the course of the nineteenth century. Porter (1997) suggests that pervasive state intervention in medical activities did not arrive in Britain until the twentieth century, but if nineteenth-century state concern for public health was more ad hoc its influence on medical confidentiality was not inconsiderable. The Common Lodging Houses Acts of 1851 and 1853 compelled the proprietor of a lodging house, on pain of a 40s fine, to notify the authorities if a resident showed signs of an infectious disease (Mooney 1999). Through the Contagious Diseases Acts of 1864, 1866, and 1869 the state designated policing duties to the medical profession, giving them the authority for 'the forcible medical examination' of prostitutes and the power to confine those with VD for up to three months (Savage 1990). The Acts were primarily intended to maintain order and control at dockyard and garrison towns, but as Lawrence (1994) notes, 'although there was a powerful medical lobby which viewed the Acts as progressive extensions of public health legislation, many doctors considered them a gross infringement of individual rights'.

Medicine, as dystopian writers of the twentieth century would emphasise, could be used as a powerful tool for social control, but medical practitioners were not always compliant.[2] The problem was one of priorities. The doctor's foremost duty had traditionally been to the patient, but increasingly the collective interest in public health required consideration. As one medical officer of health noted in 1866, the traditional ethic of the GP, which put duty to the patient first and the patient's family second and public concern thereafter, was exactly reversed in the priorities of the doctors employed in the new field of public health (John Sykes, as quoted in Mooney 1999). The state recognised the benefits of a healthy workforce and, after the panic surrounding the physical deficiencies of conscripts for the Boer War, the pressing need for a healthy armed force. Public health reformers of the mid-nineteenth century had sought to improve the sanitation and living environment of the poorer classes. Voluntary and charitable societies focused on investigation, regulation, medical inspection and control. In an era of growing economic and military competition, the submission of the individual, particularly the 'poor' individual, to scrutiny and analysis was a necessary evil in the promotion of national productivity and security.

Legislation such as the Infectious Disease (Notification) Act 1889, and the Notification of Births Act 1908 (with an amending Act in 1915) required medical practitioners to override the confidentiality of their patients in order to inform the medical officer of health for the district in cases of infectious disease[3] or the birth of a child. Pecuniary interests were explicitly added to the mix of professional ethics and moral conscience, with the levying of fines in cases where the relevant disease (or death under the Births and Deaths Registration Act 1874) was not notified, and the provision of a small fee for every case of birth notified. Simple economics would help to circumvent any moral reticence practitioners might have about overriding patient confidentiality.

The BMA did officially support the principle of compulsory notification of infectious disease, primarily for its pivotal role in combating the outbreak of epidemics. Nonetheless, in recognition of the long-held importance of confidentiality to the doctor–patient relationship, the BMA advocated that legislation should place the onus on the householder rather than the medical attendant to notify the authorities of infectious disease. Mooney (1999) argues that accompanying their belief in the importance of confidentiality, GPs also wished to defend the right of the individual against the state. Many feared that notification,

2 In addition to the obvious examples of Huxley (1994) and Orwell (1989), the literary representation of this point can be found in Zamiatan (1960), where medical men, as channels of state control, use operations to 'cure' fantasy in the population , but a medical practitioner plays a significant role in the resistance movement.

3 A list of those diseases which qualified was issued, though there were recurring debates about whether VD should be added.

along with compulsory removal of the diseased to hospital, would deter individuals from seeking official medical assistance. Not only would such reluctance to gain medical help be detrimental to public health, it would also deprive medical practitioners of income from callouts and follow-up visits. Therefore, notification was seen both as essential for the checking of epidemics, and as a potential deterrent for patients seeking qualified medical advice. Practitioners recognised the benefit that public health accrued from early information on the spread of infection, but simultaneously wished to safeguard their traditional ethic of confidentiality and the right of the individual to be free from state interference. While the state rattled practitioners' pockets – levying fines for failure to notify or paying out small sums for compliance – the thought that potential fees could be lost through patients' reluctance to call in medical assistance for fear of notification, and the loss of follow-up visits to those isolated in hospital, entailed that even those motivated by financial self-interest might find themselves in a quandary.

Penumbral Areas of Law

It was not solely in the motives for action or the projected outcomes that practitioners were pulled in competing directions. Statute laws were often sufficiently open to interpretation to envelop practitioners in grey areas of subjective judgement. For instance, infectious disease did not have to be notified if the victims could be sufficiently well-isolated in their own accommodation. Despite having an obvious bias towards the larger, multiple-roomed homes of the better-off in society, the law was open to interpretation as to what constituted adequate accommodation for quarantine. The law was malleable enough to be moulded to suit circumstance and status, a point perhaps most evident in connection with the statutes relating to abortion. The only operation to be decreed criminal by statute law, abortion provoked an array of public and private opinions and agendas. In Barbara Brookes's words 'the legitimacy of abortion as a solution to an unwanted pregnancy was judged differently according to the circumstances of conception, the age and status of the mother and the eugenic "value" of the foetus ... It was not then, abortion itself which brought universal censure, but rather particular social classifications of the act' (Brookes, 1988). From the state's point of view the decline in the birth rate in the late nineteenth century was a significant factor in increasing the pressure it put on medical practitioners to notify cases of criminal abortion that came to their attention. In this sense the doctor's dilemma was similar to that posed by infectious disease notification, with the conflicting priorities of duty to the individual and to the state clearly evident. However, while infectious diseases put the rest of the population at immediate risk, abortion could and did remain a far more private affair, often carried out by consenting women.

The permutations of the act of abortion were numerous. The pregnant woman could attempt it herself by either using instruments readily at her disposal, such as knitting needles, or purchasing a purgative remedy. She could have an operation, defined in the loosest sense of the term, carried out by almost anyone from a friend to a professional abortionist. Or, she could turn to a qualified doctor who was legally permitted to carry out therapeutic abortions in order to protect the well-being of the mother, a rather ill-defined and easily exploited loophole. While doctors felt pulled by competing obligations, it was the law that influenced which cases of abortion medical practitioners were likely to notify, though perhaps not in the way originally intended. In attempting to deter women from abortion, the law imposed severe penalties on those convicted of the crime. In doing so, it actually succeeded in deterring medical practitioners from subjecting women to further humiliation and reputational ruin at the hands of the courts. The one clear exception was in cases where the pregnant woman died as a result of an illegal abortion. In such cases the profession saw the duty to notify in more black and white terms, perceiving the benefit of bringing the abortionist to justice in order to protect other women in the future. However, as the case of Annie Hodgkiss, discussed later in this chapter, confirmed, the possibility that a patient would die suddenly, left practitioners who followed such a policy walking a somewhat precarious tightrope.

Growing Dual Loyalty Obligations

Legislative obligations aside, the changing form of medical employment was having an impact upon medical confidentiality. As already noted, a cohort of public health doctors emerged whose primary interest in preventive, rather than curative, medicine entailed a concern for the population in general rather than for individual clients. However, increasingly there were medical roles that combined therapeutic care of individuals with obvious obligations to others. Evidently, these had the potential to pull medical practitioners in opposing directions; 'the prison doctor was implicated in a punitive regime, but ethically his duty lay with the well-being of the individual convict. A similar predicament was involved with workmen's compensation schemes for industrial accidents and illness' (Porter 1997). Employment of a doctor by someone other than the patient naturally led to an increasingly complex moral maze of obligation and duty towards employer, patient, professional reputation and, particularly after the National Insurance Act of 1911, the state. The establishment of the National Insurance scheme brought further state pressure on panel doctors to fulfil surveillance, as well as therapeutic roles. Worker, employer and the state all contributed to the cost of insurance and each had an interest in the doctor's assessment of an insured patient if questions arose over malingering and paid absence from work. As Gregory and Percival had noted, a doctor's privileged position gave them access to the homes, lives and personal details of patients. The information they gained could have utility beyond its initial diagnostic and therapeutic purpose, and growing recognition of this posed a threat to traditional understandings of medical confidentiality.

> The pre-war introduction of National Health Insurance had already led some practitioners to proffer expressions about 'the first duty of the doctor [is] to his patient, without whose permission to open them the doctor's lips are absolutely closed concerning all he may come to know of his patient while in discharge of his professional duties to him'. (Cooter 1998)

As Steve Sturdy (2002) notes, both Lloyd George and Churchill believed that concerns about widespread malingering would be short-lived, as workers came to realise that individual abuse of the system would negatively impact upon the collective benefits of the insurance scheme: 'individual welfare depended upon the responsible conduct of all'. While a changing socioeconomic and political context placed new emphasis on the connection between individual and collective welfare, its ramifications for medical confidentiality were complex. The medical journals had their columns filled with practitioner enquiries as to the correct course of action to take in situations where the right course seemed unclear.[4]

GMC Memorandum on Confidentiality 1899

In 1899 the Home Office asked the GMC to provide information detailing the boundaries of medical secrecy in Britain. The invitation stemmed from a request for information on the issue which the Foreign Office had received from the Russian ambassador. The GMC produced a memorandum which considered two aspects of the subject. The first section dealt with whether a medical practitioner could be made to divulge professional confidences in a court of law. Quoting Mansfield's ruling in the Duchess of Kingston's case, the memo made clear that 'a medical man not only may, but must, if necessary, violate professional confidences when answering questions material to an issue in a court of law' (NA HO45 9988 X72989). The second section dealt with whether there were circumstances in which a doctor could disclose information outside the courts. Referring to the decision in *AB v CD* [1851], the GMC pointed out that confidentiality was an essential element of the contract between doctor and patient. However:

> The custom of the medical profession has engrafted two exceptions. (1) in cases of criminal communications, (2) where violation of secrecy is considered necessary for the protection of wife or children (to which may be added a third exception, suggested by the Court in *AB v CD*, cited above, viz. instances conducive to the ends of science, though concealment of individuals in such cases should be secured.

---

4 For queries relating to practitioners' obligations *vis-à-vis* employers and employees see for example: *BMJ*, 1896, vol. 2, 698 'Professional confidence'; *BMJ,* 1899, vol.1, 950 'Professional secrecy'; *BMJ,* 1899, vol.2, 1652 'Privilege as to medical certificates'.

The last section of the memorandum referred to the views expressed by Henry 'Hanging' Hawkins in *Kitson v Playfair* – discussed in detail below – in which he suggested that no general rule could be laid down for either the question of privilege or the notification of a crime such as abortion. The GMC were left to conclude that 'circumstances which according to the custom of the medical profession might be deemed to exonerate him from the imputation of improper violation of secrecy, might nevertheless in a Court of Law be deemed an insufficient justification'. With the benefit of hindsight, the GMC's recognition of the potential disparity between medical and legal opinion appears an early indication of forthcoming confrontation over appropriate disclosure of medical information and the boundaries of medical confidentiality.

Mixed Signals

In many ways the GMC was expressing a view increasingly held by members of the medical profession, that the courts were sending conflicting signals. As noted in the last chapter, Mansfield's ruling in the Duchess's case had drawn disapproval from certain later judges, notably Buller in *Wilson v Rastall* [1792] and Lord Chancellor Brougham in *Greenough v Gaskell* [1838]. Dissent had not faded away by the late nineteenth century. Angus McLaren's (1993) analysis of the *Kitson v Playfair* case illustrated how the threat posed to professional reputation by doctors' appearances in the courts continued to cause concern at the turn of the twentieth century. William Smoult Playfair, royal accoucheur and Professor of Obstetrics at King's College Hospital, was found guilty of slander, and fined over £9,000 pounds after disclosing to his wife that her sister-in-law, Linda Kitson, had had an abortion or miscarriage. As Linda Kitson's husband had been abroad for the previous eighteen months, the allegation carried an implicit accusation of adultery. The medical evidence was overwhelmingly on Playfair's side; though one doctor from University College London did appear on behalf of Linda Kitson to argue that the miscarriage might have followed from a legitimate conception 17 months before. However, Playfair's legal team decided not to base their defence on proving the truth of the allegation, since destroying the reputation of a female relative in open court was not appropriate conduct for a man who had turned down a knighthood in hope of elevation to a peerage. Instead, the defence sought to prove that Playfair's disclosure was a privileged communication. However, the press ridiculed the medical witnesses called to testify on the issue of confidentiality for the answers they gave under questioning from Kitson's legal team about when disclosure of patient information was appropriate.

In his summing up, Hawkins belittled the relevance of the rules which the medical profession laid down for their own guidance on medical confidentiality. There could be no absolute rule, even with regard to giving evidence in court. Rather, 'each case must be considered by its own particular circumstances and by the ruling of the judge who happened to preside on the occasion' (Justice Hawkins, as cited in Glaister 1938). Clearly this left room for divergence of judicial opinion and made it difficult for medical practitioners to know in advance where the law stood.

Glaister picked up on this point towards the end of the section on confidentiality in his early twentieth century textbook of medical jurisprudence. Citing Hawkins's stated belief that it would be a 'monstrous cruelty' for a medical practitioner to report to the public prosecutor a woman who had sought medical attention as a result of procuring an illegal abortion, Glaister noted how this point of view conflicted with that given by Lord Justice Clerk Inglis in the Pritchard poisoning case of 1865. Dr Paterson was called to attend the wife of a colleague, Dr Pritchard. On examination, Paterson felt it possible that she was being poisoned, but decided it was not his professional duty to disclose his suspicions to the police. Mrs Pritchard subsequently died. Dr Pritchard was found guilty of poisoning his wife and was executed on Glasgow Green in front of an estimated crowd of 100,000 people. This was the last public execution in Scotland (Farmer 2003). In reprimanding Paterson for his failure to notify the relevant authorities of his suspicion that Mrs Pritchard was being poisoned, Inglis emphasised the primacy of the doctor's duty as a citizen to prevent the destruction of human life over the rules of professional etiquette which frowned on breach of confidence. Thus both Hawkins and Inglis had made quite clear their belief in the supremacy of the law over professional ideals of correct conduct on confidentiality, but to contradictory conclusions. Glaister was left to surmise that 'these two opinions expressed by these high criminal judges demand the serious attention of the medical profession, although it is difficult, if not, indeed, impossible, to reconcile the two views'. While the medical columns frequently featured a range of questions about the right course of action to take on the issue of confidentiality, by the turn of the twentieth century, the most pressing issue of concern was notification of abortion.

Notification of Abortion

Beneath a query as to the best cycling saddle for a lady, the *BMJ* published a letter received from a young doctor in late May 1896, which sought advice as to his duty in a case of criminal abortion which had come to his attention (*BMJ* 1896, vol.1, 1367). The woman, who confessed that her miscarriage had been induced by illegal use of an instrument, had been in a critical condition but was presently on the mend. The practitioner wished to know if he was obliged to report the crime. The journal's response indicated that the matter had already been discussed, but 'we apprehend that it has not been finally decided, especially in view of the opinion stated to have been given to the College of Physicians by their legal adviser'.

Unlike the best bicycle saddle for a lady (the Brookes B.30), it was not so straightforward to give clear and definitive advice in response to practitioner concerns on the notification of abortion. Before going on to examine why the questions surrounding abortion were causing so much concern, it is worth pausing to note that the individual, Mr E.B. Turner, assigned the task of trying out ladies' bicycle saddles in 1896 was a solicitor to the BMA.[5] He became heavily involved with the question of medical confidentiality, eventually becoming legal adviser to the BMA PSC from its inception in 1922.

Under the Offences Against the Person Act of 1861, the law of England had established severe penalties for a woman, and any accomplice, who procured an illegal abortion. In Scotland, the same punitive view, although not endorsed by statute, was recognised in common law. John Glaister's examination of the medico-legal risks encountered by practitioners in the course of their daily work in the late nineteenth century left the reader in no doubt of a medical practitioner's vulnerability to legal action. The ease with which claims could be brought against doctors by patients or fellow practitioners was a problem exacerbated by the difficulty of disproving any accusations. Any charge would almost certainly damage a practitioner's reputation and finances but, as Glaister notes, it could prove far more serious:

> an old and much respected practitioner in Kensington, named Haffenden … was apprehended and charged at the police court with criminally procuring abortion … from the mental anxiety arising out of the ruinous nature of the charge, [he] committed suicide by poison, although in the last document he penned during his life he declared his innocence … the jury, after an absence of six minutes, gave a verdict of 'not guilty'. (Glaister 1886)

In Glaister's opinion, until *Kitson v Playfair* the law was generally understood by medical practitioners to impose on them a duty to notify the relevant authorities of cases in which abortion was suspected or had been brought to their attention. However, Hawkins's views had 'traversed that understanding' (Glaister 1938). As the fates of Haffenden and Playfair definitively demonstrated, dubiety in the understanding and practice of the law of notification could have serious consequences. With confusion and discontent growing among doctors, in 1895–6 the RCP set up a committee to consider the medical practitioner's duty in relation to criminal abortion. At their instance, legal opinion was taken from Sir Edward Clarke (1841–1931) and Horace Avory (1851–1935).

Royal College of Physicians – Avory and Clarke

Clarke was a pre-eminent common law Queen's Counsel and was MP for Plymouth from 1880–1900. He was appointed Solicitor General in 1886 and held the post until the fall of Lord Salisbury's government in 1892. When Salisbury returned to power in 1895, Clarke turned down the position of Solicitor General in order

5 Turner was also vice-president of the National Cyclists Union, and the article was part of a series the *BMJ* ran on the health benefits of cycling (see Bartrip 1990).

to continue in private practice. In 1897 he declined an offer to become Master of the Rolls as it would have precluded him from taking any part in politics. In contrast to Clarke's esteemed position within the law, Avory was still building his legal career. Having 'devilled' for Clarke as a junior counsel, Avory rose through the legal ranks to become King's Counsel in 1901. By 1910 he was a judge on the King's Bench division of the High Court, a position he used to challenge the medical profession's traditional view of confidentiality in 1914.

The opinions of Clarke and Avory constituted a large part of the report on the doctor's duty to notify abortion presented to the RCP on 30 April 1896. The discussion focused on two main areas where members of the RCP felt the correct course of action was not clear. In the first instance, they wished to clarify when the act of procuring abortion was lawful. What, for instance, was to be done in a case where a pregnant woman's life was at risk unless her pregnancy was terminated? Would abortion in this instance be legal and, if not, would the doctor be held responsible for the resulting death of the mother? This point was dealt with quite briefly by Clarke and Avory, who stated their opinion that the law did not forbid abortion during pregnancy or the destruction of the child during labour where it was necessary to save the mother's life.

The second, and altogether more complex, matter requiring clarification was what the medical practitioner's duty was once he suspected, or was made aware of, a case of criminal abortion. The question could be subdivided. Would a medical practitioner lay himself open to being charged as an accessory to the crime if he gave medical aid to a woman post-abortion? The crime tarred both the person who carried out the act, and the woman who solicited it, as felons. Therefore, by knowingly aiding a patient who was unwell as a result of a criminal abortion, a practitioner could feasibly be brought up on a charge of being an accessory to the crime. Would a doctor be liable to indictment for misprision of felony if he did not report the crime?[6] Finally, did the doctor have any privilege with regard to secrets confided in him by patients?

Taking the questions in order, Clarke and Avory stated that, in their opinion, a medical practitioner did not render himself liable as an accessory if he treated a patient whom he knew or suspected had had a criminal abortion, provided he did nothing to assist the patient to escape from, or defeat justice. This inferred that the doctor should not hinder the law, but had no obligation to actively assist justice by notifying the authorities that a criminal act had taken place. In other words, in relation to criminal abortion the physician's duty was simply to treat the patient to the best of his skill, with no active dual loyalty duty to notify the law. With regard to misprision of felony, the medical practitioner would not be liable merely because he did not give information in a case where he suspected criminal

6 Misprision of felony was the concealment of a crime committed by another, but without such previous knowledge or subsequent assistance of the criminal as would make the party concealing an accessory before or after the fact. The crime was becoming obsolete by the early twentieth century.

abortion. In a case where a practitioner was told by a patient the name of someone she was about to go to in order to have an abortion carried out, Clarke and Avory thought that the medical practitioner had a duty to warn the person, presumably meaning the named individual, that such a statement had been made.

Clarke and Avory were asked specifically what duty lay on the medical practitioner who suspected criminal abortion had been procured. Their answer, that a medical man should tend to a patient he believed to have been party to a criminal abortion, seems entirely in keeping with a humane justice system. It would be improper for an ill woman's health, or indeed life, to rest upon the single opinion of a medical practitioner as to whether she had committed a crime. In that scenario the doctor would be simultaneously judge, jury and executioner. Rather, justice required that the process should be based on evidence collected and discussed before the courts, whose obligation and purpose was to establish the criminality or otherwise of the act. However, Clarke and Avory gave no indication that a duty lay with a doctor to notify the law where criminal abortion was suspected. Rather, they suggested that a doctor who treated a woman without notifying the police would not be likely to face a charge of misprision of felony. Moreover, if a doctor became aware that a colleague was about to carry out a criminal abortion he should inform the colleague that he was aware of the fact. The RCP was left with the impression that their members should carry out abortions, before or during birth, where the mother's life was at risk; medically treat, but in no other way assist, women who came to them after a criminal abortion; and that they were under no obligation to notify the law.[7]

To their question on medical privilege, the RCP received a straightforward rejection of the idea of an existing medical privilege. In response to a request as to how to go about getting a change in the law on privilege, Clarke and Avory suggested that if they were right in the views they had expressed, no alteration of the law would probably be desired. Their general advice was that medical practitioners should exercise their own discretion as to when information should be given in particular cases. The doctor should follow his conscience.

These opinions are important, not least because they represent a specific consultation of legal opinion by the RCP on the question of confidentiality at the turn of the twentieth century. They were also referred to by Professor Robert Saundby in his early twentieth-century work *Medical Ethics: A Guide to Professional Conduct*. Saundby was an ex-chairman of both the BMA Council and of its Central Ethical Committee; in 1912 he was elected to the GMC as a direct representative of the medical profession. In *Medical Ethics*, Saundby related the opinions expressed by Avory and Clarke in their consultation with the RCP as being 'to the effect that a medical man should not reveal facts which had come to his knowledge in the course of his professional duties, even in so extreme a case as where there are grounds to suspect that a criminal offence had been committed'

7 This last point was raised by Professor Saundby in 1915, during his analysis of Clarke and Avory's opinions expressed before the RCP in 1896.

(Saundby 1907). Unsurprisingly, this view was picked up by, and provoked a reaction from, the judiciary. Perhaps more unexpectedly, the judge who raised the objection was Horace Avory, one of the two lawyers whose opinions provided the basis of Saundby's statement.

Avory and Annie Hodgkiss

Sitting as judge at the Birmingham Assizes on 1 December 1914, Avory was forced to throw out a case against Annie Hodgkiss for the manslaughter of Ellen Armstrong, who had died from the effects of an illegal abortion. Armstrong, a young unmarried woman, whose family had been patients of Dr A[8] for some time, was taken ill and admitted to the Birmingham Women's Hospital. Dr A visited Armstrong in hospital. During the visit Armstrong told Dr A that she had had an abortion and gave the name of the woman who had performed it. She explicitly asked Dr A not to tell anyone, a promise which Dr A considered binding. Armstrong subsequently, and very abruptly, died of a haemorrhage. Having carefully gone through the papers connected with the case, Avory was forced to state that, in the absence of sufficient evidence, the jury was advised to find no true bill. In addressing the jury, Avory made it quite clear that he believed that the opinion he had expressed along with Clarke in 1896 had been misrepresented in Saundby's textbook on medical ethics. Avory's implication was that in the case before him, he felt that there had been a failure on the part of Dr A to perform the duty which society had a right to expect from a medical practitioner placed in such circumstances, and notify the authorities.

This opinion was picked up by Sir Charles Mathews, Director of Public Prosecutions, who wrote to William Hempson, solicitor to the BMA, on 14 December 1914.[9] He requested that Avory's views be given wide circulation among the medical profession in order that they might correct the inaccuracy of Saundby's book.[10] If Mathews expected his letter would be met with deferential compliance, he was mistaken. Hempson's prompt reply noted that Avory's views were not in accordance with other decisions which had been passed down from the Bench at various times, notably in *Kitson v Playfair*. Moreover, the general question involved was 'of the highest importance to the medical profession and is far-reaching in point of principle'. He suggested that authoritative guidance was required and that the body which held the respect of the profession in such matters was the CEC of the BMA, to whom he was legal adviser. With Mathews'

8 The doctor involved in the case was referred to only as Dr A throughout.

9 Sir Charles Mathews (1850–1920) was Director of Public Prosecutions from 1908 until his death in 1920.

10 This letter and the following correspondence between Mathews and Hempson are all contained in the BMA CEC Minutes for 1914/15.

permission – their correspondence having been clearly marked 'Personal' – he could raise the matter for discussion by the CEC.

Mathews assented to this suggestion with one major proviso. As far as possible, discussion of the question of medical secrecy in relation to abortion should be kept out of the press in order to avoid controversy.[11] In his own words, 'what I should deprecate would be a press controversy upon the subject to which men of eminence in the medical profession might become contributors, and in which they might announce themselves as entirely differing from the views of Mr Justice Avory, and as declining to be bound by them'. It is not surprising that the Director of Public Prosecutions would advise against the sparking of a press controversy in which eminent physicians might be inclined to lead a rebellion against the law. However, Hempson was not willing to give even an implied guarantee that the topic could be entirely withheld from the medical press.[12] Evidently, both sides foresaw the far-reaching implications of the question of medical confidentiality and the potential for direct conflict over the issue. The judiciary wished to keep direct challenges to their authority out of the public gaze, but Mathews also recognised the difficulty the legal system would be faced with if it lost the ability to authoritatively demand medical evidence. Acting on behalf of the medical profession, Hempson was aware that popular opinion would be a strong factor in maintaining their position, and that public support would be crucial if any challenge to the law was to be contemplated. After further correspondence it was agreed that a meeting between Hempson and Mathews would be held to discuss the matter.[13]

This meeting took place on 22 December 1914 at Whitehall. Hempson made it clear that he did not believe Avory's views would meet with approval or compliance by the medical profession. In response, Mathews indicated that there could be no support for practitioners who claimed that statements made to them by patients should be held to be inviolable. Emphasising their dual loyalty obligations to the law, he underlined that doctors 'were citizens of the State, [and] that as such they owed a higher duty to the State in aid of the suppression of crime than to their patient'.[14] However, he conceded that solicitors, barristers and ministers of religion were not under the same obligation to disclose information, and that they were not subject to the same duty as he contended attached to the medical profession.

Hempson enquired whether the state proposed to offer protection to medical men, who disclosed information when required in accordance with their proposed public duty, from any civil proceedings which might be brought against them by patients. Mathews was reluctant to commit himself on this issue, but he 'obviously

11 BMA CEC Minutes, 1914/15. Mathews to Hempson, 17 December 1914.

12 BMA CEC Minutes, 1914/15. Hempson to Mathews, 18 December 1914.

13 BMA CEC Minutes, 1914/15. Mathews to Hempson, 19 December 1914 and Hempson to Mathews, 21 December 1914.

14 Taken from Mr Hempson's note on his meeting with the Director of Public Prosecutions, 22 December, 1914. BMA CEC Minutes, 1914/15.

recognised that such obligation of protection would not be assumed by the State'. Hempson suggested that once the BMA had given the matter its due consideration, a deputation could meet with some high state official, such as the Home Secretary, in order to obtain an authoritative ruling on the point. He reiterated that Avory's dictum did not receive support from other legal authorities of an equal or higher standing, a challenge which Mathews conceded. However, Mathews confided in Hempson that the Lord Chief Justice[15] had considered and approved the decision of Avory and that, as Chief Coroner of England and Wales, he proposed that a copy of Avory's views, bearing the mark of his confirmatory approval, should be sent to every coroner in England and Wales as 'a guiding light as to the attitude which it was their duty to adopt should similar cases arise at any inquest before them'. Hempson must have been left with the impression that, while contradictory decisions had been handed down by judges in the past, there was a growing uniformity of opinion among key legal figures that medical practitioners should be made aware of their ultimate duty to the state and their necessary contribution to the ends of justice.

BMA Central Ethical Committee and Saundby's Memo

Having been given permission to bring the question of medical confidentiality, as raised by Avory, before the CEC, Hempson arranged a meeting for 8 January 1915. In light of the fact that much of Avory's criticism of the medical profession had focused on Saundby's supposed misrepresentation of the views expressed during the consultation with the RCP in 1895, Saundby was invited to attend the meeting. He was unable to do so, but sent in his place a memorandum he had written on the subject, which he intended to submit for publication in the *BMJ* but was currently withholding pending the consideration of the matter by the RCP. His memo had been read and approved by both Dr A, the doctor in the case over which Avory had presided, and the honorary surgeon of the hospital in which the patient had died.

Referring back to the RCP's consultation with Clarke and Avory, Saundby's memorandum reiterated the difficult position medical men found themselves in with regard to their duty in relation to the 'unfortunately frequent' crime of abortion. He contended that the legal opinion stated by Clarke and Avory omitted all reference to any obligation to communicate with the police and therefore 'they may be said not unfairly to have given ground for inference that in their opinion no such obligation exists, for otherwise they surely should have included it in their statement of his duty'.[16] This seems a fair point to make. As noted above, the question which had been put to Clarke and Avory had explicitly requested advice on the duty of the medical practitioner, who knew or believed he was in attendance upon a case where criminal abortion had been procured. To say that

15 Rufus Isaacs, Lord Reading.

16 Saundby's Memorandum as contained in the BMA CEC Minutes 8 January 1915.

a doctor should treat the woman to the best of his skill and do nothing to aid her from escaping justice, without explicitly stating that he had a firm duty to inform the authorities that a criminal act had taken place, does seem to have encouraged the interpretation which Saundby took. Indeed, if Clarke and Avory's answer had not conveyed this impression to its audience, but rather intended being an avoidance of the fundamental question, presumably such an obvious omission would have been picked up by the RCP who were anxious to have greater clarity on this complex practical problem.

Saundby's memorandum indicated that the medical profession was disposed to draw a general distinction between cases in which the patient recovered or was expected to do so, and cases where death resulted or was likely to do so as a result of an illegal operation. In the former instance, the profession was 'indisposed to break the implied bond of professional secrecy'. In the latter, there was recognition of a duty to help in securing that a crime with such serious consequences did not go unpunished. In recognition of the apparent lack of consistency on this position, Saundby suggested that justification was found in the doctor's desire to avoid the scandal that would be brought upon the patient and her family if he were to report every case of criminal abortion which came to his attention. Significantly, he bolstered this justification by stating his belief that public opinion not only supported such an attitude but would be 'shocked and outraged' were the practitioner to act in another manner. Any change to this view would have to be brought about through fresh legislation, sanctioned by public opinion.

Saundby acknowledged that by making such a distinction in practice it was inevitable that there would be cases in which the death of a patient, whom the doctor had believed would recover, would occur suddenly – leaving no time for a dying deposition. Indeed, these were the circumstances of the case over which Avory had presided, and which sparked his tirade against the profession. Yet, Saundby believed such injustice as occurred in these cases could only be seen as an unfortunate consequence that could neither be blamed on the medical practitioner acting under the existing circumstances, nor be done away with until public opinion had changed. Those who read Saundby's memorandum would have been struck by two key points. The distinction between notifying criminal abortion in cases where the patient was likely to die and non-notification where the patient was likely to recover, while acknowledged as imperfect, would require legislation to change it. Moreover, such legislation would require the backing of public opinion, which in Saundby's view firmly supported the position adopted by medical practitioners.

Although Saundby was unable to attend the meeting of the CEC, the 'importance of the subject'[17] led the chairman, Reginald Langdon-Down, to request the BMA solicitor, Hempson, to attend. His opinions were recorded in a draft memorandum prepared pursuant to the meeting of 8 January 1915, by James Neal, the BMA

17 BMA CEC Minutes, 1914/15. Phrase used in a letter from James Neal, Deputy Medical Secretary to the BMA to members of the CEC, 1 January 1915.

Deputy Medical Secretary. Hempson explained that solicitors and barristers had an absolute privilege of protection with regard to statements made to them in their professional capacity, and that, by custom, courts normally recognised protection for ministers of religion. However, no other class of persons was accorded such protection by state authority or Act of Parliament. In the case of medical practitioners, Hempson reiterated the point he had put to Mathews, namely, that there was a conflict of authority on the matter. Quoting from Hawkins's ruling in *Kitson v Playfair*, Hempson noted that while this decision had given a clear indication that medical men were not to go running to the authorities in every case of illegal abortion, it was contended in 'certain quarters'[18] that medical men, as citizens of the state, owed a higher duty to the state in the detection of crime, than to their own patients. Presumably the 'certain quarters' was a reference to Hempson's prior meeting with Mathews.

Neal's memorandum made clear the CEC's stance on this apparent dichotomy. In the absence of state protection for doctors who found themselves subjected to civil proceedings as a result of notifying a case of suspected illegal abortion which was subsequently judged to be untrue, and the prospect of resultant high damages – the £12,000 damages initially awarded against Playfair was an ominous precedent – the committee felt that the state could not reasonably claim that a medical practitioner had an obligation to breach patient confidentiality without the patient's consent. Furthermore, the committee drew attention to the ill consequences that any departure from the 'usual custom of regarding the confidences of a patient as sacred' would have by deterring the general public from seeking qualified medical opinion. Any person who had been involved in a criminal act would not be able to seek medical attention for fear of personal incrimination.

As a result of its discussions, the committee made three recommendations to the BMA Council. Firstly, no information should be given under any circumstances without patient consent. Secondly, if the state could not protect doctors from legal actions that might arise as a result of disclosure, it had no authority to claim that doctors were obliged to disclose patient information. As well as ventilating the question in the *BMJ*, the final resolution proposed sending a copy of the resolutions to the appropriate Department of State.[19] In light of the committee's knowledge of the stance advocated by both the Director of Public Prosecutions and the Lord Chief Justice, its proposals were a sign of defiance. Any suggestion that the BMA Council might reject or dilute such confrontational recommendations was quashed by its adoption of them in an amended form on 27 January 1915. Far from acting in a conciliatory manner, the council's only amendment was the removal of the conditional element of the second resolution. This deletion implied that the BMA was not simply looking to protect its members' interests by seeking state protection

18 BMA CEC Minutes, 1914/15. Point 8 of the Draft Memorandum from the CEC meeting 8 January 1915.

19 The first two recommendations came to be known, and are later referred to, as Minutes 542 and 550 respectively.

from financial damages arising from civil proceedings against them. It was clearly stating that the medical profession took very seriously the duty of confidentiality and would not give it up without a fight.[20]

The final resolution underlined that the council would not limit their sabre-rattling to medical meetings. Not content with sending a copy of a resolution, denying state authority over the medical profession with regard to notification of illegal abortion, to the relevant state department, the final resolution proposed ventilating the whole question in the medical press, against the expressed wishes of the Director of Public Prosecutions. The gauntlet thrown down, initially by Avory and then by Mathews, had been firmly taken up by the BMA, which clearly had no intention of backing away from a fight.

In addition to the above decisions, the council passed a resolution empowering the CEC to take 'any further action considered desirable',[21] including sending a deputation to the appropriate state department. By mid-March, Hempson was able to report that he had, again, met with Mathews to discuss the letters which had been sent to the Lord Chief Justice and the Home Secretary by instruction of the council at the end of January. As a result of this meeting it was quite possible that the BMA would be asked to send representatives to meet the Law Officers of the Crown and that the RCP and the RCS might also be involved in such a meeting. He had given Mathews an undertaking that, for the time being, no correspondence should appear in the *BMJ* on the matter. Evidently, publication of the divergence in medical and legal opinion on the issue of confidentiality was being strongly resisted in legal quarters. At their first meeting, Hempson had made it quite clear to Mathews that not even an implied guarantee could be given that a subject of such magnitude could be kept out of the press. Moreover the CEC and council had both made it clear that the matter required ventilation in the medical press at the very least. It can only be assumed that undertaking not to publish correspondence on professional secrecy in the *BMJ* was a prerequisite to being granted an opportunity to discuss the matter with the Law Officers of the Crown. The judiciary were trying to keep the issue away from the public gaze, and were forcing the medical profession to comply with its wishes by discussing it in private. For the time being, the BMA complied. The only article in which the issue of confidentiality / professional secrecy was discussed in the *BMJ* of that year was the Supplementary Report of Council 1914–1915 in the *BMJ*, 3 July 1915 (Supplement, 4).

---

20 The content that was removed from the second resolution was reiterated in an amendment to Point 9 of the Draft Memorandum of the CEC meeting 8 January 1915. It read: 'The Committee is advised that no obligation rests upon the medical practitioner voluntarily to disclose the confidence of his patient without the patient's consent. It suggests that, if the State desires to set up such an obligation, it should at the very least preface such an endeavour by affording to the practitioner protection from any legal consequences that may result from his action.'

21 BMA CEC Minutes, 1914/15. 19 February 1915.

The CEC recommended that any deputation sent to the Law Officers of the Crown on this matter should consist of the chairman of representative meetings, chairman of council, treasurer, the chairman and deputy chairman of the CEC, the medical secretary, deputy medical secretary and the solicitor. In short, a high-ranking slice of the BMA. It further recommended that if the two Royal Colleges were also invited to send deputations, then a prior meeting between the Colleges' representatives and the BMA deputation should be arranged. Consensus among medical opinion and unity in approach would be significant assets if any serious challenge to legal authority was to be made.

In fact, it was a deputation from the BMA alone which met with the Lord Chief Justice, the Attorney General, the Public Prosecutor and other legal authorities on 3 May 1915. With a defensive qualification that no observation made by the Lord Chief Justice during the meeting could be taken as a judicial pronouncement of the law, the Law Officers reiterated their assertion that doctors had a duty to notify cases of abortion. This rule was subject to three limitations. The doctor had to be of opinion, either from examination of the patient or because of a communication from the patient, that abortion had been attempted or procured by artificial intervention; the intervention had to have been carried out by someone other than the patient herself; and the doctor had to believe that the woman was likely to die as a result of the abortion and that 'there was no hope of her ultimate recovery'.[22]

Anxious to have clarity on the matter, the CEC had the wording of the above three limitations approved by the Lord Chief Justice in a meeting with Hempson on 11 May 1915. Once again there was an explicit request from the legal side that no publication of the matter in the press or the *BMJ* should be made, as the Lord Chief Justice did not wish the question to be openly discussed until something definite had been arrived at or until he had given his sanction to it being publicly known. In fact, the Lord Chief Justice's views were published as part of the supplementary report of council in the *BMJ* supplement of 3 July 1915. The Lord Chief Justice was informed that the BMA wished to include his statements in their report of council and that this would entail a discussion of the subject at the forthcoming ARM in July. The CEC stressed that the BMA had no desire to open any further debate of the matter but they had to respond to the remarks of Avory at the Birmingham Assizes. The law could not publicly provoke discussion and then demand that the medical profession gave no open response.

The GMC, RCS and RCP

In their meeting on 28 May, the CEC also noted a letter which had been received from the registrar of the GMC, indicating that he had received a communication from Mathews relating to the notification, by medical men to the police, of illegal operations. Mathews had made reference to the resolutions which had

22 BMA CEC Minutes 1914/15. 28 May 1915.

been formulated by the BMA, and the president of the GMC requested a copy of these and any other relevant information for the GMC executive committee's consideration. With interest in the subject snowballing, it was again agreed that the RCP and the RCS should be approached in order that a meeting of representatives could discuss the duties of medical men in relation to criminal abortion.

On 10 June, the council of the RCS passed a resolution indicating that, as they had already considered the matter and sent a reply to Mathews, they could see no advantage in the proposed conference. Their reply to the BMA included a copy of their letter to Mathews. This letter gave a clear indication that they could not concur with the opinions expressed by Avory, not least because they were not given as the basis of a judicial decision. The RCS had never defined the doctor–patient relationship but it had always recognised that complete confidence between doctor and patient was essential in the treatment of disease. In their opinion, it was fortunate that such confidence nearly always existed and was of incalculable advantage to the patient and the public. No written rules could have any binding effect in what they termed a matter of 'honour and conscience'[23] and ultimately the conduct of each medical practitioner had to be decided by his own conscience and sense of duty to his patient and to the state. The letter concluded that the rarity of complaints as to the conduct of medical practitioners in criminal cases *vis-à-vis* the frequency with which they were involved in them indicated that there was no need to attempt to frame rules for the guidance of fellows and members of the RCS on such questions. 'The Council believe that in the future, as in the past, the course to be taken can safely be left to the medical practitioner.' The honourable physician and his conscience were, usually, the best judge of each situation.

On 15 June, the RCP, having had the matter under consideration by its censors board since the remarks of Avory had been brought to their attention by Mathews in early January, discussed the BMA proposal for a meeting. During the meeting it passed five resolutions. The first iterated that each medical practitioner had a moral obligation to secrecy which could not be breached without patient consent. The second and third together stated that doctors should urge a patient suffering the ill-effects of an illegal abortion to give evidence against the abortionist. This was especially advisable in cases where the patient was likely to die. If, however, she refused, the doctor was 'under no obligation (so the college is advised) to take further action'.[24] This appears to confirm Saundby's assertion that Clarke and Avory had left the RCP with the belief that they had no absolute obligation to notify criminal abortion. The remaining two resolutions recommended that doctors should obtain the best possible medical and legal advice, not only to ensure the validity of any evidence a patient might give but also to protect the doctor from subsequent litigation; and that if a patient should die in circumstances where criminal abortion was suspected, the doctor should refuse to issue a death certificate but communicate with the coroner. Having expressed the position as

23 BMA CEC Minutes, 1914/15. RCS to Director of Public Prosecutions, 2 July 1915.

24 BMA CEC Minutes, 1914/15. RCP to BMA, 2 July 1915.

they saw it, and acknowledged that they were looking to obtain further legal advice on confidentiality in relation to criminal abortion, the RCP did not see any need for a meeting with the BMA and the RCS.

It was therefore quite clear by mid-1915, that Avory's remarks at the Birmingham Assizes in 1914 had sparked discussion of the question of medical confidentiality among key bodies of the medical profession, each of which had independently come to the conclusion that they could not concur with his point of view. No general meeting of these medical bodies took place, although their opinions were shared through confidential correspondence. With legal opinion, in the form of the Lord Chief Justice and Director of Public Prosecutions, firmly in support of Avory, and opposed to any general discussion of the matter in the lay or medical press, the whole situation reached a hiatus in terms of institutional interaction by the end of July 1915. To an extent this is probably attributable to the disruption caused by the First World War, which engaged the full attention of the BMA who undertook to organise medical provision for the war effort. Andrew Morrice (2002b) suggests that the medical profession were victorious in the stand-off over medical confidentiality in 1915. If so, it was more by default – throwing the last punch before the bell sounded for the end of the round – than because of any convincing argument they made. While the First World War enveloped attention, the stated differences between legal and medical opinion on the relative merits of the doctor's duty to the patient and to the state, pointed towards a resumption of the dispute in the near future.

The only other record of the issue arising in the BMA CEC minutes for 1915, was a letter received from the assistant secretary of the Renfrewshire panel committee informing the BMA that a recent case in the Inner House of the Court of Session (the supreme court of Scotland) had very recently considered the question of privileged communications made to a Roman Catholic priest. The case concerned a paternity dispute in which one of the parties had made a statement to the priest, and while the sheriff substitute (county court judge), who originally heard the case, had decided in favour of a priestly privilege, the Court of Session reversed his judgement. This point would have been of great interest to the CEC, for not only did it illustrate that the question of confidentiality was being more generally probed, but also any argument for medical privilege would be more akin to that which had been customarily given to ministers of religion than to the privilege accorded to solicitors and barristers. The committee requested that they be informed when the case was published in the law reports.

While other issues came to dominate the debate over the boundaries of medical confidentiality, the question of abortion did not disappear. The Honorary Secretary of the Sheffield division wrote to the BMA in June 1918, seeking advice relative to her being summoned to give evidence in Court. In 1917 she attended a woman who had suffered a miscarriage in the seventh month of her pregnancy, and had returned to see her earlier in 1918 when she was again ill as a result of miscarriage, this time in the third or fourth month. Criminal abortion was suspected in both cases. The CEC suggested that when she was asked by the court to disclose information which she had obtained in the exercise of her professional duties she should protest that she could not betray the professional confidence of her patient. She should then be guided by the directions of the magistrate or judge. In light of the frequency with which similar queries, cases and advice arose over subsequent years, this short paragraph in the CEC minutes assumes an altogether more pivotal importance than the committee could have realised.

Summary

The nineteenth century was a period of far-reaching change for medical practitioners. The professionalisation of medicine, the founding of medical journals and the BMA, and the establishment, under the 1858 Medical Act, of the GMC with its authority to maintain a single register of qualified practitioners, meant that by the early twentieth century the issue of medical confidentiality was addressed by a more unified and cohesive body of practitioners. Medical ethics had evolved, in the first half of the nineteenth century, predominantly, though not exclusively, as a response to intra-professional conflict in an unregulated marketplace. After the establishment of the GMC with its power to hold disciplinary hearings and remove practitioners from the Medical Register, medicine had the beginnings of a new system of professional self-regulation and prescriptive advice on professional conduct. As noted, for medical confidentiality at least, the GMC's approach was far from perfect and practitioners were still faced with contradiction and confusion on the correct action to be taken with regard to many ethical dilemmas. This point was equally true when it came to judicial interpretations of the law. The decisions of Hawkins and Inglis sent conflicting signals to practitioners about their duties as professionals and as citizens of the state. Leaving disclosure decisions up to the individual doctor generated uncertainty. On the one hand practitioners were left unprotected from legal proceedings against them in cases where someone they had accused of performing an illegal operation was found not guilty. On the other, they received condemnation from legal authorities for their perceived failure to do their duty as citizens when they did not notify the authorities. Failure to notify deaths could cost practitioners through relatively small fines; questioning the honour of a middle class lady, as William Smoult Playfair discovered, could cost many thousands of pounds in damages; and a false allegation of facilitating abortion could cost a practitioner his reputation, his income or, in the case of Haffenden, his life.

State intervention in medicine had placed doctors in a pivotal role in public health through notification acts and, post-1911, partially state-funded health care. The rise in the number of situations in which medical men were employed by someone other than the patient they were directly treating led to conflicting obligations for practitioners. The medical journals attempted to respond to questions about the disclosing of medical information about employees to their employers; whether a prospective bride should be forewarned of her fiance's contagious VD; or what to do in cases of suspected abortion. Such complex problems, by dint of the recognised importance of the particulars of each case, did not easily permit of standardised advice. As with the GMC rulings and the legal opinions, the effect produced was uncertainty for medical practitioners.

Lord Mansfield's decision in the Duchess of Kingston case distinguished between information demanded in court and breach of confidence outside the witness box. While there was no change in the practitioner's duty to give evidence in court, the nineteenth century saw an extension of the law's demands on doctors as the state tightened its grip on them as public servants of general welfare and justice. However, practitioners still largely remained individual competitors in a challenging marketplace. Herein lay the crux of the conflict. While the state, and the elevation of medicine into a more regulated profession, pulled practitioners towards collective goals, traditional values and the competitive marketplace clung on to them and held their focus on the individual interests of both patient and practitioner. State interest in the collective would need more than fines and small fees to change doctors' traditional belief in the primacy of their duty to the patient. As the judiciary frequently reminded them, doctors had duties as citizens of the state. However, as many practitioners emphasised, while certainly citizens, they were not direct employees of the state.

It is clear that the question of medical confidentiality was an important one in the early twentieth century, involving high-status individuals and interest groups. Avory, who triggered debate in late 1914, had been involved in the consultation with the RCP in 1895–6. The interpretation of his remarks by Saundby's textbook drew severe criticism from legal quarters. The attempts by the Director of Public Prosecutions, with the informal support of the Lord Chief Justice, to cajole the medical profession into putting duty to the state above duty to the patient, met with opposition by each of the medical bodies approached: the BMA, the RCS, and the RCP. Although no meeting took place between these three bodies, it is clear that they did communicate their opinions to each other, and there was further institutional interaction when BMA representatives met with the Lord Chief Justice, Attorney General, Public Prosecutor and other legal authorities to discuss the question in May 1915. The strong desire by the judiciary to keep intra-professional discussions out of the press, and the BMA's initial reaction, are worthy of note when it is considered that both sides claimed to be acting in the interests, or with the support, of the public.

The hiatus in institutional interaction on the question by mid-1915 did not equate to a definitive resolution of the question. The CEC minutes record that the question continued to arise in subsequent months and years. Although professional secrecy was involved in matters ranging from the payment of farm labourers' wages to the admission of individuals to mother and child homes, the issues of criminal abortion and VD recurred time and again. While abortion had been most prominent in the 1895–6 and 1914–15 discussions, VD came to dominate the debate over medical confidentiality in the early interwar years. The medical profession were joined by the newly established Ministry of Health in seeking to challenge the judiciary, and overturn the 150-year-old precedent of the Duchess of Kingston's case.

Chapter 4
The Ministry of Health

> Truth, like all other good things, may be loved unwisely, may be pursued too keenly, may cost too much. (Knight Bruce in *Pearse v Pearse*, quoted by Minister of Health in correspondence to Lord Chancellor, 3 June 1920, NA MH78/253)

The First World War exposed large numbers of civilian doctors to medical practice in a military context, providing many with their first experience of the contrasting approach to medical confidentiality in the military compared to private practice. In his analysis of the role of doctors in combating malingering, Roger Cooter states 'common soldiers and sailors were not of course private patients; nevertheless, civilian doctors carried over into the military norms of confidentiality and trust, sufficient for many of them to find the business of exposing malingerers deeply repellent' (Cooter, 1998). In private practice, the perception that a doctor could be trusted to keep his patients' secrets was an asset in securing him business in a competitive medical marketplace where reputation directly affected income. While the importance of medical confidentiality had long been emphasised in writings on professional ethics, by the early twentieth century the traditional approach to the issue was coming under increasing pressure. The impact of poor health on the industrial and military competitiveness of the country ensured that growing emphasis was given to a public health agenda, which often required notification of cases of infectious or contagious disease to the local Medical Officer of Health. The emerging specialism of public health brought with it new categories of doctors whose priorities differed from those of private practitioners. In Roy Porter's words 'a cohort of doctors emerged, beholden not to individual clients but in the guise of guardians of the health of the populations generally' (Porter 1997).

Royal Commission on VD

While public health measures typically required the breaching of patient confidentiality in order to notify cases of contagious or infectious disease, VD was viewed differently. The comparative merits of notification and compulsory treatment of VD were frequently advocated, particularly in Scotland, but the balance fell in favour of the importance of protecting confidentiality – save during the two World Wars, when there were large increases in cases and specific regulations were passed to facilitate contact tracing. Attempts to address the problem of VD initially reflected broader attempts to clean up cities, with an emphasis on female prostitutes as vectors of the disease (Hall 2001). Growing awareness of the extent of the problem and its potential impact on national efficiency brought calls for

Government action, eventually resulting in a Royal Commission on VD, set up in 1913. The Commission issued its final report in 1916, strongly advocating the view that confidentiality of diagnosis and treatment was essential to the success of public health measures intended to check the rapid spread of such diseases among the population (Hall 2001, 126).

Encouraging individuals who suspected they may have contracted VD, a physically and socially stigmatic set of diseases, to seek medical assistance, depended on giving assurances that diagnosis and treatment would be confidential. The Commission's view on this was reflected in Article II (2) of the VD Regulations of 1916, which stated that: 'All information obtained in regard to any person treated under a scheme approved in pursuance of this article shall be regarded as confidential.' This represented endorsement of the importance of confidentiality by the Local Government Board, which implemented the scheme, and the Ministry of Health, which took over responsibility when it came into being in 1919. The particular importance of confidentiality in VD treatment came across in Parliamentary debates. For example, Walter Long, the President of the Local Government Board, stated:

> There is a feature attached to these diseases which does not belong to the ordinary troubles of health. The patient does not like it to be known that he or she is suffering from this disease; they like to conceal the fact; they do not want it notified. Therefore if we are really going to deal with our suffering population, we must take care not only that there is proper provision for their treatment, but that everything is done that can be done to get it without notification … What I am imploring them [hospitals running VD treatment clinics] to do is to take the patients in and welcome them from wherever they come, to ask them no questions, and seeking in no way to identify them with this horrible misfortune that has overtaken them. (Hansard, Parliamentary Debates, House of Commons (84), 239)

In order to avoid delays in implementing the VD treatment scheme, the Local Government Board did not seek parliamentary support for the incorporation of the Royal Commission's recommendations into new statute law. Rather, using powers provided by the Public Health Act 1913, the Local Government Board declared VD a national emergency, allowing it to insist that local authorities adopt the measures for treatment contained in the 1916 VD Regulations (Evans 1992, 421–2). While this minimised delays in the short run, the lack of statutory backing had significant repercussions for the debate over confidentiality in subsequent years.

The publication of the report of the Royal Commission on VD in 1916 brought new issues to be contemplated by the BMA CEC. Paragraph 205 of the report recommended that the law should be amended to allow that a communication made *bona fide* by a medical practitioner to a parent, guardian or other person directly interested in the welfare of a woman, or man, with the intention of delaying or preventing them from marrying a person with an infectious form of VD, should be treated as a privileged communication. Significantly, this proposal had the support of the President of the Probate Division.[1] The parliamentary subcommittee of the BMA medico-political committee asked the CEC to consider the implications of paragraph 205 in relation to their previous consideration of the question of medical confidentiality. The CEC concluded that in light of council minutes 542 and 550 of 27 January 1915, it was 'very strongly' of the opinion that medical practitioners could not make such disclosures as were contemplated in paragraph 205 of the royal commission report without the consent of the patient (BMA CEC Minutes 6 June 1916). Furthermore, no amendment to the law which would allow such a communication to be privileged was required, 'unless and until the duty of making such communications is imposed on medical practitioners as a statutory obligation'. The council adopted the CEC's recommendations on this matter and passed a resolution indicating that it would be left to the chairman of the council to include a reference to the decision in the report, which was to be submitted to the ARM for 1916. This he did, and an amended version of the recommendation was put as a substantive motion to the 1916 meeting.[2] The resolution was lost. Uncertainty over correct action mirrored earlier concerns regarding notification of criminal abortion. What to do in the case of a syphilitic fiancé became a regular test, often revealing continued uncertainty.

Ministry of Health

The Ministry of Health, established in 1919, was a symbol of state interest in the welfare of the post-war population. Dr Christopher Addison, the first Minister of Health, was a staunch promoter of a social welfare agenda within Lloyd George's coalition government, including a highly ambitious scheme of slum clearance and house construction. Addison owed much of his political progress to close links with Lloyd George, having used his medical background to secure sufficient medical support to allow Lloyd George to implement his National Insurance scheme prior to the First World War. As Addison's biographers (Morgan and Morgan 1980) note, in addition to his own wartime experience at the Ministries of Munitions and Reconstruction, the nascent Ministry of Health had the 'formidable administrative team' of Sir Robert Morant as permanent secretary and Sir George Newman as chief medical officer; as well as the 'outstanding civil servant' Sir John Anderson as second secretary.

Medically trained, Newman took the M.D. at Edinburgh in 1895 the same year he received a diploma in public health from Cambridge. His keen interest in

1 Royal Commission on Venereal Diseases. Final Report of the Commissioners, (London: His Majesty's Stationery Office, 1916), para. 205.

2 The amended version read as follows: 'That in the opinion of the RB no amendment of the law to provide that a communication such as is contemplated in Recommendation 25 of the Royal Commission on Venereal Disease shall be privileged is called for.'

public health resulted in his appointment as Chief Medical Officer to the Board of Education's newly established school medical service in 1907, where he developed an early working relationship with Morant while drawing up plans for the medical inspection of schoolchildren. Newman also served on a number of health-related committees during the war before becoming Chief Medical Officer of Health in 1919, a post he held until 1935. Morant had been Permanent Secretary of the Board of Education from 1903 until leaving to become Chairman of the National Health Insurance Commission in 1911. He therefore had considerable experience of government interaction with the medical profession prior to his appointment as Permanent Secretary at the Ministry of Health in 1919. The same can be said for Anderson, who was Secretary of the National Health Insurance Commission from 1913 until he moved to the Ministry of Shipping in 1917. He became Additional Secretary to the Local Government Board in March 1919 and to the Ministry of Health when it took over the responsibilities of the Local Government Board in July 1919. Though formidable, Addison, Newman, Morant and Anderson did not last long as an administrative unit. In October 1919 Anderson left to become Chairman of the Inland Revenue. His absence was heightened by the sudden death of Morant in March 1920. Almost exactly a year later, Addison himself was moved to become Minister without portfolio. The disruption caused by the loss of such experienced personnel did not help the nascent Ministry of Health in its attempts to challenge the law over medical privilege in the early interwar years.

In taking over the Local Government Board's responsibilities, the Ministry inherited its VD treatment scheme, complete with the guarantee of confidentiality given in the 1916 VD regulations. While the Ministry's concern for public health typically entailed breaching confidentiality in order to gather statistics or isolate cases of infectious disease, in the case of VD, the Royal Commission report had emphasised that, unlike other notifiable public health threats, the rapid spread of VD would be best tackled by protecting the confidentiality of diagnosis and treatment.

Confidentiality of VD Treatment

The Ministry's attention was first drawn to the question of medical confidentiality by a series of letters querying the legal position of doctors when asked to disclose information at a patient's request. This situation most frequently arose with VD medical officers, whose testimony regarding the presence or transmission of VD could benefit their patients in divorce proceedings. In late October 1919, Colonel Bolam from the VD treatment centre at Newcastle Upon Tyne Royal Victoria Infirmary wrote to the Ministry of Health. Bolam, it should be noted, was also Chairman of the BMA Council, a direct representative on the GMC and a member of the consultative council of the Ministry, becoming a key adviser to the Ministry on VD during the interwar years, though he gave no indication that he was writing in any of these other official capacities. He indicated that a number of awkward medico-legal questions were arising relative to the disclosure of information about patients attending VD clinics, and suggested that a definite plan was needed for dealing with such cases (Bolam to Ministry of Health, 28 Oct 1919, NA MH78/253). The policy adopted by staff at the Newcastle hospital was not to disclose information about the patient to any third party, either in writing or verbally.

Bolam's question related to the importance of confidentiality in the effort to combat VD as laid out in Article II (2) of the Public Health (Venereal Disease) Regulations 1916. Francis Coutts, the Senior Medical Officer in charge of the Ministry's work on tuberculosis and VD, referred Bolam's letter to Machlachlan, who suggested that although the breaking of confidence was to be done at the patient's request this should not impact upon the doctor's duty under the 1916 regulations.[3] Having drafted a letter along these lines, Machlachlan requested the Ministry's legal adviser, Sir Maurice Linford Gwyer, review the position. Gwyer took the opposite view, interpreting the 1916 regulations as simply restating medical etiquette on the point. Etiquette would not impose any obligation upon the doctor to refrain from disclosing relevant medical information at the patient's request. Indeed, he noted that moral and social duty may require it of him. The VD regulations could not override the law, which stated that any doctor subpoenaed to give evidence in court must answer all questions put to him, though he may appeal to the judge for exemption. Gwyer believed that 'most judges will take a reasonable line in such a case and not adhere too rigidly to the strict letter of the law' (Gwyer to Machlachlan, 7 November 1919, NA MH78/253), a viewpoint he was forced to revise in light of subsequent test cases. He suggested that, ultimately, there could be no hard and fast rule as to when confidentiality should be held inviolate.

Gwyer's opinion formed the basis of Coutts' reply to Bolam in Newcastle. Recognising the growing importance of clarifying the extent of confidentiality under the VD regulations, a further 50 copies of Coutts' letter were made and it became the Ministry's stock response, to queries on confidentiality in the months that followed.[4] In recognition of this it is worth quoting in full.

> I have referred your letter of the 28th October to our legal adviser who is of the opinion that it is difficult to lay down any general rule for the guidance of the medical staff of Venereal Diseases Clinics. You are of course aware that the Public Health (Venereal Diseases) Regulations, 1916, provide that all information obtained in regard to any person treated under a scheme approved in pursuance of the regulations shall be regarded as confidential. This provision

---

3 There were six Senior Medical Officers, each with responsibility for a sub-section of the Ministry's portfolio.

4 For example, it was sent in response to a request, similar to Bolam's, from Arthur Griffiths, Secretary to the East Suffolk and Ipswich Hospital on 17 November 1919; and again to Hubert Sumner, Secretary to the Birmingham and Midland Hospital for skin and urinary diseases on 9 December 1919.

imposes an obligation on the medical officer not to disclose to third parties any facts which his examination of a patient brings to light, but a disclosure at the request of a patient would not constitute a breach of the regulations.

The question whether such a disclosure should be made in any particular case must depend on circumstances. Where a patient bona fide contemplates legal proceedings, or where legal proceedings have actually been begun, it would not be unreasonable for the doctor, when so requested by the patient, to indicate the nature of the evidence which he would be prepared to give, if subpoenaed for that purpose. He should always insist upon a subpoena for his own protection, and his evidence should be strictly confined to matters of fact, including such inferences as may legitimately be drawn from those facts.

The question whether the doctor should give a written statement to the patient's solicitors must depend on the facts of the case. Where these are complicated or obscure, it may not be unreasonable that the solicitors should be made aware what evidence the witness is prepared to give; and if they are not prepared to take the risk of calling a witness who has given them no proof of his evidence, a refusal on the part of the doctor might lead to a denial of justice to the patient. But written statements by the doctor should be the exception rather than the rule, and certificates should not be given in any case. They are inadmissible as evidence in legal proceedings and are clearly capable of abuse.

Our legal adviser is further of the opinion that the medical officer would be well advised to confine his disclosure of information, even though he has the patient's consent, to the patient's solicitors where proceedings have begun or are bona fide in contemplation, and to the parent or guardian in the case of a minor. The responsibility for making use of the information will then be on the person to whom it is communicated, and the doctor would of course in every case take all reasonable precautions to satisfy himself that it is not required for any but proper and legitimate purposes.

If a medical officer is subpoenaed to give evidence against the interest of his patient he must of course answer all relevant questions put to him, but he may properly appeal to the court for protection if a question involves him in a conflict of duties.

I hope that the above may be of some assistance to you. (Coutts to Bolam, 15 November 1919, NA MH78/253)

Garner v Garner

While medical confidentiality had come to the Ministry's attention as an area of dubiety in 1919, the widespread reporting of the case of *Garner v Garner* ([1920] 36 TLR 196) pushed it into prominence on the agenda. Articles in *The Times* on 14 and 15 January, and in the *Morning Post* of 16 January, heightened concern at the Ministry. Clara Garner was seeking a divorce. A disparity in English divorce law meant that, while a husband had only to prove his wife's adultery, a wife was required to prove an additional offence, for example, evidence of her husband's cruelty towards her. The transmission of VD from husband to wife could provide evidence for both these clauses if it was shown that the husband had contracted VD from an extramarital relationship (adultery) and then infected his wife (cruelty). With this in mind, Clara Garner had subpoenaed Dr Salomon Kadinsky of the Westminster hospital to give evidence on her behalf.

Appearing in court, Kadinsky was reluctant to breach the government pledge of secrecy, which stated that all VD treatment was to be regarded as strictly confidential. Before being sworn as a witness he produced a note from the chairman of the house committee of the Westminster hospital which cited the emphasis placed on secrecy by the government regulations on VD. The judge, Alfred McCardie, refused the protest, stating that ,'in a Court of Justice there were "even higher considerations than those which prevailed with regard to the position of medical men"' (*The Times*, 14 January 1920). Kadinsky took the oath and testified that Clara Garner suffered from syphilis.

Gwyer was quick to grasp the importance of the reporting of the case in *The Times*. Consistent with his earlier stance on the subject, he noted that the doctor had been summoned in order to give evidence on his patient's behalf. The question of confidentiality therefore arose along the same lines as before: did the VD regulations impose an absolute obligation on doctors not to disclose patient information, even when the patient consented to disclosure? As Coutts' earlier letter to Bolam made clear, the Ministry's interpretation of the regulations permitted disclosure at the patient's request. Newman agreed with this view, suggesting that the leader in *The Times* had completely missed this point, thereby wrongly stating that the government's VD treatment scheme was futile. In the paper's words: 'the endeavours which have long been made to root out a hidden plague in the community must be allowed to rank among the pious futilities of the Government' (*The Times*, 14 January 1920). Newman did note, however, that a case could arise in which a doctor was subpoenaed and compelled to give evidence contrary to the wishes or interests of his patient. No scheme for the treatment of VD could avoid this legal requirement.

While senior personnel at the Ministry were content with McCardie's ruling in *Garner v Garner*, there was some condemnation in legal quarters of the decision to compel the medical witness to disclose patient information. In an article entitled 'Doctors and Professional Privilege', the *Solicitors Journal* questioned whether McCardie should not have had the courage to override the many legal precedents of rejecting medical privilege in court. Not only, it argued, did the lack of professional privilege place medical practitioners in a very awkward position, but on grounds of public policy 'it seems very undesirable that a doctor should be compelled to disclose facts about the health of a patient when the State has itself invited such patients to undergo treatment in one of its venereal hospitals under a solemn and well-advertised pledge of absolute secrecy' (*Solicitors Journal*, 24 January 1920). The article cited many cases in which privilege had been claimed, including the Duchess of Kingston's trial, and drew analogy with other professions whose members regularly received confidential information, notably lawyers and clergymen. Instances in which the latter were not compelled to give evidence by dint of judicial discretion, were highlighted as being closely analogous to the treatment that doctors should receive. The piece ended by suggesting that 'now wider safeguards than that seem desirable'.

In the aftermath of *The Times*' provocative slant on the McCardie ruling and its potential impact on the efficacy of the government's VD treatment scheme, Gwyer proposed that a letter, intended to clear up the 'misapprehension' of McCardie's decision, should be circulated to the VD clinics and treatment centres. Newman agreed, recommending that copies should be sent to all county and county borough councils and inserted in the press. To this end a letter was drafted, predominantly by Gwyer, and a copy was sent to Alfred Cox, Medical Secretary to the BMA, for comment. The accompanying note, signed by Morant, iterated the Ministry's belief that such a letter was required to counter the potential harm that the press coverage of *Garner* had caused. He suggested that the BMA, with whom 'I am most anxious that this Ministry should always work in touch', would probably have a committee already looking into the issue, and any comments would be welcomed (Morant to Cox, 21 February 1920, NA MH78/253).

Cox's reply indicated that the BMA had had the matter under consideration on a number of occasions, notably when a deputation met with the Lord Chief Justice, Home Secretary, Solicitor General and Public Prosecutor in 1915. This collective of legal and political opinion had tried to convince the BMA deputation of the important duty upon medical men, as citizens, to disclose information about suspected criminal practices. However, the deputation had 'stoutly resisted' the proposal to use doctors as private detectives, arguing instead for a form of medical privilege to be granted. No doubt recalling the legal objections to press involvement in 1915, Cox indicated the general support of the BMA, and the specific backing of Dr Langdon-Down, Chairman of its CEC, to the Ministry's proposed letter being inserted in the medical press. Cox was also supportive of the suggestion that Addison might bring the matter to the broader attention of the government (Cox to Morant, 26 February 1920, NA MH78/253).

The delay involved in corresponding with the BMA raised a question as to whether the insertion of a letter in the press, reopening the issue a month and a half after the case had been reported in *The Times*, might be counterproductive. However, Morant believed the ill-effects of the press reports may have had a lasting impact upon the efficacy of the VD treatment campaign across the country. While the facts of *Garner* were in favour of the Ministry's stance, another case could easily arise in which the circumstances posed a more genuine threat to the confidentiality of patient information. Thus, by clearing up the present misapprehension of the regulations for doctors, by way of inserting a letter in the medical press alone, greater clarity could be maintained for the future.

An edited version of the draft letter, signed by Newman, and dated 31 March 1920, was subsequently circulated to medical officers at VD treatment centres and in counties and county boroughs. A copy of the letter was also included in Newman's first annual report as Chief Medical Officer. The report contained a section devoted to the question of professional privilege in relation to the work of VD clinics, in which it was again stressed that while there was an obligation of secrecy this could not override the law. Echoing Gwyer's earlier optimism the section concluded: 'If called upon to give evidence which violates the rule of professional confidence the doctor may properly appeal to the court for protection and to such an appeal the court would no doubt, so far as the law permits, give full and sympathetic consideration' (Newman 1920).

Three weeks after Newman's circular, the Ministry received another letter requesting advice on what course should be adopted when a medical officer was subpoenaed and compelled to give evidence in court. The sender, Hugh Woods of the London and Counties Medical Protection Society, requested that a deputation of members might be received at a meeting to discuss the issue and its clear importance to the overall success of the VD treatment campaign. Gwyer advised that the meeting was desirable, as the question's growing importance indicated that it might be worthwhile to 'guide' medical opinion into 'moderate and reasonable channels from the outset' (Gwyer to Newman, 26 April 1920, NA MH78/253).

Accordingly, Addison, accompanied by Sir Arthur Robinson,[5] Newman and Gwyer, received the deputation from the London and Counties Medical Protection Society. The deputation stressed their belief that a privilege, akin to that of the legal profession, was now required for medical practitioners. Any such privilege should only be applicable to evidence in civil cases and would not impact upon doctors' obligations in criminal proceedings. Addison expressed his agreement with their views, suggesting that in order to achieve their mutual goal legislation would be required. He assured them that he would give the matter his consideration, and the meeting's minutes record that, after the deputation had left, he instructed Gwyer to draw up a note on which he could see the Lord Chief Justice[6] (Minutes of meeting with London and Counties Medical Protection Society, 6 May 1920, NA MH78/253).

---

5 Robinson had joined the Ministry following the death of Morant the previous month.

6 Rufus Isaacs, Lord Reading.

Approach to the Lord Chancellor

As requested, Gwyer drew up the memorandum and it was sent, together with a copy of the VD regulations and Newman's circular, to Sir Claud Schuster, Permanent Secretary to the Lord Chancellor, on 3 June. The accompanying letter asked for the memo to be passed on to the Lord Chancellor,[7] with a request that he advise Addison on what action should be taken to secure a form of privilege for medical practitioners in court which would ensure the confidentiality of VD patients. Gwyer put forward a number of arguments for the extension of privilege to medical practitioners in civil proceedings, citing the importance of confidentiality to the VD treatment scheme and the lenient treatment received on numerous occasions by members of the clergy appearing as witnesses in court. He argued that the basis for legal privilege as stated by Knight Bruce in *Pearse v Pearse* provided just as much justification for medical privilege:

> Truth, like all other good things, may be loved unwisely, may be pursued too keenly, may cost too much. And surely the meanness and the mischief of prying into man's confidential consultations with his legal adviser, the general evil of infusing reserve and dissimulation, uneasiness, suspicion, and fear, into these communications which must take place, and which, unless in a condition of perfect security, must take place uselessly or worse, are too great a price to pay for truth itself. (Addison to Birkenhead, 3 June 1920, NA MH78/253)

There followed some brief correspondence between Schuster and the Ministry regarding further copies of the memo being sent, at Birkenhead's request, to the Lord Chief Justice, the Master of the Rolls[8] and the President of the Probate, Divorce and Admiralty Division[9], for their consideration and comment, and to ask Reading to raise the matter at a judges meeting (Schuster to Barter, 9 June 1920, Barter to Schuster 11 June 1920, NA MH78/253).

Having initially written to the Lord Chancellor at the beginning of June 1920, Birkenhead's failure to furnish the Ministry with the requested opinions prompted Barter to write again in early December (Barter to Schuster, 3 December 1920, NA MH78/253). Still there was no response. It took a letter from the ever-dependable Gwyer in late January to obtain a long overdue, and highly unsatisfactory, response (Gwyer to Schuster, 25 January 1921, NA MH78/253). Writing the following day, Schuster indicated that he had, as yet, only received a written reply on the question from the President of the Probate, Divorce and Admiralty Division. In addition, he had had several discussions of the matter with the Lord Chief Justice. Neither had been particularly favourable

7 F.E. Smith, Lord Birkenhead.

8 Lord Sterndale.

9 Sir Henry Duke.

to the proposal and the matter had been postponed until a meeting of the chief judges could be arranged to discuss it. Additional delays were foreseen in relation to the imminent change of Lord Chief Justice as Reading was vacating the post in order to become Viceroy of India.

This reply, while breaking the lengthy silence from legal quarters on the subject, was unsatisfactory for a Ministry keen to proceed in promoting the cause of medical privilege amidst mounting controversy and pressure. In a written response to Birkenhead, Addison again emphasised the prejudicial effect that the perceived lack of confidentiality was having on public health measures (Addison to Birkenhead, 4 February 1921, NA MH78/253). Adverse reports of the Ministry's medical record card system, appearing in *The Times*, had failed, once again, to take note of the facts. The system of record cards, introduced as an integral part of the National Insurance scheme, had been put on hold in 1917 due to 'the great pressure upon the time of practitioners, occasioned by the withdrawal of so many of their number for military service' (Interdepartmental Committee on Insurance Medical Records 1920). Before recommencing with the new system, Addison had engaged an interdepartmental committee to advise on ways in which the forms used for the reports could be improved (*The Times* 13 March 1920, 8). The new record card system was implemented along the exact lines of the recommendations contained in that interdepartmental committee report, including one that received a lot of negative press attention.

> A practitioner is required to afford to the Medical Officer … or to such other person as he may appoint for the purpose, access at all reasonable times to any records kept by the practitioner under these terms of service and to furnish the Medical Officer with any such records or with any necessary information with regard to any entry therein as he may require. (*The Times* 26 November 1920, 12)

The scheme was designed to allow the Ministry of Health to collect more accurate statistics on the health of insured patients. The medical records of a patient would be put inside an envelope with their details on the outside for identification purposes. In the event of the records having to be sent to a Medical Officer, the patient's file would be placed within a windowed envelope for transit, a point of grave concern for *The Times*: 'thus a messenger who handles these cards may find it difficult not to see whom they concern. The whole thing is public and open to the last degree' (*The Times* 26 November 1920, 12). In an attempt to alert the public to the threat that the new scheme posed to the confidentiality of insured person's health records, *The Times* published a series of articles related to this 'medical inquisition'.[10] Amidst arguments that the scheme discriminated against the confidentiality of panel patients, and fine rhetoric about confidentiality being 'the breath of medical practice' (*The Times*

10 *The Times* 26 November 1920; 24 December 1920; 26 December 1920; 30 December 1920; 31 December 1920; 1 January 1921; 3 January 1921.

18 February 1920, 10), the reporting strayed into scaremongering. Referring to the fact that a Medical Officer could appoint someone to act on his behalf one article suggested that 'there is absolutely nothing in the regulation so far as can be seen to prevent one of the new advisers nominating, say, his wife to the post of scrutiniser of these most private and confidential documents' (*The Times* 26 November 1920, 12).

Addison's letter to Birkenhead pointed out that the newspaper campaigns, 'inspired by motives which have very little connection with a desire to promote the efficiency of our medical services', were creating a deal of uneasiness among the more 'ignorant' of insured individuals and were an encouragement to those doctors 'who never lose an opportunity of vilifying the panel system'. All this was simply adding to the importance of the question of medical confidentiality and Addison concluded by stating:

> I entertain no doubt that if the Cabinet should agree to the introduction of legislation amending the present law public opinion would be wholly with us, but in a matter so nearly affecting the practice and procedure of the Courts, I should be glad to know that I am assured of your support. (Addison to Birkenhead, 4 February 1921, NA MH78/253)

The Ministry's anxiety that the question should be dealt with as early as possible did nothing to change Birkenhead's measured approach. Replying on the Lord Chancellor's behalf, Schuster restated that circumstances, primarily the change of Lord Chief Justice, could not permit the reporting of a consensus of legal opinion on the matter (Schuster to Addison, 9 February 1921, NA MH78/253). It would, after all, be highly improper to proceed without consulting the principal judicial officers who would be materially affected by any change in the law.

In fact, Birkenhead was preoccupied debating with the Prime Minister, Lloyd George, about who should be appointed Lord Chief Justice. On the day that Schuster wrote to Addison on his behalf, Birkenhead was himself preparing a 'lengthy typewritten document' to try and dissuade Lloyd George from appointing A.T. Lawrence to the vacant position (Rowland 1975, 533). His protestations failed and, in order to keep his Liberal ally Sir Gordon Hewart (the Attorney General) in the Cabinet, Lloyd George appointed the 77-year-old Lawrence to the position on the understanding that he would be replaced by Hewart before the next change in government (Birkenhead, 1959, 402–7).

Schuster's response, coupled with the numerous earlier delays, clearly tested Addison's patience. He wrote to Birkenhead on St Valentine's Day 1921 expressing his keen disappointment and emphasising, once again, the pressing nature of the matter, which was, he stated, certain to be raised in Parliament very soon. However, Addison's attempt to pressurise the Lord Chancellor into support of the Ministry's proposed alteration to the law was dealt a severe blow by Birkenhead's, atypically immediate, response:

> Dear Minister of Health,
>
> You must allow me to point out that it is perfectly futile of you to write me such letter on grave legal matters as that which I received from you this morning. The changes which you desire are far-reaching and highly disputable. I am myself at present opposed to them. The President of the Probate, Divorce and Admiralty Division is very strongly opposed to them. The delay, therefore, to which you make such querulous reference, until the Lord Chief Justice is appointed and possibly the new Attorney General, is entirely in your favour, as it may conceivably, however improbably, supply you with two Judges who agree with your views.
>
> Nothing in the meantime is to be gained by concealing you from my own view that it is highly doubtful whether you will ever obtain the modification of the existing law which you desire, and that it is even more doubtful whether such a modification, if admitted, would not be extremely pernicious.
>
> In conclusion, I have only to add that there will be no avoidable delay in consulting the new official, or officials and that you will be immediately informed of the result.
> Yours very truly,
>
> Birkenhead. (Birkenhead to Addison, 14 February 1921, NA LCO2/624)

Unperturbed by what Gwyer termed the 'very strange' reply from the Lord Chancellor, Addison subsequently met with Birkenhead who undertook to raise the matter within two weeks of the appointment of the new Lord Chief Justice, discuss it with the other judges, and report back to the Minister. Gwyer, ever the optimist, suggested that Addison should not read too much into Birkenhead's unfavourable stance on their proposal since 'the letter scarcely represented his considered judgement, and indeed bore the appearance of having been written in a moment of pique' (Gwyer to Machlachlan, 5 April 1921, NA MH78/253). Clearly the Ministry of Health had not given up hope of convincing the judiciary of the benefits of medical privilege. One month later, a communication from Schuster indicated an imminent meeting between Birkenhead and Lawrence. In light of the circumstances of the elderly Lawrence's appointment as Lord Chief Justice, there was, perhaps, not much ground for hope. Shortly afterwards, Schuster confirmed that Lawrence was in full agreement with the informally expressed views of his predecessor, as well as those of the President of the Probate, Divorce and Admiralty Division and, of course, Birkenhead himself. Clearly, this did represent the considered judgement of the judiciary and its foundation could not be as easily belittled as Birkenhead's previous response. To Birkenhead, the unanimous legal opinion meant Addison's proposal could be taken no further.

The attempt to state that the question was closed seems to have spurred the Ministry of Health – not content to have what they could and could not achieve dictated to them by the judiciary – into greater action. Besides, not all avenues had been exhausted. In a handwritten note on the back of Schuster's letter, Sir Arthur Robinson suggested that the only way to take the matter forward would be by formally referring the question to the Cabinet as a matter of difference between the Ministry and LCO. He requested that before suggesting this to Addison, information on medical privilege in other countries should be obtained.

International Comparisons

In late May, Gwyer set out his reasons for believing the matter should be pursued (Gwyer to Newman and Robinson, 31 May 1921, NA MH78/253). He argued that the question of medical privilege in this context was ultimately one of policy, and consequently legal opinion, while carrying great weight, could not be regarded as conclusive. Furthermore, the LCO had not given detailed reasons for their position. Gwyer suggested that the Society for Comparative Legislation should be consulted in order to furnish the Minister with the information on the standing of medical privilege in other countries, before any approach was made to the Cabinet. On the question of raising the matter with Cabinet, he noted a recent precedent when proposals to make housing bonds a trustee security under the Housing (Additional Powers) Act, 1919 were met with unanimous opposition from the judges of the Chancery Division. In that instance, the Cabinet did not accept the judges' opinion as final and the proposal went on to become statute. Newman agreed with Gwyer's view that the question should not be left, believing there were 'strong medical grounds for the course proposed' (Newman handwritten comment on Gwyer's memo, 3 June 1921, NA MH78/253).

The Society for Comparative Legislation was contacted and Mr Bedwell from the Society replied to the Ministry on 13 June 1921. He opined that the dominant influence of Roman Catholicism in the European countries made them ill-suited for current purposes but he believed that the United States might prove more fruitful. He was not aware of a collected work that contained information on the policy adopted in other countries, but he suggested that it would not take long for someone from the Ministry to research the matter in the Middle Temple library, where he himself was the librarian. Bedwell's advice seems to have been taken as the Ministry's file contains several pages of notes on legislation regarding medical confidentiality in countries ranging from New Zealand and Canada to many of the American states. Gwyer used this information in a memo he drew up for the Cabinet (Ministry of Health memorandum for Cabinet Meeting June 1921, NA MH78/253). In relaying it to Robinson, he indicated that he had been in touch with Miller-Gray of the Scottish Office who had informed him that while there was no privilege for medical men in Scotland, it was felt that 'doctors should not be pressed to give evidence about their patients unless absolutely necessary' (Gwyer to Robinson, 17 June 1921, NA MH78/253).

While the Ministry sought out ways to develop their case at the highest levels of government, the growing problems for Lloyd George's coalition saw the Prime Minister take Addison away from Health to become Minister without portfolio. Having waited for the appointment of the new Lord Chief Justice only to see the position filled by the elderly Lawrence, whose primary function was to keep the seat warm for Hewart[11], by April the Ministry was adjusting to a new Minister of Health. Lloyd George's removal of Addison, ostensibly because of the difficulties connected with the cost to the public purse of his ambitious housing program, came at a bad time for the Ministry. The founder of Imperial Chemical Industries, Sir Alfred Mond, took over as Minister when the department was gearing up to persuade Cabinet of the case for medical privilege. A delay in making the approach to Cabinet was out of the question. Indeed, the issue gathered increased urgency when it became apparent towards the end of July that Lord Dawson of Penn intended to raise the issue in the House of Lords and suggest that it be referred to a select committee of the two Houses of Parliament.

Dawson had chaired the thirty-first meeting of the Consultative Committee on Medical and Allied Services at the beginning of July, in which the question of medical privilege had been prominent among a number of issues the Ministry had requested the committee to examine and report back on. The minutes of the meeting express at some length the discussion that took place, including the appearance of Gwyer midway through to offer his advice. Going against Gwyer's opinion, the committee finally passed the following resolution, by 11 votes to 3: 'In the opinion of the Council it is in the public interest that medical practitioners should not be compelled in proceedings in courts of law to disclose communications made to them by their patients.' (Minutes of the Consultative Council on Medical and Allied Services, 1 July 1921, NA MH78/253) The three dissenters on the committee agreed with Gwyer that the protection afforded to medical men should be limited to civil cases.

Dawson's belief that medical privilege should extend to both civil and criminal proceedings went against the Ministry's view of the issue and the prospect of his raising the issue in Parliament threatened to jeopardise their proposal relating solely to civil cases. Mond wrote to Birkenhead later the same month (Mond to Birkenhead, 21 July 1921, NA MH78/253). He noted Addison's previous correspondence and indicated that he, too, was keen to arrange a meeting to discuss the matter. He stressed that the perceived absence of a complete guarantee of secrecy under the government's VD treatment schemes had led to something approaching a crisis. However, in contrast to Dawson and the majority of members of the Consultative Council on Medical and Allied Services, the Ministry sought legislation that would permit a level of privilege to medical practitioners in civil cases alone – a position for which there were a number of respectable precedents.

11 Hewart took over from Lawrence after a year.

A short bill could be passed along the lines of legislation in force in New Zealand, which stated:

> A physician or surgeon shall not, without the consent of his patient, divulge in any civil proceeding (unless the sanity of the patient is the matter in dispute) any communication made to him in his professional character by such patient, and necessary to enable him to prescribe or act for such patient.
>
> Nothing in this section shall protect any communication made for any criminal purpose, or prejudice the right to give in evidence any statement or representation at any time made to or by a physician or surgeon in or about the effecting by any person of an insurance on the life of himself or any other person. (Sections 2 and 3 of the Evidence Act (1908) New Zealand)

If Birkenhead concurred, there would be no need for a joint committee to discuss the matter and the Ministry could explain the situation to Dawson. If not, then Mond was keen to discuss the situation with him. Clearly, the new Minister for Health was trying to contrast Dawson's more extreme position, with talk of select committee investigations and a universal medical privilege, with the Ministry's comparatively moderate and reasonable position.

In the end, the Ministry persuaded Dawson to temporarily withdraw his motion (*The Times* 28 July 1921, 10). Robinson indicated that Dawson had been 'made to see the difficulties' during discussions at the Ministry (Robinson, 23 July 1921, NA MH55/184). Nonetheless, the Ministry still faced mounting pressure to clarify the position of medical confidentiality in connection with VD treatment. Two letters on the subject were received in the autumn of 1921, the first from the Monmouthshire County Council Association and the second from the County Councils Association. Both referred to the inconsistency between the Ministry's advertisement posters for VD treatment centres, which clearly stated that all proceedings would be strictly confidential, and the recent highly publicised legal rulings which falsified that claim (Hughes to Ministry 19 July 1921, Johnson to Ministry 5 November 1921, NA MH78/253). Either, the letters demanded, the Ministry must have secrecy recognised by the courts, or the literature would have to be withdrawn.[12] The second letter had been forwarded on from the Ministry of Health in Cardiff who, believing the issues raised to be of widespread concern, suggested that a reply would be better coming from Whitehall (Ministry of Health, Cardiff to Slator, 9 November 1921, NA MH78/253). The Ministry in Whitehall's reply simply stated that they had the matter under consideration.

The delay in tabling his motion for discussion did not deter Dawson from continuing his campaign for medical privilege. Consecutive issues of the *Law*

---

12 By contrast, when the explicit guarantee of secrecy was removed from public propaganda following the Second World War, complaints to the Ministry of Health demanded it be reinstated (see Chapter 9).

Times on 25 March and 1 April 1922 covered at length a debate on professional secrecy opened by Dawson at the Medico-Legal Society. The debate effectively summed up the central tension involved in discussions of medical confidentiality. While disagreeing on the extent, the Ministry of Health and the Consultative Council on Medical and Allied Services both argued that medical privilege was necessary for practitioners to carry out their professional duty and promote public health. Meanwhile, the judiciary emphasised the doctor's civic duty to aid in the administration of justice. Both sides claimed that their course of action best served the public interest.

If the complexities involved in weighing the duties against each other could not provide a satisfactory resolution, no simple solution would be found by focusing on the consequences. After all, who could definitively state that the end of public justice was more important than that of public health or vice versa? Despite differing standpoints, all those attending the Medico-Legal Society's debate were agreed that answers were urgently required. Lord Justice Atkin suggested that the topic was 'on the whole the most important that had ever engaged the attention of the society, because it was one that intimately concerned not merely medical men, and not merely lawyers in their capacity as ministers of justice, but the public at large'. Medical confidentiality was to continue to engage Atkin's attention as he lent the weight of his support behind attempts to gain medical privilege through private members' legislation in 1927 and 1936 (see Chapter 7).

Dr Elliot: The Ministry's Medical Martyr

In early June 1921, John Elliot, Medical Officer to a VD clinic in Chester, wrote to the Ministry of Health in urgent need of advice (Elliot to Coutts, 3 June 1921, MH78/253). He had been subpoenaed to appear as a witness in a divorce case and give evidence against a patient. He was keen to know if he had no other choice but to give evidence in the pending trial. Replying the following day, Coutts explained the position as the Ministry currently understood it. Having been subpoenaed, Elliot must attend the court but could protest against being required to disclose confidential information received during his work at the VD treatment centre, making clear that it was in the public interest that such matters should remain confidential. If the appeal for exemption was not granted, Elliot was left with only two options: have the protest recorded and then answer questions; or refuse to give evidence. If the latter course was adopted, he ran the risk of imprisonment for contempt of court, which, while being of personal discomfort, would 'no doubt very effectively draw attention to the hardship of the position' (Coutts to Elliot, 4 June 1921, NA MH78/253). Perhaps, Coutts continued, Elliot could furnish the Ministry with details of when the trial was to take place in order that they could send a shorthand writer to take notes on the court's actions, and Elliot himself could drop by the Ministry to discuss the best way to put any protest he wished to make. Coutts also suggested that Elliot might wish to get in touch with legal counsel, though it was unlikely he would be permitted to use them in court.

Elliot's next letter stated that the importance of the case was such that he felt he might not have the confidence to put the protest effectively so he had corresponded with Honaratus Lloyd K.C. (Elliot to Coutts, 5 June 1921, NA MH78/253). Clearly passionate about the issue, Elliot claimed to be of a mind to decline to answer any questions and face the consequences, though he reserved any final judgement until he had talked the matter over with Lloyd. The case was *Needham v Needham* and, while he felt sure he would have the support of the whole profession, he hoped he would also have the support of the Ministry, as far as it was possible for them to give it. This, it turned out, was an important qualification.

On receiving this letter, Coutts sent a note to Gwyer indicating that, although Elliot had engaged the services of a lawyer, it appeared he might be a willing – and timely – martyr in the Ministry's cause of medical privilege.

> I think it is very probable that if we gave him direct encouragement he would decide to decline to give evidence and thus make it a test case. I recognise however, that we could not well do this officially, and it is a great responsibility to advise him unofficially in this direction. (Coutts to Gwyer, 6 June 1921, NA MH78/253)

A great responsibility indeed; but also a great opportunity. Having received a negative response from Birkenhead on the proposal to extend a form of legal privilege to doctors, the Ministry was keen to continue its promotion of what it believed was a justified and necessary cause. The coincidental arrival of Elliot's plea for help pushed the door, seemingly closed by the consulted legal opinion, once again ajar. The circumstances seemed ideal. In the course of researching the matter over the previous months, the Ministry had frequently come across references to the informally recognised privilege granted to clergymen when appearing as witnesses in court. Memoranda in the Ministry's file noted precedents in which the judge ruled against the disclosure of confidential information by a clergyman.[13] The suggestion was that judges were reluctant to imprison clergymen for refusing to disclose information confided in them, recognising that no form of punishment the court could impose would be sufficient to counter such witnesses' sense of a higher duty. The Ministry now seemed keen to test whether the same leniency would be shown to a doctor who, in face of similar consequences, resolutely stood by his belief in the ancient and venerable principle of medical confidentiality. Elliot could provide them with their test case, but first he had to be persuaded of the contribution his potential, even likely, sacrifice would make to the greater good of the cause. Yet the matter was more delicate. The guiding hand of the Ministry must leave no obvious fingerprints on the wary Dr Elliot's back as it encouraged

---

13 Best C J in *Broad v Pitt*, 3 C & P 519; Alderson B in *R v Griffin*, 6 Cox 219.

him into the spotlight of public attention. Or, put less poetically, into prison for contempt of court.

However, the Ministry were not the only ones advising Elliot. Lloyd's counsel to him, as stated in Elliot's next communication, was that while initially refusing to give evidence, if the court maintained its demand Elliot should comply (Elliot to Ministry of Health, undated, NA MH78/253). In addition to appearing as a witness, Elliot was required to bring the hospital records with him and the Secretary to the Infirmary was also likely to be subpoenaed. Writing on a Tuesday, Elliot was to meet with the Infirmary's Chairman, Secretary and Solicitor on the following day before travelling to London on Thursday to meet with the London & Counties Medical Protection Society, from whom he had requested counsel. He understood the trial could be called on Friday. With so many demands upon him it is little wonder Elliot concluded by stating, 'I don't quite know what to do'. The only other communication the Ministry received from Elliot, before his appearance in court, was a telegram from Chester simply stating, 'Trial Tomorrow Coming to town will call Ministry Seven Ock' (Post Office Telegraph, Elliot to Ministry of Health, NA MH78/253).

The Daily Chronicle, which ran two stories relating to the *Needham v Needham* trial on 10 June 1921 and a follow-up article gauging the medical profession's reaction on 11 June, eagerly recounted Elliot's performance in court. The reports noted his prolonged attempt to have medical privilege recognised by the court, arguing that the 1916 VD regulations were statutory authority for him not to disclose, and that it was on this understanding that he and others had taken up posts as medical officers at VD clinics. The judge, Justice Horridge, flatly stated that such regulations held no jurisdiction in the King's courts. Despite further protests that the confidential relationship between doctor and patient was one of the principles held dearest by the medical profession, and that it was essential to public health measures to combat VD, Horridge ordered Elliot to assist in the administration of justice and answer all questions. Elliot acquiesced. In sweeping style the *Daily Chronicle* announced to its readers:

> It is clear that if there is no guarantee of professional secrecy in certain kinds of clinic the whole object of the Ministry of Health acting in the interests of the public is likely to be defeated. The matter requires legislation. (*Daily Chronicle* 10 June 1921)

As had been the case in the aftermath of *Garner*, it was the legal journals that seemed to take the dimmest view of the judge's ruling. In the *Law Journal* of 18 June 1921, criticism was made of Horridge's demand for the medical witness to provide a statutory basis for medical privilege. No such statutory proof could be had for the privilege enjoyed by the lawyer or the minister of religion, though both were customarily recognised. The grounds for both were the interests of public policy in carrying out the administration of justice. But public policy clearly emphasised the need for unfettered communications between patient and doctor under the advertised pledge of secrecy for the VD treatment scheme. Adverse legal decisions could deter individuals from seeking treatment under the government's scheme and, clearly, this was not in the public interest. The article concluded: 'a strong judge is required to create a precedent that would be beneficial to the public as well as fair to medical men.'

This point was not lost on the Ministry of Health. A memo from Coutts to Newman indicated that, together with Gwyer, he had met with Elliot on 9 June to discuss the line of argument that should be taken. They had decided that counsel from the London and Counties Medical Protection Society should be used, if possible, to put forward Elliot's case. This request had not been granted by the judge, though Coutts clearly believed that Elliot had presented their case well. Although he eventually acceded to give evidence, after entering his protest, Elliot stated that he would have been willing to go to jail if it had only been for a few days but the risk of imprisonment lasting six months was too great.

The Ministry's problems were clearly mounting. Elliot, their potential martyr, had failed to convince the judge of the need for medical privilege. Moreover, he had flinched in court at the prospect of a prolonged imprisonment. But losing their medical martyr was only the beginning of the Ministry's predicament. The detrimental impact that the ruling, coupled with the sensationalist press reports of it, could have in deterring VD sufferers from seeking treatment at the Government's scheme of confidential clinics was exacerbated by the possibility that VD medical officers were themselves becoming disillusioned with the system. Coutts noted that Elliot was seriously contemplating giving up his position at the VD clinic, and another letter received from a VD medical officer in Oxford, made clear the strong feeling that 'this ruling of Mr Justice Horridge puts us in an altogether false position with our patients' (Gibson to Coutts, 10 June 1921, NA MH78/253).

The prospect of losing medical officers from VD clinics, on top of everything else, was potentially catastrophic. Coutts proposed that the issue should be pressed, that strong leading articles on the subject should appear in the medical journals, and that the Ministry should meet for discussions with the RCP, RCS and the BMA (Coutts to Newman, 13 June 1921, NA MH78/253). He suggested some of the daily newspapers might also be willing to take the matter up. Concurring with Coutts' assessment of the seriousness of the situation, Newman immediately forwarded the memo on to Gwyer with a note stating: 'You will wish to see this in view of your memo for the minister. I think we ought to try and act at once. It is important we should not lose our VD officers.'

A week later, Hugh Woods, secretary to the London and Counties Medical Protection Society wrote to the Ministry, inviting them to meet the costs the Society had incurred in their support for Elliot.[14] He insisted that the Ministry must act in order to ensure that medical officers, who took up their posts believing that confidentiality would be observed, would see the regulation protected and enforced. It could not be expected that busy practitioners would risk prolonged

14 These amounted to £32 15s.

imprisonment for carrying out what they believed was their recognised duty. If the legislature failed to deliver such protection then 'it may be necessary for some members of our profession to incur martyrdom of the kind with a view to awakening the consciousness of the public' (Woods to Ministry of Health, 20 June 1921, NA MH78/253). The onus was on the Ministry to provide the circumstances in which medical officers could maintain their duty of secrecy, which the Ministry's regulations rightly imposed upon them. A further letter on the 5 July indicated that Dr Hallam from the syphilis and skin clinic at the Royal Infirmary, Sheffield, had been subpoenaed to produce all records, notes and memoranda relating to a patient from his clinic. Hallam was responsible to the Ministry for these records and so advice was being sought on whether he should produce them. Woods ended on an ominous note, stating that the very existence of these types of clinics was involved in the question.

The Ministry sent a negative reply with regard to the request for expenses. It claimed to have no funds for this purpose, and it had been made clear to Elliot in the meeting before the case that, while the Ministry sympathised with his position, it could offer him no financial assistance. As for Hallam, if he had been subpoenaed he must attend (Slator to Woods, July 1921, NA MH78/253).

In fact, Hallam was exempted from attending court. In a series of letters in early June, Hallam and his colleague, Dr Mouat, both of whom had been subpoenaed to appear in the case of *Atwood v Atwood* in the divorce court, requested advice from the Ministry to which, they felt, they were responsible for the medical records of patients.[15] The information required by the court related to a patient who had been treated for gonorrhoea at the VD clinic in Sheffield. Mouat was in charge of the treatment of this particular disease while Hallam specialised in treatment of cases of syphilis. Consequently Hallam had had no contact with the patient concerned. The Ministry advised Hallam to write to the solicitor in charge of the case and explain these circumstances to him, and in a brief note to the Ministry from the London and Counties Medical Protection Society, it was noted that Hallam's subpoena had been withdrawn. Mouat, however, could only be given the advice, by now somewhat worn and hollow, that he must attend as a witness under subpoena but could attempt to claim that the information requested was privileged. If the judge refused, he must give evidence unless he was willing to risk imprisonment for contempt of court. It was a sign of how little progress had been made on the issue by the Ministry that they included a copy of Newman's letter circulated to medical officers at VD clinics, which had been written in February 1920.

Alfred Cox wrote to the Ministry on the 23 June to say that in light of Horridge's ruling in *Needham* the BMA Council had passed the following resolution:

> That the Council of the British Medical Association has learnt with great concern of the position created by the recent decision of a Judge that the medical

15 NA MH78/253. Mouat to Newman 2 July 1921; Ministry to Mouat 4 July 1921; Hallam to Newman 4 July 1921; Coutts to Hallam 5 July 1921.

> officer of a venereal disease clinic must give evidence in a civil case as to the medical condition of a patient under his care at a venereal disease clinic, thus violating the confidence between doctor and patient and the direct undertaking given by the Local Government Board that all proceedings at such clinics should be absolutely secret and confidential. In drawing the attention of the Ministry of Health to these facts the Council of the Association would urge that such legislative steps should be taken as would render such an occurrence impossible in the future.

The Association further requested that Mond receive a deputation from the BMA Council to discuss the matter in the hope of inducing him to take steps towards securing the required legislation. The proposed meeting did not take place due to the proximity of the BMA annual general meeting. However, the Association was able to report that another resolution of relevance had been adopted amidst overwhelming support:

> Resolved: That the Association use all its power to support a Member of the British Medical Association who refuses to divulge, without the patient's consent, information obtained in the exercise of his professional duties, except where it is already provided by Act of Parliament that he must do so.

John Elliot may not have provided the Ministry with the martyr it secretly wanted but he did bring the question of medical privilege in civil proceedings back into the spotlight, sparking debates in the popular press, medical and legal journals. The recurring references to him and the *Needham* case ensured that his prolonged protest had secured publicity for the cause. In an article titled 'Should doctors tell?' in the *Daily Chronicle* of 19 November 1921, Elliot received a number of tributes for his role in bringing the matter to greater public attention. The Ministry, while still suffering in the aftermath of failing to gain ground towards securing medical privilege, could be pleased by Elliot's performance. Furthermore, they need not give up all hope of a martyr. In the same article that praised the efforts of Elliot, Dr H. W. Baley of Harley Street[16] was quoted as stating:

> I regard the confidence between patient and doctor of so much importance that if I were put into the witness box I would go to prison rather than give away my patient. A doctor should not be obliged by the law to give away his patient except in cases of crime.

16 It is possible that this was Hugh Wansey Bayly, Organiser and Medical Officer in charge of the Venereal Department at St George's Hospital; and, together with Lord Willoughby de Broke, co-founder of the Society for the Prevention of Venereal Disease. See (Hall 2001, 128) and entry in *Who Was Who*.

Given his address, it is probable that Baley was utilising the press attention surrounding the case to advertise his high ethical standards. As doctors were banned from officially advertising their services, Baley's portrayal of himself as an honourable gentleman was no doubt intended to attract paying patients to his practice – mirroring the intentions of Caesar Hawkins in the Duchess of Kingston's trial 150 years before. Baley adopted the same tactics in the aftermath of a similar case in 1927.[17] Given the negative response from the Law Officers of the Crown, the possibility of a Harley Street martyr must have been a pleasing prospect for the Ministry. More importantly, both the BMA and the London and Counties Medical Protection Society had started to echo the Ministry's initial thoughts on the merits of medical martyrdom.

---

17 For a detailed account of this see Chapter 7.

Chapter 5
The BMA

While no single organisation could claim to represent the opinions of the whole of the medical profession, there are a number of reasons for examining the BMA's position on medical confidentiality in the early decades of the twentieth century. Although the RCP and the RCS were both involved in the question, it was the BMA which was at the forefront, both in 1915 and in the early interwar years, in sending delegations to meet with the Ministry of Health and the law officers of the Crown. This was, in part, because the most controversial issues, in particular the government-sponsored VD treatment scheme, were more likely to affect GPs and medical officers engaged at public treatment centres than high-ranking private practitioners. The specific disputes certainly engaged the attention of the BMA membership, and there are strong grounds for seeing the BMA as the body that represented general medical interest by the interwar years.

The BMA had gained much valuable experience in the debate over the implementation of the National Insurance measures before the war. This experience of negotiating with government and attempting to represent the medical profession at large was an important learning curve for the Association. As Peter Bartrip points out:

> Even if the BMA is deemed to have lost the national insurance contest in terms of not achieving everything it desired and of having to make a humiliating climbdown, it won in terms of acquiring recognition as the voice of the profession. It thereby ensured that no future government would be able to ignore it ... It had won a place at the top table for all future negotiations relating to the health of the nation. (Bartrip 1996, 163)

Recognised as a key medical body with which government would negotiate, the BMA's major contribution in organising the medical profession in support of the war effort further improved its status by the early interwar years: 'it emerged from the war with a much enhanced reputation both in the eyes of the authorities and of the profession at large' (Bartrip 1996, 181). Coupled with the fact it had been involved in the debate over confidentiality both before and into the interwar years, the BMA provides an important insight into the medical perspective on the controversy over medical privilege and the confidentiality of VD treatment.

However, it should also be stressed that the BMA was not a homogenous mass with a single opinion. Consultants and GPs, both of whom were represented in the organisation, often appeared to be at loggerheads, a point highlighted by the rise of medical guilds around the turn of the twentieth century (Bartrip 1996, 142).

Moreover, as the BMA of the early twentieth century reformed to become a more democratic organisation – instituting an annual meeting of representatives from around Britain to discuss and vote on policy resolutions – it became clear that the opinions of the membership were not always in agreement with those of its governing council. Therefore, while the BMA had appeared relatively unified in its resistance of the legal challenge to confidentiality in 1915, it was an organisation with the potential to provide a range of medical opinions on the debate.

In broad terms, the BMA's internal debate was dictated by the calendar with the focal point being the ARM held each spring. At these meetings the representative body of members from around the country would examine policy resolutions brought before them by the BMA Council. For the question of confidentiality, the Council relied on the CEC to clarify the issues and recommend resolutions which they could approve and present to the ARM for ratification by the representative body. At the best of times, the sheer range and complexity of issues that the CEC had to consider and take into account on the question of confidentiality made their task of developing policy resolutions difficult. The intensity of the debate over confidentiality in the early interwar years added further complications.

With Cries of 'No' and 'Yes' – The Central Ethical Committee, 1920

Having taken a stand on the boundaries of confidentiality in 1915, by 1920, when the debate was reignited, the BMA had to think seriously about the practical implications of their position. What support would the Association be willing to give a member who got into difficulty as a result of challenging the courts on medical confidentiality? As noted in the last chapter, the focus of debate had shifted from abortion to VD. In some respects this strengthened the BMA's position. By the terms of the Venereal Diseases Act of 1917 all but registered medical practitioners were prohibited from treating VD, the medical profession therefore had a monopoly on treatment. It was thus easier for the BMA to make a case for confidentiality of treatment based on a professional code of ethics which guided all those legally permitted to carry out such treatment.

In 1920 the BMA Council engaged a standing subcommittee of the CEC to examine the question of confidentiality with specific regard to VD. This resulted in a draft memorandum drawn up by the deputy medical secretary, George Anderson. Opening with a reiteration of the BMA's previous resolutions on medical confidentiality it quickly became evident that the siege mentality of 1915 had not diminished: 'the main attack on professional secrecy appears likely to come from the bureaucratic side of Government especially from that concerned with the administration of the law' (BMA CEC SSC minutes, 9 November 1920).

The law's steady encroachment into the confidentiality of the doctor–patient relationship, partly by legislation and partly by judicial decision, defined it as the opposition. Previous attacks, notably by the Lord Chief Justice in 1915, had been temporarily resisted but could be renewed at any time. The publicity caused by

Justice MacCardie's decision in *Garner* in January 1920 suggested that conflict would resume sooner rather than later. However, allies were at hand in the form of 'certain departments of the Government' (Memorandum by Deputy Medical Secretary, BMA CEC, 9 November 1920), presumably a reference to the Ministry of Health. Their support would be expected in any stand the BMA made against further encroachment into the traditional boundaries of medical confidentiality.

In his memo, Anderson acknowledged that the doctor's duty of confidentiality was not absolute. Three main exceptions had been insisted upon by the state. Firstly, in a court of law when the court had ruled that information of a confidential nature had to be disclosed. Secondly, under the provision of an Act of Parliament, such as in notification of infectious diseases. Thirdly, where a doctor's duty as citizen overrode his professional duty, for example, where he was made aware of information which could prevent a crime, or grave danger to another person, or where disclosure would safeguard the interests of the patient – as in cases of mental disorder.

The first two exceptions were sufficient justification for a doctor to breach confidentiality. However, it was recognised that some practitioners might choose to disobey an order of the court and face the consequences. The CEC felt it would be impossible for the BMA to lay down any general rule as to what action should be taken in such cases. Each would have to be decided upon its own merits. The third exception appeared to pose more problems as there was a greater likelihood of differing opinions about the doctor's duty in individual cases. Again, no general rule could be stated but it was suggested that the doctor should try and persuade the patient to consent to disclosure. If unsuccessful, the doctor should revert to his conscience and, if time permitted, he could appeal to a judicial committee such as the CEC. The BMA would then have to back any action taken by a practitioner who had exactly followed the advice given by the CEC.

With regard to the question of VD, the ARM of 1920 passed a resolution which bound doctors not to disclose information without patient consent, but it was qualified by the first of the exceptions above (Minute 74, BMA ARM 1920). This meant that a practitioner was absolved if he disclosed information at the demand of a court. Cause for greater concern were cases in which the onus lay with the practitioner himself to make the decision, for example, in cases of proposed marriage where syphilis was likely to be transmitted from one party to another and to any children resulting from the marriage. A common theme in the debate, the case of the syphilitic fiancé was cited by Hempson in a speech to the ARM in 1920, by Birkenhead in his published essay 'Should a Doctor Tell?' (Smith 1922) in 1922, and matches the synopsis plot of the contemporary film 'Should the doctor tell?'[1] Anderson suggested that generalisation on the best course of action in such cases was impossible. More than the Ministry of Health or the Lord

1 Two versions of the film were made: a silent movie in 1923 written by G.B. Samuelson and P.J. Ramster; and a sound and picture version in 1930 written by Samuelson and Edgar Wallace.

Chancellor, the BMA found it difficult to isolate the problem of confidentiality in VD treatment from the rest of medical practice and Anderson's memo referred to other issues that had raised questions on the boundaries of medical confidentiality in recent meetings of the CEC. But, while queries about confidentiality arose in many different contexts, VD was rapidly becoming the most acute difficulty.

The general advice given by the CEC emphasised the duty of members to maintain the confidences of their patients, and the committee searched for ways to obviate the practitioner from making the ultimate decision to breach secrecy. Doctors were absolved of their duty if their medical evidence was demanded by a judge in court, though they were still advised to begin by attempting to plead privilege. Similarly, they could give medical information when required under statute law. In both situations, the consent of the patient was taken to be implicit on the basis that individuals knew of these exceptions to confidentiality when they consulted the practitioner. Greater complexity arose in areas where a breach of confidentiality was requested or seemed necessary outside a legal context. The tendency was again to emphasise a secondary role for the practitioner in the decision-making process. If information was required by an insurance company, or similar body, the practitioner should first gain the patient's explicit consent; or if a health certificate was being issued, this could be given to the patient, thereby placing the responsibility firmly away from the practitioner.

Yet, what was the doctor to do if the patient did not take the responsibility of making the decision, or acted in an irresponsible manner? If it was, as the CEC persistently stressed, impossible to lay down comprehensive rules of practice in such situations, then the belief that practitioners should proceed according to their conscience was unlikely to produce uniformity of practice. Increasingly standardised medical knowledge and education in medical theory and education did not mean that doctors shared a single opinion on questions of conscience. Confirmation of this came during Hempson's speech to the ARM in 1920 (*BMJ* 24 April 1920). Reciting the hypothetical case of the syphilitic fiancé, Hempson asked whether his audience would not ensure that the father of the innocent girl was informed of the health threat from the man she was to marry. The members of the representative body replied with cries of 'No!' and 'Yes!'. Clearly doctors were not of one mind and the dichotomous response was later picked up and used by the judiciary as evidence of the practical difficulties in legislating on medical confidentiality.

Beyond their faith in conscience as a guide, there seemed to be an underlying inconsistency in the CEC's approach. If the practitioner was best placed to be the judge of when to disclose information in cases too complex for fixed guidelines, it is unclear why he should be attempting to minimise his role in other cases. This inferred a reluctance to take responsibility for disclosure decisions wherever possible, and where it was not possible to defer to another decision-maker, the onus was on individual rather than collective responsibility within the profession. Confirmation of this came with the CEC's decision that the BMA would not be prepared to support its members in maintaining medical confidentiality until a general guiding policy had been laid down. This was a rather empty statement since Anderson's memo, summarising the committee's deliberations on the question, had given a clear indication that no general rules *could* be laid down. Driving home the CEC's reluctance to commit BMA resources, Anderson indicated that, even if guiding principles were arrived at, and all members made aware of them, it was still doubtful whether the BMA could in any way support its members in challenging the law – the facts relative to each particular case would have to be considered before it could contemplate giving any support. However, the CEC did endorse some general measures. It was deemed desirable that publicity should be given, in the columns of the *BMJ,* to the CEC resolutions on the subject and that an article should appear annually in order to guide the BMA membership. Thus, having been strong in its vocal defiance of the law's attempts to encroach into medical confidentiality in 1914–15, when faced with the practicalities of the position, the BMA seemed considerably less sure of itself.

'For They Did Not Wish to be Anarchists'[2] The CEC, 1921

Having hinted in 1920 that a renewal of the legal assault on medical confidentiality was imminent, the BMA Council was, by October 1921, having its attention drawn by Hempson to the cases of *Needham v Needham* and *Devonshire v Devonshire and Eve*. The latter case involved a married couple in Ilford who were now estranged. The wife had a stillborn child and the husband denied paternity. The medical officer of health for Ilford, Dr Burton, notified the birth, including details of paternity according to the terms of statute law. Subsequently, the husband filed for divorce on grounds of adultery and the judge demanded Burton's testimony as evidence, overruling protests from both Burton and the Ilford Urban District Council. In both *Devonshire* and *Needham*, medical practitioners had been called upon by judges to divulge patient information in court, but it was *Needham* that provoked a BMA Council resolution sent to the Ministry of Health.

> The Council of the BMA has learned with great concern of the position created by the recent decision of a judge that the medical officer of a VD clinic must give evidence in a civil case as to the medical condition of a patient under his care at a VD clinic, thus violating the confidence between doctor and patient and the direct undertaking given by the Local Government Board that all proceedings at such clinics should be absolutely secret and confidential. In drawing the attention of the Ministry of Health to these facts the Council of the Association would urge that such legislative steps should be taken as would render such an occurrence impossible in the future. (BMA CEC 25 October 1921)

2 Reported statement of E.B. Turner at a special meeting of the BMA Council held to discuss the question of professional secrecy. BMA CEC Minutes 31 March 1922.

Accompanying the resolution was a request that Mond receive a deputation from the Association at an early date.[3] In referring to *Needham*, it was made explicit that doctors were not the only ones under the impression that the treatment of patients within the government VD scheme was to be strictly private and confidential: 'every member of the public' was under the same belief (BMA Council to Ministry of Health 23 June 1921, CEC Minutes 25 October 1921).

While John Elliot's appearance in *Needham* clearly impacted upon the Ministry and the BMA Council, it struck a nerve with the membership of the BMA. Coming just a few weeks before the ARM at Newcastle in 1921, Elliot's ordeal became a significant point in the development of BMA policy. Drawing on the recommendations developed by the CEC in 1920, the Council put forward a motion with two distinct elements to the representative body at Newcastle. Firstly, members should not *voluntarily* disclose patient information, but if they chose to claim privilege in court, or failed to comply with existing legislation, they could not expect support from the BMA. Secondly, all attempts to add *new* exceptions to the general rule of confidentiality held by the profession, would be resisted by all lawful methods, and the BMA would support, by all means in its power, any practitioner who was penalised through such encroachment. The CEC and Council were therefore advocating a staunch defence of the status quo.

As a consequence of *Needham*, the representative body were of an altogether different mind. Rejecting the Council's motion, they voted to replace it with Minute 45. This stated that practitioners who refused to divulge information without patient consent, except where required by statute law, should receive the support of the full power of the BMA. Such a policy would allow doctors to directly challenge judicial denial of privilege for medical witnesses which, as previously noted, was a common law precedent dating back to the Duchess of Kingston's trial. Elliot's court appearance had raised the hackles of the BMA membership who were of the opinion that doctors should not be forced to divulge in court. A resolution was passed making clear the extension of the position (Minute 48, ARM Newcastle 1921). However, as the resolution had not been published in the *BMJ* two months prior to the meeting, Hempson indicated that it could not be adopted as BMA policy. A further resolution was duly passed urging that the Council should act upon Minute 45 as a resolution of the representative body and submit it to the next representative meeting with the view to it becoming fixed as BMA policy (Minute 51, ARM Newcastle 1921). With obvious discontent among the representative body, the Council referred the whole question back to the CEC.

With the prospect of a more confrontational policy than they had advocated, the CEC had to consider the consequences of the post-Newcastle position. While doing so they received a relevant enquiry from Dr Burton, the medical officer of

3 It was further resolved that the deputation should consist of the Officers of the Association, together with the Chairmen of the Medico-Political, Insurance Acts, Central Ethical, Hospitals and Scottish Committees. Dr Dain and Dr Garstang were subsequently added to this list.

health for the Ilford Urban District Council who had been forced to produce the notification of birth card in *Devonshire* in February 1921 (CEC 25 October 1921). In June the Ilford Council had sought advice from the Ministry of Health on how to address the confidentiality question involved in local authority officials being subpoenaed to give information in court. Initially, the Ministry had reiterated their standard advice to plead privilege and be directed by the judge. When further prompted by Ilford Council, the Ministry had stated that any further protection would require legislation. This was unlikely to be forthcoming and they were unable to agree with Ilford Council's proposal that all local authority documents should be protected on grounds of secrecy. Burton's letter to the BMA included correspondence showing he had taken the matter as far as was possible in a local context, and he was keen to know if the BMA could suggest any other method for dealing with the problem in future.

The CEC's reply, reiterating the complexity and difficulty of the question – a standard addendum for both the BMA and the Ministry – stated that, with the whole matter under consideration, the BMA was currently being guided by the representative body's resolution from the Newcastle ARM (CEC SSC 10 November 1921). Burton was incensed by this reply. He felt that the CEC had no understanding of the problem from the medical officer of health's point of view. What was required was simply that official documents in their possession were given the same recognition of privilege as was given to documents held by other government offices (see Chapter 8). The CEC were going about things in the wrong way. If documents that were compulsorily given to a medical officer were not awarded a privilege of confidentiality, then it was unlikely that GPs would be given concessions regarding the production of other, non-compulsory, documents. Burton pointed to Dawson's proposed motion in the House of Lords, which the government had persuaded him to drop temporarily, leading to fears that the whole question would be 'conveniently shelved' (CEC 10 November 1921). He hoped that there were enough medical men in the House of Commons to ensure that this would not happen. Burton was clearly keen on the possibility of legislation being debated in parliament, a point of view that was certainly not in line with the thoughts of either the Ministry of Health or the CEC by mid-1921.

With pressure mounting, the CEC subcommittee met in early December 1921. The meeting examined a memorandum written by Langdon-Down designed to provide focal points for discussion, and clarify the post-Newcastle position. The intention behind Resolution 48 differed from that behind the Council's proposed position in so much as it aimed to establish a new principle which 'if the speeches and feelings manifested at the Representatives Meeting may be taken as a guide, is, that absolute inviolability shall be accorded to professional confidences, whereas no such intention was in the mind of the Council in the early part of this year' (CEC 5 December 1921). Despite disagreeing with Resolution 48, Langdon-Down recognised that the BMA would be bound by it for the year. Moreover, Council was obliged to resubmit the same resolution to the following ARM with a view to it becoming established BMA policy. *Needham* had ended with Elliot caving under pressure from the court to break confidentiality because he was not guaranteed support for himself and his practice. If a similar case were to arise under the position adopted by the representative body in 1921, the member involved *would* be guaranteed the full support of the BMA, making a test case more feasible, but at a time when the whole question of confidentiality was being politically sidelined by the withdrawal of Dawson's motion in the House of Lords. However, while Resolution 48 had to be resubmitted to the 1922 ARM, the Council could also offer alternative resolutions. Having seen their proposals thrown out in Newcastle, and given the practical implications of Resolution 48, the CEC felt it wise, yet again, to reconsider the whole question as a matter of principle.

Fundamentally, all were agreed that patient information should not be unnecessarily divulged. The professional position of the medical practitioner placed him in circumstances where he obtained private and intimate information about patients in order to provide them with the best advice and treatment. Such information was given on the tacit or expressed trust that it would not be further broadcast by the doctor, which in Langdon-Down's opinion was the reason that any breach of confidentiality met with fierce opposition. In his own words: 'the strong feeling that the doctors hold about this is just due to this, that it hurts the deepest feelings of decent honourable men that they should divulge information received under such circumstances' (CEC 5 December 1921).

The reference to the medical man as a decent and honourable individual confirms that many still saw the question primarily as one of honour. The potential detriment that any perceived breach of confidence would have on the willingness of people to seek treatment and the implications for public health were, in Langdon-Down's eyes, subsidiary claims. He cited the relevant section of the Hippocratic Oath, concluding that these guiding principles were so much a part of daily practice that it was a shock to the practitioner to find that there were exceptions to it. But exceptions there were, both by Act of Parliament and also 'as a matter of history the demands of the Court have been greatly acceded to for 150 years past in the public interest and without a sense of dishonour to the profession' (CEC 5 December 1921), another clear reference to the Duchess of Kingston's trial, with the emphasis firmly placed on honour.

It was generally recognised that no change could be brought about in statute, and Langdon-Down believed that the representative body's desire to make professional privilege absolute would have to be sought through public support for the position leading to a change in custom. In other words they would have to set a new common law precedent. While recognising the power of custom, he pointed out that the profession had been against the notification of infectious diseases when it was first introduced but had changed its attitude over time. In the same vein, the question of professional secrecy had been reopened by another infectious disease, VD, the dire consequences of which had led a section of medical opinion to believe that it, too, should be notified in the interests of public health. But the outrage sparked by the legal cases earlier in 1921 stemmed from the stark realisation that the rules laid down by a government department had no more legal authority, without an Act of Parliament to back them, than the rules of professional secrecy which generally guided the medical profession.

Langdon-Down recognised that the question boiled down to a dual loyalty conflict: a doctor's duty to the patient and to the law. In court, the practitioner should follow his own convictions in deciding what action to take. If he disclosed at the demand of the court, he would do no dishonour to himself or his profession. If he chose not to disclose, he should explain his reasons to the court. Recognising that there were exceptions to the rule of professional secrecy, Langdon-Down believed that the judge, rather than an external body like the BMA, was best placed to decide when medical evidence was material to a case.

Concern that patients would boycott treatment *en masse* unless the state granted the medical profession absolute privilege, was, in Langdon-Down's view, unfounded. If doctors gossiped about patients it would certainly undermine trust. But to see confidentiality broken for the purposes of giving evidence in a small number of cases in court would have a negligible impact on the number of patients seeking treatment. If legislation protected the proceedings at VD clinics, there would be growing pressure to extend its application beyond a single class of patients, and a law advocating absolute confidentiality could have dire consequences for the profession. Such a law was in force in France and, Langdon-Down believed, medical practitioners objected strongly to it, fearing that wrongdoers could use a medical man as shield and accomplice. A more sensible alternative would be to make clear to the public that proceedings at VD clinics were no more confidential than normal doctor–patient consultations.

The medical profession should not seek privilege in order to be perceived as having equal status with lawyers or the clergy. Medical evidence was of undoubted value in court, and any claim should be based on much more 'public spirited motives'. Referring to *Kitson v Playfair*, he suggested that, rather than being a legal endorsement of medical secrecy, the high damages which had been levied against William Smoult Playfair had been a result of the injuries which he had caused to Linda Kitson, not punishment for breaching professional confidence. It is worth noting that this view of the decision was contrary to the interpretation subsequently adopted by the BMA PSC in 1922.

The Chairman of the BMA Council, Robert Alfred Bolam, believed medical practitioners should not be compelled to divulge patient information in court. For Langdon-Down, this position would not only be largely against the public interest, but would also be the most invidious one for the medical practitioner. As the law currently stood, a practitioner contravened the law if he chose *not* to disclose patient information in court. Such action demonstrated courage of conviction not to disclose patient confidences, even if found to have been misplaced in a particular case. However, if the position was reversed and the practitioner had to violate the law in order to make a disclosure, then mistakes would prove much more costly for the doctor, who could have kept his patient's confidences at no risk to himself. In addition, Bolam's position entailed that the decision of what was in the public interest would be taken away from the public figure of the judge, and placed in the hands of the individual private practitioner.

As an alternative, Langdon-Down advocated that the public should be more clearly informed that while medical practitioners were bound by a strict rule of confidentiality, it was not absolute. If the widespread coverage of controversial cases in the press was not enough to draw the public's attention to this fact, then the BMA's discussion, and publication, of resolutions which emphasised that no *voluntary* disclosures should be made, would alert them to the exceptions. By proceeding along these lines the public would become aware of the limitations to medical secrecy, and when doctors were forced to divulge information, there would be no dishonour to themselves or their profession.

Those who wished to challenge the common law hoped to be seen as martyrs for the cause: 'the public which might be moved to sympathy by spontaneous individual self-sacrifice on the altar of principle would be equally moved by organised martyrdom with the support of the Association' (CEC 5 December 1921). Public opinion was a powerful weapon and if the public was anxious to support the profession on the subject of confidentiality it could make its voice heard. But, in Langdon-Down's view, it was not just the public's support that seemed lacking: 'ministers who were so eager to act, draw back and common sense asserts its way'; suggesting that the Ministry of Health's appetite for challenging the law had been satiated by Elliot's appearance in *Needham*. He suggested that the CEC should prepare a report for Council, stating that while it firmly upheld the traditional rule of professional secrecy it recognised that there had to remain exceptions to it.

In other words, Langdon-Down was aiming at a compromise that stressed both the importance of the doctor's duty of confidence and the need to take account of the consequences of maintaining or breaching confidentiality. The CEC would suggest that the BMA should not be too quick to oppose all future legislation, as was implied by Minute 48, for the simple reason that new measures might be in the public interest. Rather than seeking to set a new common law precedent on medical privilege, the BMA should aim to assert, to the public and the authorities, the importance of medical confidentiality and emphasise that it should only be overridden in extreme circumstances. This could be done by giving BMA support to practitioners believed to have been unreasonably dealt with, regardless of whether in a civil or criminal case, after due consideration of all the circumstances. As a start, and consistent with the demands that were coming in to the Ministry of Health, the pledge of secrecy in the advertisements for VD clinics should either be withdrawn or clarified to make its limitations known.

Having advocated that Minute 48 be amended to reflect the points in Langdon-Down's memorandum, five resolutions were proposed. The first acknowledged that from the widest view of the public interest, both social and medical, there had to be exceptions to the general rule of professional secrecy. In order to safeguard the honour of the profession, the existence of these exceptions, with definitions where possible, should be made clear to the public. Recognising that exceptions were necessary, the second resolution stated that the BMA should not adopt a policy which promised undiscriminating and unquestioning support to any member who disobeyed the order of a court. Therefore, Minute 48 should not be confirmed. The third proposal was that the principle of professional secrecy should be maintained at the highest possible level with the widest view of public interest. If a case arose in which a member was called upon to disclose information obtained in the exercise of his professional duties, which was, in the opinion of the Council or the CEC, contrary to the highest public interest, the BMA should support that member with its full power. Such support would take the form of awakening public opinion to the threat to the public interest, and organising it in defence of the doctor. Resolution four stated that it was undesirable to move in a direction which might result in an absolute imposition of medical confidentiality on doctors. It was also undesirable that rules on confidentiality, such as those governing VD clinics, should be given legal backing. Rather, if retained, such rules should be accompanied by an explanation that they were subject to the exceptions which applied to other medical secrets. The fifth, and final, resolution simply stated that if, contrary to resolution two, Minute 48 was officially adopted as BMA policy, it should be amended by deleting the word 'already'. Essentially this would leave the acceptability of future legislation that challenged the boundaries of medical confidentiality still open to debate by the BMA as and when it arose.

A second meeting of the subcommittee took place in December 1921 at which a memorandum by Francis Crookshank was received. In addition to his role as a member of the CEC and later the BMA PSC, Crookshank was vice-president of the Medico-Legal Society. No doubt with Burton's query after *Devonshire* in mind, Crookshank raised an important point which had not been sufficiently dealt with by Langdon-Down. New forms of information gathering were challenging the established practice of the courts. Under statute law, and on threat of penalty, individual members of the public were compelled to give information, affecting their private interests, to public officials. According to the developed pattern of legal practice, such information could then be demanded in court, and medical practitioners could be compelled to give it, even for only private interests. Whether this position was in the public interest was a matter for debate. In Crookshank's view, a distinction should be drawn between information voluntarily given to a private practitioner and information imparted, either by statutory compulsion or under a pledge of secrecy from a public body, to a doctor acting as a public official. He was keen to point out that the problems raised were not simply narrow questions of professional privilege but rather wider questions of public policy and public right. This was an important point, for it further illustrated the growing influence of state interest in medical information. Doctors were increasingly being used as instruments of the state for the gathering of information. The early twentieth-century doctor had a duty to pass on information about births, deaths, infectious diseases, criminal abortions, incapacity of insured workers and the medical records of insured patients for statistical purposes. The question of medical confidentiality therefore went right to the heart of the medical profession's role in twentieth-century society.

The CEC subcommittee accepted both Langdon-Down and Crookshank's memoranda with a few amendments.[4] The most significant change to Langdon-Down's proposals was the complete omission of one of the proposed resolutions. The subcommittee backed away from resolution four:

> That it is undesirable that steps should be taken that might lead to the imposition of the duty of secrecy on the profession by law and that consequently it is undesirable that rules such as those governing the procedure at VD clinics in this matter should be given the force of law and if they are retained it is desirable that they should be accompanied by an explanation that they are subject to the exceptions which apply to other medical secrets. (CEC Minutes 19 December 1921)

This was a significant omission and there was no explicit explanation given as to why it was left out. It is probable that having found the recommendations put forward by Council to the ARM of 1921, so out of touch with the representative body's thoughts on the matter, the subcommittee were reluctant to fly in the face of the stated general opinion. The four resolutions they were recommending clearly advocated a more moderate position than that proposed by Resolution 48. They noted a general rule of secrecy which had necessary exceptions, which in itself entailed that the BMA could not, indiscriminately, give its support to members who disobeyed a court's ruling to disclose information. Support would be given, where considered appropriate, to aid a practitioner who had acted in the best interests of the public. These were general resolutions backed up by claims of best interest to the public. But proposed resolution four had gone right to the crux of the controversy of medical confidentiality in 1921. It dealt not only with the question of gaining recognition for medical privilege in court – the topic of Dawson's sidelined motion in parliament and the demand of the Newcastle ARM – but also with the controversy surrounding the rules of confidentiality governing VD clinics, the very issue that had triggered the interwar debate on medical confidentiality.

The CEC passed its recommendations on to the Council and in March 1922 a special meeting of Council was held. The key points for discussion centred on the divergence between the resolutions passed at the ARM in Cambridge 1920 and that in Newcastle 1921. Such differences had to be cleared up and a clear definition of the BMA's position, particularly with regard to the conditions and extent of the support it would give its members, had to be agreed before the ARM in Glasgow 1922. Two distinct sides emerged during the meeting. Langdon-Down put forward the views of the CEC, summarising the arguments developed in their December meetings. He placed particular emphasis on the need to make patients aware of the limits to confidentiality and to remind doctors that secrecy was claimed in the interest of the patient/public, not the profession. The French penal code prevented

4 The key points of Crookshank's memo were included as notes qualifying the proposed resolutions.

doctors from disclosing information, a system which many French doctors found 'irksome' (CEC 31 March 1922). He concluded by reiterating his opinion that the judge was best placed to decide whether or not a doctor's evidence was necessary. However, recognising that judges were not infallible, provision would have to be made for cases where 'judges misunderstood their function'.

Council was not enthused by the CEC's proposals. Ernest Fothergill saw no dissonance between the 1920 and 1921 resolutions. Fothergill was a long-serving member of Council and a constant thorn in the side of the CEC. His proposals on confidentiality had a tendency to conflict with CEC recommendations. He regarded Resolution 48 as little more than a rider to the resolution passed by the 1920 ARM. Nobody would expect the BMA to give its support to anyone who flippantly refused to give evidence, but only in circumstances where it was a clear matter of conscience. If this was accepted, the question was the extent to which the Association would be willing to support such a practitioner. Naturally, in Fothergill's opinion, such support would have to be financial – providing for the practitioner's family, maintaining his practice, and enlisting public support for his cause.

This motion was seconded by Guy Dain. Dain was, in 1922, at the outset of a long and successful career in the BMA. Serving on many committees, he went on to chair both the representative body and Council, and was a direct representative to the GMC from 1934–1961. He was also a member of the Council on Medical and Allied Services and had supported the majority resolution, given to the Ministry of Health in July 1921, that doctors should not be compelled to disclose patient information in court (see Chapter 4). Dain drew a clear distinction between medical confidentiality and medical privilege. The former was a general rule not to disclose, while the latter only had relevance in a court of law. If a doctor claimed privilege it should be for his patient, just as the lawyer's privilege was for his client. In terms of the comparison, the doctor's evidence was more important because it related not only to what he had been told, but also to facts he had learnt by virtue of his skill, for instance that a person was suffering from a particular disease. Dain disagreed with Langdon-Down's opinion that the judge was best place to decide whether medical evidence should be disclosed. He felt, in many cases, the doctor was best placed to weigh up the potential benefit the evidence would have relative to the detriment it would cause the patient. While the BMA should not advocate absolute privilege on all occasions, there were cases where the evidence practitioners were called on to give was of relatively minor importance. In such cases the doctor's refusal to disclose should be upheld.

Dawson was a further supporter of Fothergill's motion. He believed that there had been some confusion between confidentiality and privilege. The question was whether the medical profession was going to insist upon a form of privilege over and above that accorded to a member of the public. Dawson believed that doctors should demand a measure of special privilege, though in the interests of the state, this should not extend to absolute privilege. He suggested that the limits and applications of the privilege should be discussed by medical and legal representatives, but noted that while his legal friends tended to favour a privilege which was only applicable in civil cases, Dawson himself did not favour such a clearly drawn distinction. He had no qualm in stating quite frankly his opinion that lawyers had carved out for themselves an 'astonishing measure of privilege', which had smoothed the legal profession's procedure and secured its place. The priestly privilege derived from the distinction maintained between the priest in his religious capacity and as an ordinary man. What he learnt in the former he felt justified in asserting he did not know in his latter capacity. No judge would run counter to such a claim. Yet, by virtue of their work, doctors were even more involved with the intimacies of human life, receiving secrets relative to a patient's health and otherwise. Echoing the founding fathers of modern medical ethics (Gregory 1772, Percival 1803), Dawson painted a vivid picture of a patient lying on his sickbed, unburdening his mind by confessing certain secrets to his medical attendant. These, not infrequent, confessions were made in moments of weakness and they should be protected by a special privilege granted to medical practitioners in courts of law. Dawson requested a 'strong, unequivocal' statement on these lines from the BMA.

Dawson's remarks found support from James MacDonald. MacDonald had preceded Bolam as chairman of Council from 1911 until 1920. Like Dawson and Dain, he was a member of the Council on Medical and Allied Services and had supported their majority resolution in July 1921. MacDonald explained that he would be prepared to go further than most in exalting the interest of the individual patient, even above public interest, in the cause of medical confidentiality. Henry Brackenbury, a future chairman of both the representative body and Council, was somewhat more reserved. He indicated that the Newcastle resolution's call for a guarantee of unlimited support for a practitioner who refused to disclose in court was excessive. The circumstances and extent of support should be clarified, and a more exact definition be given of when disclosure was the correct course of action. This latter point was perceived, by Sir Thomas Jenner Verrall, as being an exceptionally hazardous route to take. Verrall, who served on the Council from 1893 until his death in 1929, felt that the decision had to be left to the circumstances of each case as it arose.

Drawing on the importance of circumstances, Charles Buttar, the representative member for Kensington, reiterated those in which the ARM in Newcastle had approved controversial Resolution 48. Disturbed by the recent events of *Needham*, the representative body had passed a strong resolution which might, now that more consideration had been given to it, require modification. Buttar believed that there was no middle course to be followed: either the profession contended for an absolute principle of professional secrecy or they ceded the question by default. He pleaded that the BMA stand by the principle of absolute inviolable secrecy, suggesting that if it were necessary for medical men to stand in contempt of court in nine out of ten cases, the resultant protest would be so great as to ensure they did not remain in duress for long.

Bolam indicated that a committee might be set up to consider the matter. This view was supported by Edward Turner (of bicycle seat fame) who suggested that a small committee would have a better chance of arriving quickly at one clear-cut and decisive recommendation. As far as the general law of evidence went, he believed that conscience should be the guide as to whether or not to disclose. However, doctors should still respect statutory obligations 'for they did not wish to be anarchists'. The Council unanimously agreed to refer the matter back to the CEC for further discussion and a more exact formulation of the 'conditions under which, the extent to which, and the ways in which the Association would be willing to support any of its members who refused to divulge' (CEC 31 March 1922). The CEC was to be bolstered for this purpose by the cooperation of the aforementioned speakers.[5] Bishop Harman[6] suggested that the extended CEC should carefully consider a recent article by William Brend[7] in the *BMJ* (14 January 1922, 64–6). In this manner, the CEC was augmented and evolved into the BMA PSC which met for the first time in April 1922.

Summary of 1921 Developments

Clearly 1921 was a trying year for the BMA and its policy on professional secrecy. *Needham* had brought publicity to the question of confidentiality, or rather the obvious lack of it for patient information when demanded as evidence in court. Even when such information had been given under an expressed, and widely advertised, pledge of secrecy. Its timing, falling as it did just before the ARM at Newcastle, brought a backlash of opinion. The representative body voted to disregard the considered advice of the CEC and Council, and adopt a far more extreme position, which called for the recognition of an absolute privilege of confidentiality except in matters already covered by statute. They further demanded the full, unquestioning, support of the BMA for any member who fell foul of the system as a consequence of maintaining confidentiality in this way. The result, Resolution 48, was referred back to the CEC for debate, on the understanding that it was to be resubmitted to the ARM in Glasgow 1922, where its acceptance would result in it becoming the established policy of the Association. This was a clear indication that the more moderate approach being advocated by the CEC and Council, was not in keeping with the majority of members' opinions in the aftermath of Elliot's publicised ordeal in court. In fact, growing discontentment characterised the atmosphere surrounding the issue throughout 1921. Burton and the Ilford Urban District Council were clearly not satisfied with either the Ministry of Health or the BMA's

5 Dawson, Turner, Verrall, Dain, Fothergill, MacDonald.

6 Nathaniel Bishop Harman went on to become Treasurer of the BMA and the Association's direct representative on the GMC. Specialising in problems of the eye, he was an advocate of notification of cases of *ophthalmia neonatorum*. He was also the grandfather of the future government minister, and deputy leader of the Labour party, Harriet Harman.

7 Brend was trained in both law and medicine and was a lecturer on forensic medicine at Charing Cross Hospital Medical School.

approach to the whole question. Furthermore, there were clearly some who felt that the opportunity for change was slipping away with the enforced sidelining of Dawson's motion in the House of Lords. Elements of the BMA showed signs of disappointment at the lack of action from 'certain government departments'. The CEC were not impressed by the reversal of the 1920 Cambridge resolution and the widespread support for the more extreme position advocated in Resolution 48. The divergence of opinion between certain key figures of Council and the CEC was prominent in the special meeting to discuss the five CEC proposals, based on Langdon-Down's assessment of the best way forward, in early 1922. This dispute resulted in the matter being referred back, once again, to the CEC. But the importance of arriving at a clear policy, and the pressure of time before the ARM in Glasgow 1922, saw some important characters drafted in to augment the CEC. The PSC, as the expanded group came to be known, included both doctors and lawyers, and the members held a wide range of opinions on professional secrecy. It is perhaps of little surprise to learn that before too long individuals felt obliged to break away and publicise their opinions elsewhere. In a pamphlet which reprinted a speech on professional secrecy that he had given to the annual meeting of the South Midland Branch of the BMA in late June 1922, Crookshank stated:

> My diffidence in dealing with this subject arises from the fact that, with your President, I have been, until recently, a member of the Central Ethical Committee of the British Medical Association, which, as you know, has given much attention to the questions involved. Unfortunately, I lately felt compelled to dissociate myself from the work of that committee owing to my inability to find my own views in harmony with the policies advocated by some of those in greater authority. (Crookshank 1922, 3)

The PSC, charged with the task of bringing order out of chaos, became the focus of attention.

The Guiding Light of Conscience – the First Meeting of the BMA Professional Secrecy Committee, 1922

With pressure of time before the ARM in Glasgow, the first meeting of the PSC took place at the end of March 1922. Members were to discuss the CEC recommendations put forward to Council, two further memoranda, one from Fothergill and another from Dain, and Brend's article in the *BMJ*. Specifically, the committee was to focus upon the extent to which, and the ways in which, the BMA should support any of its members who refused to disclose medical information in court. Other than the specific emphasis on the doctor's obligation in court, the remit matched that given to Council by the representative body at Cambridge in 1920 (Minute 76 ARM 1920), testament to the frustrated efforts of the BMA to achieve meaningful progress towards a fixed policy for the guidance and support of its members in the intervening period. Yet, time was of the essence, as Council wanted a final report before its meeting on 26 April.

Fothergill's memo was first. As he had made clear at the special meeting of Council, he advocated rejecting the recommendations which the CEC had put forward.[8] He believed that they had been formulated in order to establish the law in the strongest possible position and that they failed to take sufficient account of the situation which had arisen in the Newcastle ARM. He reiterated his belief that the Cambridge and Newcastle resolutions were not antagonistic. By suggesting that they were, and believing the desire for privilege to have stemmed from 'professional dignity, pride and jealousy',[9] the CEC had disregarded it and stressed a more moderate position (PSC 31 March 1922). However, given the strength of feeling expressed at Newcastle, the attempt to return to the earlier position threatened to set the debate on a circular trajectory.

In Fothergill's opinion this could be avoided, as the CEC report had already given the solution to the confusion over professional secrecy: *conscience*. In 1896, Avory had called the same factor 'discretion'; a report of the CEC had also referred to it as 'moral obligation'; and, in order to sum up the collective meaning of these terms, Fothergill cited the words of Tredgold :

> The quality of mind which enables a man to feel that he has obligations to society which makes him sensible of the ideals of honour and honesty; of compassion and chivalry; of patriotism and altruism; and which not only restrains the individual from doing wrong, but impels him to do right. (PSC 31 March 1922)

Fine words indeed, but, in practice, a phrase such as 'patriotism and altruism' could pull the doctor who wished to serve both state and patient, in opposing directions. Fothergill suggested that Resolution 48 should not be interpreted as giving carte blanche to members to disregard the demands of a court. Rather, no support should be expected by, or given to, a practitioner who refused to disclose based on a desire to flout the court or appear heroic. The backing of the BMA should only be given to practitioners who had weighed the matter carefully and acted in the interest of the current patient and other patients' future concerns. Fothergill's intention was quite clear. He wished to separate out the egoistic attention seeker from the principled martyr, but, beyond this broad division, it is difficult to see how the sanctioned motive applied when a practitioner found himself in a case where both parties were his patients. The interest of one patient did not always match with the interests of other patients.

Fothergill turned to Brend's article on professional secrecy. This set out four conditions which should be fulfilled before the BMA provided support to

8 His objections were split into those which he saw as fundamental objections, and those which were concerned with detail. Only the former will be given overt consideration here.

9 This remark, made by Langdon-Down was quoted by Fothergill.

a member who refused to give evidence in court (*BMJ* 14 January 1922, 66). Firstly, communications must originate in a confidence that they would not be disclosed. Secondly, the element of confidentiality must be essential to the full and satisfactory maintenance of the relation between the parties. Thirdly, the relation must be one which, in the opinion of the community, 'ought to be sedulously fostered'. Lastly, the injury that would result to the relationship by disclosure of the communications must be greater than the benefit thereby gained for the correct disposal of litigation. Fothergill proposed an addition to Brend's four criteria, namely, that the doctor in question would be required to decline the court's request using language agreed and approved by the ARM. He believed that such a declaration could follow the lines of that used by the French: 'That as the facts on which he is being interrogated were brought to his knowledge whilst acting in his professional capacity and therefore were obtained in confidence he, in the exercise of his conscience finds himself unable to disclose them without his patient's consent' (PSC 31 March 1922).

These, it will be noted, were hardly revolutionary words having been the standard advice given out by the BMA and Ministry of Health over the preceding two years. Fothergill's next step was to outline the forms of support that a practitioner who fell into difficulty with the court, as a result of following the above advice, would receive. Support was required on three fronts. Firstly, there was the tricky issue of finance. In no doubt of the scale of the problem, Fothergill queried whether the funds of the BMA could be used, or if a separate fund, which demanded a subscription based upon a percentage of each member's practice, would be required. Secondly, on a local level, each branch would have to have a centrally approved system of support in place, in order to continue the work of a member's practice during any period of imprisonment. Lastly, on a central level, the medico-political committee could educate and focus the press, public, legal and government opinion in favour of the member, while also aiding the local branch in the maintenance of the member's dependants and practice. Having taken account of his proposals, Fothergill believed the BMA would be in a position to suitably amend Resolution 48 for resubmission to the ARM in Glasgow, and that either before or afterwards, a committee of medical and legal practitioners, along with some laymen, should be formed to discuss the whole question.

Next on the meeting's agenda was Dain's memo. The maintenance or violation of professional secrecy was, in his opinion, a moral issue and consequently should be a matter for individual conscience. Distinguishing between the general rule of medical confidentiality and the question of medical privilege, Dain accepted that there were exceptions, statutory and moral, to the former. In the case of medical privilege he drew attention to the acceptance of a level of privilege for both priest and lawyer. The high profile cases in which doctors had been forced to break professional confidences in the early 1920s had made clear that they had no privilege in court. According to Dain, when a doctor felt bound by conscience not to disclose, the lack of support from the BMA, evident in the account given by Elliot post-*Needham*, made it nigh impossible to resist the court's demands.

Recognising the impact that guaranteed support would have on doctors who found themselves bound by conscience to maintain secrecy, the two previous ARMs had passed resolutions advocating BMA support (Minute 76 in Cambridge 1920 and Resolution 48 in Newcastle 1921).

Many had tried to draw a distinction, according medical privilege in civil cases but not in criminal cases. In the latter, the state required the violation of secrecy for the purposes of public justice, whereas in the former, one individual was seeking the breach of another individual's medical confidentiality for their own ends. The civil cases in which disclosure was most often required were those involving divorce, and, in Dain's opinion, these could largely be avoided if the law of divorce was altered to give equality to the sexes. As previously noted (Chapter 4) medical evidence was used to prove adultery and cruelty, both of which were required for a woman to divorce her husband. But Dain's prediction, of a drastic drop in the demand for medical testimony if women had parity of proof in divorce proceedings, was perhaps overly optimistic. Evidence from VD doctors could be subpoenaed in order to prove adultery alone. Indeed, that was the basis on which Elliot had been subpoenaed to give evidence in *Needham*.[10] Parity in the divorce law would remove the need for women to prove more than their husbands' adultery, but this would not necessarily reduce the number of cases in which medical evidence was demanded.

Dain disagreed with Langdon-Down that the judge was best placed to decide whether a patient's confidence was to be breached. A judge might regard the doctor's testimony as an easy method of establishing facts, without considering the damage to public confidence in the medical profession. In other words, the convenience of the court might be enough for a judge to require medical evidence, particularly when a doctor's testimony could save the court time and bother. Dain's final point related to the semantics of Resolution 48. He noted that it committed the BMA to use all its *power*, not all its *resources*, which suggested, to him at least, that the support would not be monetary but rather would equate to local and national influence. Thus, like Fothergill, Dain interpreted Resolution 48 as being applicable only to *bona fide* members who based their refusal to disclose on a conscientious objection, in keeping with the essentials laid down by Brend's article. However, unlike Fothergill, Dain clearly did not feel that the BMA should provide financial support.

Dr Stevens put forward two notices of motion to be considered. Firstly, in the absence of patient consent, a practitioner was not justified to disclose, even in a court of law, professional confidences which might damage the good name or reputation of the patient, or might involve him in any harm other than of a purely financial nature. In cases where a refusal to disclose was considered to be justified and yet the practitioner still fell foul of the court, Stevens urged the BMA to make suitable representation to the Home Office, and ventilate the issue in the *BMJ*.

---

10 In Scotland *ophthalmia neonatorum* was a notifiable disease. (Davidson 2000, 178; Jenkinson, 2002, 164).

Secondly, he suggested that the Hippocratic Oath should be published in the *BMJ*, along with examples of the forms of obligation to which medical graduates were required to subscribe in universities and colleges in England, Scotland and Ireland. As in 1915, the *BMJ* was once again being invoked as a weapon in the debate on confidentiality. However, it is also interesting to note the specific exclusion of financial harm from the justifications for protecting a patient's confidences. Argument was made in Chapter 2 that doctors' ideals of honour were not always easy to distinguish from their financial interests. Here, Stevens drew a clear distinction between the hurting of a patient's reputation and any damage done to his financial interests. Stevens was emphasising that reputation mattered, money did not – at least as far as patients were concerned.

Having considered the report of the proceedings of the special Council meeting, the memoranda from Fothergill and Dain, the article by Brend, and the notices from Stevens, Dawson proposed the following motion: 'that the proper preservation of professional secrecy necessitates a measure of privilege being recognised for medical witnesses in Courts of Law above and beyond what is accorded to the ordinary witness.' (PSC 31 March 1922) The proposal was unanimously resolved. Crookshank proposed that the term 'privilege' not be construed as meaning 'legal privilege'. After considerable discussion this was withdrawn and replaced by a further proposal by Crookshank that the term 'privilege' *should* be construed as meaning 'legal privilege'. Wallace Henry put forward an amendment which clarified that the measure of privilege aimed at was that no registered medical practitioner would be compelled to disclose professional confidences without patient consent. This amendment was carried, also as a substantive motion, by ten votes to four. Clearly then, despite many months of focused discussion, the select membership of the PSC were having difficulty establishing exactly what the privilege, which they all wanted, actually was. Unanimity was restored with a proposal by Arnold Lyndon. Lyndon joined the BMA Council in 1922 and served on it until 1935. He also served on the council of the Medical Defence Union and on the Standing Joint Committee of the Medical Defence Union and Medical Protection Society. He suggested that for the time being the BMA should support in every way possible any member who, in the opinion of Council or the CEC, was considered justified in refusing to disclose professional confidences. It was further resolved that Stevens' motion for the publication in the *BMJ* of the Hippocratic Oath and the examples of forms of obligation should be forwarded 'for the favourable consideration of the Editor'.[11]

In adopting Lyndon's proposal, the PSC seemed to be broadly agreeing with the representative body's feeling as expressed in Resolution 48, but with two key exceptions. Rather than advocating unqualified support for any member who refused to breach secrecy in court, which Resolution 48 technically permitted, Lyndon's proposal only granted support where an arbiter deemed the member's actions to have been justified. This led, naturally, to the second qualification; that

11 The editor of the *BMJ* at the time was Sir Dawson Williams.

the arbitration of whether a member's actions fell into the 'justified' category should be undertaken by BMA Council or the CEC. If accepted, this would not only remove the potential threat of indiscriminate demand on BMA resources, it would also give control of BMA policy on confidentiality back to the more moderately-minded Council and CEC.

The Second Meeting of the BMA Professional Secrecy Committee

The second meeting took place a week and a half later, with only a fortnight left before the Council deadline. Brend had been asked to furnish the committee with information relating to the privilege granted to doctors in some states in America, particularly focusing on the objections which had been made to the privilege, and who had made them. After the unanimous acceptance of Lyndon's proposal at their previous meeting, Alfred Cox had drawn up a draft report to be considered by Council before being put to the 1922 ARM. Memoranda were also received from Fothergill and Hempson.

Cox's draft report examined whether the claims of communal interest, as expressed by a judge, overrode those of the individual patient. Council supported the representative body's belief that it was in the best interests of the community, and in keeping with the best traditions of the medical profession, to support a medical practitioner who refused to give out information without patient consent. The obligation of confidentiality was long-standing, having found expression in the Hippocratic Oath, and had even been 'fitfully' endorsed by the law when high damages were awarded to patients whose confidence had been violated – presumably another reference to *Kitson v Playfair*. The BMA had always resisted demands from the law that doctors should disclose more information, particularly in relation to abortion. Their grounds for resisting the law's advances were simply that:

> for the good of the greater number it is essential that nothing shall be done to prevent persons who are ill from consulting doctors in the fullest confidence that their secret, even if it be that they have connived at the commission of a crime, is safe with the doctor. (PSC draft memo, 11 April 1922)

Such firm assurance of the sanctity of the doctor–patient relationship, even in the context of past crime, is strongly reminiscent of the RCP's discussion with Avory and Clarke, and Saundby's comments in *Medical Ethics* which had incurred the wrath of judicial opinion in 1915. This represented a return to a more fundamental position than either the BMA Council or CEC had shown since the 1915 confrontation. Having launched out with a strong stance against the law in the pre-war debate the higher echelons of the BMA had recoiled to a more moderate position in the discussion of the early 1920s. The draft report was even keen to point out that the notification of infectious diseases, while recognised as the only exception to confidentiality, placed the responsibility on the relatives and friends of the patient as well as the doctor, to notify the authorities. Furthermore, the law of notification was well known, so implicit consent to notification could be taken from the patient's willingness to consult medical opinion.

Seemingly advocating a strong stance in favour of maintaining medical confidentiality, the draft report then muddied the issue by stating that everyone was aware that there were occasions on which individual practitioners would feel their duty to the state or other individuals compelled them to breach the confidence of their patient. In keeping with the opinions expressed by Fothergill and Dain, this was taken to be a matter of morals, governed by individual conscience, and therefore could not be covered by general rules. Having dealt, in broad terms, with the issue, Cox turned to the tricky question of how the widespread belief in the fundamental importance of medical confidentiality might be reconciled with the right of the state to demand evidence in court. The privilege given to lawyers was required for the legal system to work and so was in the interests of the general public as well as clients. Although there was no official privilege granted to priests, the courts understood the importance of secrecy such men attached to information given to them in their religious capacity. Demanding information from priests would only incite a passive resistance 'which would be stronger than the law', so priests were understood to enjoy a greater degree of privilege, despite potential detriment to the administration of justice.

By contrast, the case against medical privilege amounted to the detrimental impact it would have on the detection or prosecution of crime. Yet, Cox pointed out, the same argument could be levied against the priest and lawyer. The crux of the medical case for privilege revolved around the belief that:

> It is better that injustice should be done or crime left undetected on rare occasions than that fear of public disclosure should be placed in the way of perfectly free communications between patient and doctor. If this free communication is impeded disease would be left untreated and not only the individual but the community would suffer. (PSC draft memo 11 April 1922)

Council was aware that there was a conflict of roles between the practitioner as citizen, with his duty to the state, and the practitioner as doctor, with his duty to the individual patient. For this reason, they advocated that there should not be an absolute privilege for the medical profession on a par with lawyers and priests. Rather, the dual loyalties conflict could best be resolved by granting a modified privilege that prevented the court from compelling a medical practitioner to divulge information without the consent of his patient. It is not clear how this would substantially differ from legal and religious privilege, for presumably neither group would have much difficulty in aiding the demands of justice if their client gave them consent to do so. Indeed, the suspicion that this was more of a comprehensive privilege than the report made it out to be is highlighted by its similarity to BMA Council Minute 542 of 27 Jan 1915: 'the Council is of opinion that a medical practitioner should not under any circumstances disclose voluntarily, without the patient's consent, information which he has obtained from that patient in the exercise of his professional duties'. As noted in Chapter 3, this was agreed at a time when the BMA was seeking to establish itself in a strong position in maintaining confidentiality against the wishes of the law.

Having established the extent of the privilege to be sought, Cox turned to assessing the level of support the BMA would be willing to give its members. The PSC had adopted Lyndon's recommendation from the previous meeting. Thereby, only individuals whom Council or the CEC deemed to be justified in refusing the court's request were eligible to receive BMA support. The criteria for assessing whether a case was justified were fourfold. The first three were lifted directly from Brend's article in the *BMJ*, but the fourth differed. Brend had emphasised that the damage disclosure would cause to the doctor–patient relationship would have to be greater than the benefit gained through the correct disposal of litigation. In other words, the predicted consequences would determine whether BMA support was justified. By contrast, the PSC argued that the practitioner must persuade Council that the information came to his knowledge in his professional capacity and consequently he considered himself 'morally bound to plead inability to disclose them [the patient's confidences] without his patient's consent'. This change – from Brend's fourth criteria, which had been endorsed by Fothergill at the previous meeting, to the draft report's new fourth criteria – indicated a clear shift in the way the committee was thinking about privilege. There was a move away from consequentialist arguments which had failed to convince the judiciary that the benefits to public health of maintaining medical confidentiality in court could outweigh the loss of medical testimony to the legal process. The justification for lawyers' privilege was that, without it, individuals would not have necessary access to legal advice for fear their adviser would be subsequently subpoenaed to give evidence, thereby hindering the work of the justice system. A similar argument had been put forward by advocates of medical privilege, who argued that without guarantees of confidentiality, many with VD – especially those who were married – might refrain from seeking necessary medical treatment to the detriment of public health. However, instead of modelling their claims on the consequentialist model of legal privilege, the PSC was now attempting to align the doctor's position with that of the religious adviser: an individual morally bound to secrecy whose strong conviction of duty made him immune to the discipline of the court. Too late for Elliot of Chester, the BMA was setting a course for medical martyrdom.

Elliot had succumbed to the court's demand because of the absence of practical professional support. Cox's draft report indicated that support would now be available on three different levels. The local division would be responsible to Council for successfully maintaining the doctor's practice. The BMA would organise public opinion through the press and parliament. It would also provide legal advice, and their funds would be made available because 'the cases will be test cases on a matter which affects the honour and interests of the medical profession'. The draft report ended on a rather positive note, suggesting that any enforced imprisonment of a practitioner would probably be short; the courageous act of going to prison, rather than betraying a patient's confidence, would probably enhance a practitioner's long-term prospects, and if any additional funds were needed these could easily be raised by special appeal. Thus, the final paragraph read somewhat like a BMA manifesto for medical martyrdom.

Elliot had been willing to endure prison for a short period, and here Council was suggesting that imprisonment would not last long. As well as promising publicity for the cause, legal advice, and BMA funds, additional sources of support could be drummed up as required, so potential martyrs need not worry about how their family would survive or whether their practice would be damaged. Indeed, far from proving detrimental, it was suggested that martyrdom could enhance a practitioner's long-term prospects, presumably by attracting patients who had been impressed by the high ethical standards displayed. The similarities between the underpinning philosophy of these conclusions and Caesar Hawkins' stance in the Duchess of Kingston trial are stark. Just as Hawkins had used his forced appearance in court to advertise his ethical approach to medical practice, in the full knowledge that such a high profile trial would be closely followed by patients, both actual and potential, so the PSC were reassuring members that martyrdom for the cause of medical confidentiality would reap benefits for the individual concerned. The organisation of public opinion, through multiple channels of press and government, would do for the medical martyr's reputation, what galleries packed with spectators and the *Gentleman's Magazine* had done for Hawkins 146 years prior. Save, perhaps, for the elevation to a knighthood.

Having considered the draft report, the PSC turned to a memo by Fothergill on the conditions and terms of BMA support. Fothergill proposed three additional criteria for support to the four set out in the draft report the committee had just considered. The first addition placed an obligation on a member who sought BMA support to get in touch with Council as soon as it was likely that he would be called upon to breach confidentiality without patient consent. He would also have to agree, in writing, to act in accordance with Council's decision. Fothergill's second addition stipulated that the member would have to be a fully paid up subscriber to the Medical Secrecy Defence trust fund (to be set up) and could not be involved as a defendant in any ethical procedure at any level of the BMA. Lastly, he would also have to be a member of a recognised medical defence society which could aid him should he feel morally bound to make a disclosure without patient consent.

Therefore, unlike the draft report which advocated the use of BMA funds, Fothergill advocated the setting up of a Medical Secrecy Defence trust fund which would provide financial assistance of up to a year and a half's purchase value of the doctor's practice as assessed by an independent accountant. As Bartrip (1996) notes, the significant rise in the BMA subscription charges in 1914 had been a contributory factor to a decline in membership around this time, and the Association's finances had been hit hard by the National Health Insurance struggle and the First World War.[12] In order to avoid adding greatly to members' costs, it was proposed that members who paid 3 (or 5) shillings into the Medical Secrecy Defence trust fund before February each year would have that amount discounted from their annual BMA membership subscription. The fund could also be bolstered by a donation from the medical insurance committee and by approach to some of the recognised medical defence societies. Fothergill, of course, would not have been aware of the London and Counties Medical Protection Society's request to the Ministry of Health to be recompensed for their financial support of Elliot the previous year. Yet, Fothergill echoed Cox's assertion that the financial loss to a temporarily imprisoned practitioner would be both small and consequently offset by a boom in his practice. He also agreed that BMA support should take the form of local practical support, publicity/opinion support, and financial support for dependants, and suggested Resolution 48 should be amended accordingly.

Fothergill's other major point of interest echoed Crookshank's enquiry as to whether a doctor holding a public position should be required to give information in a private interest case. Building on what he had stated in his earlier memo, he suggested a medico-sociological committee be formed to consider this and other questions, and report either to Council or direct to the ARM in Glasgow. If this was unsatisfactory, as an alternative he suggested approaching the relevant departments of government with a view to 'the implied pledge being incorporated in an Act of Parliament and not being left to orders issued by a Department' (Fothergill memo PSC 11 April 1922). This referred to the regulations issued in conjunction with the government VD treatment clinics, which Elliot had unsuccessfully tried to cite as his justification not to disclose in *Needham*. The judge had ruled that regulations, even when issued by government departments, did not have force in a court of law. Encapsulating the same pledge of secrecy in statute law would prevent the forced disclosure of information received by a doctor working in a government approved scheme for the private interest of a divorce case. However, as the previous two years had shown, and as subsequent attempts at legislation would confirm (see Chapter 7), getting statutory recognition for any form of medical privilege was no easy task.

The final item on the PSC's agenda was a memo by Hempson. He was at pains to dispel the belief that there was a distinction to be drawn between medical confidentiality and privilege. In his view, what was being sought was recognition, within the law courts, of the generally endorsed practice of doctors maintaining their patients' confidences. There were four stages to the achievement of this objective. Firstly, doctors needed to standardise their position on medical confidentiality. Secondly, the general public had to be made aware of the medical profession's concerted attitude. Thirdly this, along with its traditional basis, had then to be instilled into the mind of the law. Lastly, support would be needed for members who suffered as 'martyrs to the cause' (Hempson memo PSC 11 April 1922).

12 Subscription rates rose by 68%, from 25s to 42s (Bartrip 1996, 194).

Having set out his thoughts on the way the BMA should proceed, Hempson addressed a point which had thus far been overlooked. In formulating their position by consideration of the doctor's obligation to his patient, the BMA had failed to consider the consequences for relations within the profession. Having previously worked as solicitor to the Medical Defence Union, Hempson had seen many cases where doctors had been cited to give testimony in investigations of malpractice. If an individual who brought a case of malpractice against a practitioner had consulted four additional doctors but only called the two whom he knew would give favourable evidence on his behalf, what would be the position of the two doctors who were not subpoenaed by the plaintiff? Even if subpoenaed to appear by the defendant (accused practitioner), it is unlikely they would have the consent of the patient (plaintiff) to give testimony against his case. What advice and support could the BMA offer members in such circumstances? The example seemed to leave the doctor with two options: either break the patient's confidentiality in order to give testimony in favour of the defendant; or maintain confidentiality to the detriment of a fellow doctor. The first option, allowing breach of confidentiality without patient consent to protect a doctor's reputation, could readily be interpreted as prioritising the interests of the medical profession over ethical considerations of patient confidentiality. The second option would only permit practitioners to give evidence *against* each other, posing a threat to professional harmony and unity. While the illustration given involved a civil case, the same issues would be raised if a doctor stood trial on a criminal charge.

Hempson foresaw a further difficulty in the BMA's proposed policy. If conscience was the measure of justification for pleading privilege in court and the support or otherwise of the BMA was to be determined by Council in light of the facts of each case, it was feasible that a practitioner could refuse to disclose in court on grounds of conscience, only to find that Council later disagreed with his position. The merits of an act of conscience could at times only be assessed after the event. Moreover, conscience could take different practitioners in different directions. Behind the fine rhetoric of Tredgold's definition of conscience lay the fact that 'in man there are varying degrees of "conscience" according to his birth, his upbringing or his station in life'. Individual conscience was not a fixed yardstick with which to measure, or on which to rely.

In a sub-appendix to the printed minutes of the meeting, Langdon-Down tried to draw together the threads of agreement which had emerged in the PSC's discussions. Four things were required. First, the maintenance of the public's interests as patients, although it was recognised their interests as citizens sometimes needed priority. Secondly, doctors sought to maintain professional dignity in court, both in their actions and in the court's level of respect for them. Again, it was realised that the public's interests, as patients or citizens, was of prior importance. Thirdly, the profession wished to avoid 'being called upon to do violence to our consciences, whether in their civic or their professional capacity' (Langdon-Down memo, 11 April 1922). This simply highlighted the dual loyalties dilemma faced by a profession bound by a strong sense of conscience and duty, caught between the traditional obligation to private patient and the growing obligations to collective interests. Lastly, anarchical methods of achieving the profession's goals were to be avoided.

The prolonged debate had brought Langdon-Down to the conclusion that legislation was too rigid and ill-adapted for the ends on which the BMA were now focusing. Absolute privilege was not sought, so the difficulties faced by practitioners would best be removed by emphasising to the public that medical confidentiality was subject to certain exceptions. He suggested that a compromise was the best solution. Practitioner's should not antagonise judges, but make clear to them the importance of maintaining patient confidentiality. Therefore, while the doctor had a duty to disclose medical evidence to prevent 'grave injury to the State, the patient or other persons', so judges should recognise a duty on them not to compel a breach of medical confidence unless absolutely necessary. If there was evidence to show that the judiciary was not cooperating, then the matter could be taken back to the law officers of the Crown. Thus after numerous meetings, memos and proposals, widespread debate, and the setting up of a PSC to advise the BMA, the CEC chairman suggested that the solution lay, more or less, with a better advertised version of the status quo. Like children arguing over a toy, both the courts and the medical profession could get what they wanted. But first they would have to learn to cooperate.

Sibling Rivalry and the 'Spoilt Child of the Professions'

Langdon-Down's desire to promote compromise no doubt stemmed from many years considering the question as chairman of the CEC. It may also have been influenced by recent events at the Medico-Legal Society. Lord Dawson of Penn had delivered a controversial address on medical secrecy to the Medico-Legal Society in the period between the special meeting of Council and the first meeting of the PSC (*The Lancet* 1922 vol.1, 619). While much of his speech merely reiterated well-rehearsed arguments over abortion, VD, and precedents from the Duchess of Kingston onwards, he raised the stakes in his assessment of the privilege given to lawyers. Dawson stressed that doctors' sole aim was gaining privilege in the interest of patients. However, he saw no such altruism in the law: 'for generations the law has occupied a favoured position; it is, in fact, the spoilt child of the professions.' Moreover, extension of a privilege to the profession of medicine was not opposed because it would be detrimental to state interests, but because it would be inconvenient to legal procedure. Such comments turned the evening's debate from a considered discussion of the problem at hand into an inter-professional argument, which spilled over to a further meeting of the society the following week.

The propensity of some doctors to see the issue in terms of relative professional prestige proved too much for Crookshank. His resignation from the CEC was acknowledged at its next meeting in April 1922. A later communication gave an indication of his reasons: 'I view with very great apprehension certain tendencies which seem to me to be forcing the BMA into an attitude of disharmony rather than of "co-operation", in respect of the interests of the social organism, and particularly, this matter of privilege.' (Crookshank to CEC 30 May 1922) Clearly passionate about the issue, Crookshank continued to speak his thoughts, notably at the aforementioned meeting of the South Midland Branch of the BMA in June 1922, which was later published (Crookshank 1922).

Others were also feeling the heat in the run-up to the ARM in Glasgow. While Crookshank's concern was that doctors' egos were distorting and undermining the social role of the profession, Hempson was worried that the medical profession's own interests were being overlooked: 'above all things we want to be careful that our altruistic conceptions for the guidance of the profession in aid of the public weal, do not place the Profession itself in circumstances of difficulty.' (Hempson to Cox 4 April 1922) Clearly he felt his point on the doctor's obligation in malpractice cases had not been satisfactorily resolved. Cox, having drafted the PSC's final report to Council, had even graver doubts:

> I have never felt less comfortable over anything than I do over this … I have tried to make it, within the limits of a short report, as convincing to myself and others as I could. But frankly I am not convinced that the line we are suggesting will stand criticism … it is quite hopeless to try to build up a series of rules and regulations and to try to make it look watertight. The attitude rests on sentiment and tradition and it is no good trying to invest it with logical consistency. (Cox to Hempson 6 April 1922)

The Annual Representatives Meeting, 1922

Given the trepidation which had gripped elements of the CEC since the representative body's drive to make Resolution 48 official BMA policy, the 1922 ARM in Glasgow was a relatively painless affair. The annual report of Council had already softened up members by setting out why the general position advocated by Resolution 48 was unjustified and indicating the circumstances in which the BMA would be willing to give support (*BMJ* supplement 1922 vol.1, 134). Prior to the ARM, the CEC requested that Council withdraw paragraph 110 of their report (CEC 30 May 1922). This paragraph set out the four criteria that the PSC had agreed should be satisfied before a member could claim BMA support, the last of which had demonstrated a shift from consideration of the consequences of doctors' actions back to an emphasis on duty. As Langdon-Down's proposed amendment during the Glasgow meeting was to show, the CEC were worried that an emphasis on doctors' duty of confidentiality, with no thought of the consequences, may stir memories of Elliot's ordeal in *Needham* and push the BMA back towards indiscriminate confrontation with the law.

Council appear to have heeded the request, as paragraph 110 was not discussed. Rather, two proposals based on the PSC's resolutions were brought before the representative body. The first was intended to quash the controversial resolutions of the previous year. It stated:

> That Minute 48 of the ARM 1921 be rescinded, and that it be the policy of the Association to support in every way possible any member of the BMA within the UK who, in the opinion of the Council or the Central Ethical Committee acting on behalf of Council, after due consideration of the circumstances is deemed to have been justified in refusing to disclose any information he may have obtained in the exercise of his professional duties. (Minute 60, BMA ARM 1922)

Langdon-Down guided this through without amendment.[13] Having reined in the difficulties of the previous year, the second council resolution aimed to guide the representative body into a more moderate agenda for change:

> That the Annual Representatives Meeting 1922, express the opinion that the proper preservation of professional secrecy necessitates a measure of special consideration being recognised for medical witnesses in courts of law above and beyond what is accorded to the ordinary witness. (Minute 63, BMA ARM 1922)

This proposal caused more of a stir. Buttar suggested that it was essential that information should not be given without the consent of the patient. Fothergill coupled this onto the Council's original motion and the representative body agreed it (Minute 65). On putting this hybrid forward as the substantive motion, two amendments were proposed. The first suggested the omission of 'without the consent of the patient concerned'. Clearly there were some who still believed the privilege should be the doctor's rather than the patient's. The amendment was lost.[14] No doubt concerned that the motion was heading towards too rigid a position, Langdon-Down proposed the insertion of, 'save to prevent grave injury or injustice to the state, the patient, or other members of the community' (Minute 67). This amendment was also rejected and Fothergill's hybrid adopted.

The BMA's new position was that doctors required a special degree of privilege in court and patient consent to disclosure was essential. Bearing in mind Cox's view of the impossibility of developing watertight rules, CEC members' hearts might well have sunk at the prospect of the matter being referred back to them in order to determine and define what the 'special degree of privilege' should be. The injunction that no information should be given without patient consent was too rigid without Langdon-Down's amendment. Yet the representative body was not finished. They rejected a proposal to press for a government committee enquiry into medical secrecy, but resolved that an appropriate BMA committee

13 Though there were seven dissentients. BMA ARM 1922 Minute 62.

14 Proposed by A. Blackhall-Morison member for Marylebone. Minute 66.

should examine a proposed scheme for the modified notification of VD.[15] Thus, the 1922 ARM, in addition to rescinding Resolution 48, had delivered more or less the Council's agenda. The BMA were neither advocating unlimited support for anyone who took the road to courtroom martyrdom, nor were they opting for Langdon-Down's vision of a better advertised status quo. Rather they were somewhere in the middle, with a belief that doctors should have privilege not to disclose without patient consent.

Away from the debates over medical privilege, there was evidence that little had changed in the CEC's staunch defence of medical confidentiality outside the courtroom. When a stillborn child was found parcelled up and left on the banks of the river Wensum in Norwich, the city police wrote to doctors in the area requesting that they notify the police if approached by a woman showing signs of having recently given birth. On learning of this, the CEC were quick to resolve that the police should be informed that BMA members were advised to ignore the request and should 'in no circumstances' give the information asked for (CEC SSC minutes, 10 July 1922). Whatever their position was in relation to medical privilege, doctors were not to be used as detectives.

By autumn 1922 the BMA Council had established that the CEC were willing to consider applications for non-disclosure in court by members and advise whether the BMA would support their claim (CEC SSC minutes 31 October 1922). The CEC were also asked to ascertain the views of the legal profession and the RCP and RCS (CEC SSC 14 November 1922). Everything seemed to be heading towards a concerted effort to shore up the boundaries of medical confidentiality against legal encroachment. By four months later the whole question had been shelved.

Moved to Inertia – the BMA Put Privilege on Long-Term Hold

Several factors contributed to this change. The ARM 1922 had resolved that a committee should consider the proposals for a modified form of notification of VD. In September an *ad hoc* committee was formed.[16] The core problem to be addressed was that many patients attending VD clinics were not completing their course of treatment. In 1920, only 20,000 out of 162,000 patients had continued treatment until cured or in a non-infectious state (Turner memo, Special Committee on VD, 19 September 1922). Seeing this as a waste of state money, it was being suggested that all people who sought free treatment should be compelled to complete the course under pain of notification to the local health authority 'who

15 The first proposal by C.W. Cunnington member for Hampstead; the second by Bishop Harman. BMA ARM 1922, Minutes 69 and 73 respectively.

16 The committee consisted of the Officers of the Association, together with Drs H.G. Dain, E.R. Fothergill, T.W.H. Garstang, Mr N. Bishop Harman, R. Langdon-Down, J. McGregor-Robertson, E.B. Turner and Sir Jenner Verrall. BMA Special Committee on the Notification of VD 1922–23.

would have power to warn him, and if still recalcitrant, take proceedings to ensure the completion of his treatment'.

The committee were not in favour of notification but decided to obtain the views of BMA divisions through a postal questionnaire. The results were overwhelmingly against notification. There was unanimous rejection of general notification, by name and address, of cases of VD. The medical officer in charge of the VD clinic in Leicester and Rutland suggested that such a policy would close the clinic as no one would attend (Special Committee on VD 11 January 1923). There was limited support for modified notification if patients stopped treatment early, 17 divisions were in favour as opposed to 51 against. However, a five-year survey in Australia had shown that modified notification had failed to affect attendance rates at clinics. By July 1923, the committee had little difficulty in advising Council that any form of notification of VD was not a favourable option at that time. Yet, consideration of modified notification alone must have been a brake on the drive for privilege. Doctors would be hard pressed to justify keeping evidence relating to VD from the courts if they were considering notifying cases outside the courtroom.

In the meantime the CEC, having consulted with Dawson, were having problems following Council's instruction to open negotiations on privilege with the legal profession. Their main concern was the level of opposition they were likely to face from the judiciary. As the 1915 debate had shown, the BMA were not averse to fighting their corner against unsympathetic legal minds. This time, however, they were up against Lord Chancellor Birkenhead. In autumn 1921 Birkenhead had written an essay on medical secrecy which he circulated to all judges and Lords of Appeal. Designed to provide a definitive argument against the granting of medical privilege its impact filtered beyond legal circles and it was published under the title 'Should a Doctor Tell?' in a collection of essays (Smith 1922). Clearly rattled by its contents, the CEC stated the essay was 'an indication of the opposition which the medical profession may be likely to encounter in its plea for such special consideration' (BMA Council agenda 14 February 1923). They recommended to Council that in light of Birkenhead's views the best way forward would be to consult with the RCP and RCS in order to develop a consensus of medical opinion before approaching the law. However, when Council met to discuss this proposal in early 1923 they decided to recommend that no further action be taken for six months. No explicit reason is given and it can only be assumed that members shared the CEC's concern over Birkenhead's rallying of the judiciary. Council's inaction on the matter was extended indefinitely in September, and by 1924 their resignation was evident: 'Council has come to the conclusion that no useful purpose would be served by proceeding further with it at present.' (CEC 25 September 1923 and Council Annual Report 1923–4) The drive for special consideration, and the battle to overturn a 150-year-old precedent denying medical privilege in court, had retreated past the Rubicon.

Chapter 6
The Lord Chancellor

> There are few gentlemen in practice who cannot cite abundant instances of the errors into which persons every day fall, who are led away by a kind of legal will-o'-the-wisp, 'a case in point': for the discovery of a case in point is often of greater prejudice than benefit, inasmuch as, by the overawing force of authority, it suspends the operation of a person's own natural good sense… . 'A case in point', therefore, can never be relied on, without knowing the spirit of legal decisions at the period when it derived its birth… . (Amos 1829, 17)

As noted in the last two chapters, the Lord Chancellor – F.E. Smith, the First Earl of Birkenhead – had a significant influence in resisting the growing calls for medical privilege from both the Ministry of Health and the BMA. Indeed, as Chapter 7 reveals, his views on the issue continued to feature in the minds of those advocating medical privilege during debates over private member bills in 1927 and 1936.

A Barometer of Legal Views

The Lord Chancellor's file on the debate over medical privilege in the early interwar years opens with the memorandum sent from Christopher Addison requesting, 'if he could be advised what steps could most suitably be taken to secure the end which is contemplated in the memorandum, namely, that such privilege should be extended to medical men in legal proceedings as will secure absolute secrecy for persons who attend VD clinics' (NA LCO2/624 Barter to Schuster 3 June 1920). Taking action on this, on 14 June 1920 Birkenhead wrote to the Lord Chief Justice, the Master of Rolls, and the President of the Probate Divorce and Admiralty Division in order to gain their views on the issue. It was Henry Duke, the President of the Probate Divorce and Admiralty Division, who was the first, and as it turned out the only, one to respond (NA LCO2/624 Duke to Birkenhead 3 July 1920). He saw Addison's correspondence as making two related demands. Firstly, a form of privilege should be extended to doctors on grounds of equality of treatment of learned professions. Secondly, that communications between doctors and patients with regard to the treatment of VD should be protected from disclosure even in court.

To the first of these arguments Duke was at pains to point out that the privilege which prevented lawyers from disclosing information was in fact the clients' privilege and not the lawyers'. The complexity of legal procedure meant that individuals caught up in legal proceedings needed access to those who had expert knowledge of the law in order to receive a fair trial. Therefore, claims for medical privilege based on equality of learned professions were misplaced. Moreover, there were rigorous restrictions upon legal privilege that prevented its use to the detriment of the public interest.

With regard to medical evidence relating to the treatment of a patient with VD, again Duke saw no reason for an exception to be made. If the law compelled diseased individuals to confide in a doctor then such involuntary confidences should not be voluntarily disclosed. However voluntary communications to a doctor, in keeping with all other communications save those which sought to obtain legal advice in relation to legal proceedings, should be available to litigants in a dispute.

Perhaps unsurprisingly, Duke's letter to Birkenhead dealt with Addison's request purely from a legal point of view. The language he used focused on compulsion and voluntariness in a legal sense only. The law might not compel someone suffering from VD to confide in a doctor but the severe ill-effects of the disease could leave an individual with little choice. When set within the context of the publicised government VD treatment scheme and its guarantee of confidentiality it is clear that there was pressure exerted on sufferers to seek treatment. This left Duke's tight legal definition of voluntariness in somewhat murkier waters. His view of the information being voluntarily given to the doctor by the patient also appears too simplistic. A doctor consulted for one set of symptoms might, during the course of examination, find evidence of an unexpected second disease. The knowledge of the second disease arose from the doctor's expert knowledge and diagnostic skill rather than the patient's disclosure. Arguably, by consenting to examination the patient had volunteered the information, despite the fact that the second disease was not the reason for the consultation. However, such a broad interpretation of voluntary disclosure could discourage those who were in any way concerned that signs of VD might be diagnosed from seeking any medical consultation. Hence why confidentiality had been given such emphasis in the regulations and advertisements connected to the clinics.

In the same vein, Duke's interpretation of the public interest was also limited. His argument that the absence of secure access to legal advice could mean the denial of justice to individuals was accurate and well-rehearsed. However, it did not take account of the similar argument that denying individuals, suffering from a disease with the social and physical stigma of VD, access to confidential treatment, not only put their own recovery in jeopardy but also risked exacerbating an already significant public health problem. In Duke's mind the public interest was served when legal justice was administered; but for those concerned with health, on an individual and communal basis, the public also had a vested interest in not jeopardising the schemes set up to tackle the scourge of VD.

One final point is also noteworthy. By distinguishing between information given voluntarily and that given under legal compulsion, Duke's thoughts resonated with some views expressed within debates and correspondence in the BMA. Statute law required the notification of births, deaths, specific infectious diseases and abortions but offered no protection against subsequent disclosure of such information in legal proceedings. As noted in Chapter 5, Dr Burton and the Ilford Urban District Council were required to provide evidence in *Devonshire v Devonshire and Eve*, a divorce case in which Burton was forced to testify regarding details of paternity recorded on a notification of birth form he had completed in accordance with statute law. By contrast, Duke's views seemed to advocate that information legally required to be given to the doctor should not be disclosed. However, even this was not clear cut, as his words implied that the doctor should not volunteer such information, but did not rule out the possibility that he could be compelled to disclosure.

Considering the scale of the problem that was demanding the time and efforts of the BMA and Ministry of Health at this time, it is noteworthy that there is very little to be found in Birkenhead's file on confidentiality between Duke's letter of early July 1920 and May the following year. A copy of the Public Health (Venereal Disease) Regulations of 1916 and a copy of the Interdepartmental Committee on Insurance Medical Records report of 1920 sit amidst sporadic correspondence with the Ministry of Health. It appears that Addison's frustration at Birkenhead's delay in furnishing him with an adequate response to his original request was not unfounded. When it finally came, Birkenhead's terse response indicated that the whole question was a 'grave legal matter', a description which further emphasised the judiciary's examination of medical confidentiality purely in terms of the law. As noted in Chapter 4, part of the delay was caused by the change of Lord Chief Justice. Having replaced Lord Reading, Lawrence was sent a copy of Addison's original memo and a copy of Duke's thoughts and asked to furnish his own opinion on the medical privilege being sought. In keeping with his predecessor, who had never formally set down his position before leaving office, Lawrence broadly agreed with the views of Duke. His only major addition to the argument was to take issue with Addison's belief that doctors did not claim privilege in criminal proceedings, as he himself had had to threaten doctors with prison for withholding evidence material to a criminal case. This is an interesting point for it echoes a recurring motif of discontent among the judiciary that medical practitioners could, and sometimes did, hinder legal work. Medical privilege, even if initially only granted in certain classes of civil cases could seep further through the system of courts, eroding as it went the law's ability to draw on such a rich source of evidence.

Gathering Legal Ammunition

Until this point, the LCO had been measured, verging on lackadaisical, in responding to calls for medical privilege. The announcement that Lord Dawson was about to initiate a debate of the issue in the House of Lords with the aim of getting it referred to a select committee, sparked it into action. On 8 July 1921, Schuster, Birkenhead's personal secretary, wrote to David Davies in the Lord Chief Justice's office asking that he prepare a detailed brief which would shed light on the nature of the legal privilege and show how this differed from the proposed privilege for medical practitioners (NA LCO2/624). On the same day Schuster also wrote to Sir Archibald Bodkin in the Director of Public Prosecutions department asking whether, in light of Dawson's motion, he could supply Birkenhead with 'ammunition'. Davies replied the next day indicating that he would create a file on medical privilege. Bodkin's reply, enclosing a file of relevant ammunition, arrived two days later.

In collecting information for the forthcoming debate, the LCO came across a speech made by Hempson, solicitor to the BMA, which drew comparison between the position of a doctor and that of a priest. While it was acknowledged that a priest's obligation of confidentiality was absolute, Hempson had expressed the view that the doctor's obligation depended to a large extent upon his own personal relations and inclination. However, from a legal point of view, if Hempson believed there were times when a doctor, as a citizen or friend, may feel it necessary to disclose a patient's condition then, 'the claim of privilege must fall to the ground, and … the obligation of secrecy really meant no more than an honourable understanding that a doctor would not gossip about his patient's affairs' (NA LCO2/624 Davies to Schuster, 11 July 1921).

Many doctors certainly saw the question of medical confidentiality in terms of honour. Langdon-Down, chairman of the CEC, realised as much when he stated, 'the strong feeling that the doctors hold about this is just due to this, that it hurts the deepest feelings of decent honourable men that they should divulge information received under such circumstances' (BMA CEC Minutes 5 December 1921). Alfred Cox, medical secretary to the BMA, also came to express a very similar view: 'it is quite hopeless to try to build up a series of rules and regulations and to try to make it look watertight. The attitude rests on sentiment and tradition and it is no good trying to invest it with logical consistency.' (Cox to Hempson 6 April 1922) Yet the BMA did not meet with the Lord Chancellor. While the BMA and the Ministry of Health met to discuss medical confidentiality, and the Ministry corresponded with the LCO, the three bodies never met together. Thus, three different interest groups each had multiple persons of profile expressing opinions on particular aspects of a complex issue, but at no point did they all sit down in a room together and debate the matter. Then again, as the Lord Chancellor's file indicated, the BMA's meeting with the Lord Chief Justice in 1915 had not led to cooperation and progress.

With Dawson's proposed motion in mind, the LCO set about examining the law relating to the production of medical information in legal proceedings.[1] A clear distinction was made between the production of medical evidence in serious criminal cases and other cases. In the latter set of cases, no medical information was to be made available, save the name and address of a medical officer who could give evidence if subpoenaed. Medical reports were not in themselves evidence and

1 NA LCO 2/624 Document entitled 38/Gen No./946 Disclosures and production of records.

only became so if there was a meaningful discrepancy between what a medical officer had written in a medical report and the testimony which he subsequently gave in court. If both sides in a case consented, a medical report could be read as evidence in order to save the time and expense of compelling its writer to appear in court. A medical officer should not give any information except on subpoena and even then he could plead professional privilege although 'this will probably be overruled by the court'. It is not clear when these guidelines were written but, as the BMA and Ministry of Health were only too well aware, the previous 18 months had firmly underlined this last point.

In serious criminal cases all ordinary restrictions could be waived, with both the defence and the Director of Public Prosecutions having access to all information, including medical records. The court itself could request to see such documents even if the defence had not asked for them. In cases where the DPP, or the police acting on his behalf, requested medical documents on the understanding that they would not be produced in court, this was deemed permissible. However, the DPP could use general information, such as the fact that an individual had been in hospital or been treated by a doctor or had suffered a particular disease, 'unless this is of such a nature as a patient might reasonably wish not to be disclosed'. Who determined which diseases fell into the category of reasonable objection was not indicated. Police enquiries made without the authority of the DPP, and enquiries by private prosecutors, were to be treated in the same way as other cases falling outside the serious criminal category. There should be no disclosure of medical records but, if possible, the name and address of a medical officer who could provide relevant comment would be made available.

Broadly speaking then, a distinction was drawn between the law's demand for medical information in serious criminal cases and other forms of judicial or police investigation. In the former the courts could demand all forms of medical information including medical records, while in the latter a medical officer could be subpoenaed to appear before a court to give testimony. No criteria for categorising cases was presented, so presumably the judge decided if a criminal case fell into the category which allowed the court unrestricted access to medical information. This is an important point, for one of the judiciary's main objections to the proposed medical privilege was the power it gave individual doctors to determine when they would give medical information. This, legal authorities argued, hindered the interests of justice and could lead to inconsistency in practice. While some cases would be easily classified in the category of serious crime, others might rely more on judicial discretion. The power to determine when a patient's desire not to have details of his or her illness disclosed was 'reasonable', left the judiciary in a similar position vis-à-vis individual and public health as medical practitioners would be in relation to justice if medical privilege were allowed. The law permitted the judiciary an amount of discretion with regard to matters of health in connection with justice, but it would not countenance medical practitioners having a level of discretion in matters of justice connected with health. No doubt status played an important role in this distinction. Judges were public officials while doctors, although increasingly involved with the state, were still largely private vendors of medical expertise. While judges focused on public interest, private interests might cloud the doctor's vision and skew judgement on the admissibility of medical evidence.

It is natural that the judiciary would regard the interests of justice as paramount, but they must have been aware of the potential damage to the public health effort caused by forcing doctors from the VD campaign to appear in court and publicly breach the government pledge of confidential treatment. A further explanation for their reluctance to consider medical privilege was the perception that even without medical privilege, doctors had a tendency to stifle the ends of justice rather than betray a patient's confidence. The judiciary were still harbouring concerns raised during the 1914–15 debate. Birkenhead's file contains Avory's charge to the grand jury from the trial of Annie Hodgkiss in 1914 which had sparked confrontation with the BMA. It had culminated with the Lord Chief Justice's failed attempt to impose on the medical profession their overriding duty to aid the law in the administration of justice, even if that meant contravening patient confidentiality. Lawrence, the new Lord Chief Justice, had recounted his experience of doctors attempting to claim medical privilege as witnesses in criminal trials. In preparing for Lord Dawson's debate, Birkenhead wrote to the metropolitan police office at New Scotland Yard requesting details of cases 'in which there either has been, or may have been, a failure of justice due to the refusal of doctors to communicate with the police when they become aware that an illegal operation has been performed' (NA LCO2/624 Bigham to Schuster 13 June 1921).

If Birkenhead was going to defend the law against medical privilege then he needed hard evidence that legal opposition to medical practitioners withholding information was well founded. The case of Annie Hodgkiss was one well-known and controversial example but the metropolitan police were being asked to provide a series of cases to show that the problem was a recurring one. Trevor Bigham of New Scotland Yard was only too willing to comply. Sending details of five cases from 1913–19, Bigham added, 'I could, I have no doubt, give you many further cases if you desired, but I think these are quite sufficient to satisfy you as to the general line taken by the medical profession and as to the practical difficulties the police have to contend with in consequence' (NA LCO2/624 Bigham to Schuster 13 June 1921). Doctors were too often an obstacle in the administration of justice. In the past, their shortcoming had been their failure to notify the police in cases of criminal abortion before the mother died, a point which had been discussed at length in 1915 and was reiterated by Bigham in his letter. To extend a form of privilege to doctors that allowed them to withhold medical testimony once a case had reached court would exacerbate the problem. Rather than allowing doctors greater leeway, Bigham followed Lord Chief Justice Reading's line of thought from 1915 and advocated greater emphasis being put on the medical practitioner's duty to assist the authorities.

Evidently, one of the major barriers to addressing the question of medical privilege was that the various sides were talking past each other. The Ministry of

Health's priority lay with the potential detriment a lack of medical privilege was causing to the effectiveness of their VD treatment scheme, and thereby public health. They were therefore only seeking privilege for doctors in civil cases. The Lord Chancellor, backed by other members of the judiciary and police, was concerned with preventing doctors becoming more of a hindrance to the criminal justice system. Meanwhile, the BMA were in internal turmoil, with its Council and CEC engaged in a game of tug of war with the representative body over the use of BMA resources to challenge the law on medical privilege. There were pockets of interaction on the issues. Bodkin wrote to Schuster to inform him that he, along with Blackwell of the Home Office and Newman from the Ministry of Health had, two weeks prior, had a long meeting to discuss the attitude of VD clinics to the use of their information in legal cases (NA LCO2/624 Bodkin to Schuster 11 July 1921). He offered to send details of this to Birkenhead, along with pronouncements on confidentiality in the divorce courts from McCardie in *Garner* and Horridge in *Needham*, and a leader in *The Times*. In an aside, Bodkin qualified his own suggestion that the documents he was sending might tire Birkenhead, by stating 'but it seems quite impossible that the Lord Chancellor can ever get weary!' Seemingly the unhurried approach, which had so infuriated Addison, had been replaced by a greater sense of urgency as Birkenhead gathered the pieces from which he would assemble his case for the debate on 27 July. As Schuster observed, 'the Chancellor attaches great importance to the question and to this particular occasion and wishes to deliver an important and conclusive speech' (NA LCO2/624 Schuster to Blackwell 18 July 1921).

A letter from the Home Office to the Lord Chancellor indicated that the memo, which Bodkin had prepared subsequent to the meeting between the Home Office and the Ministry of Health, had not gone down well with the latter (NA LCO2/624 Blackwell to Schuster 15 July 1921). It appeared that the Home Office believed general agreement had been reached that it would be 'convenient' and 'reasonable' for a doctor to give a statement to the police in all instances where he had medical information about an individual connected to a case. The Ministry of Health denied assenting to such a proposal. In their view, a doctor should inform the police of information which would exonerate an accused individual, but in all other cases it should be left to the doctor's discretion to voluntarily supply information to the police.

With the Ministry of Health and the Home Office finding it difficult to reach agreement, Alfred Mond wrote to Birkenhead six days before Dawson's motion was due for discussion (NA LCO2/624 Mond to Birkenhead 21 July 1921). Having read Addison's correspondence with Birkenhead, Mond was keen for a meeting to agree a Cabinet line on the question. He indicated that he was under considerable pressure from doctors and that he had come to the conclusion that there was a very strong case for medical privilege, akin to that of lawyers, in civil cases only. This, he suggested, would be 'only fair' to doctors and in keeping with several 'respectable precedents both abroad and in our self-governing dominions'. It would also be essential to the interests of the Ministry's VD policy: 'the essential foundation of which is the secrecy of the transactions. If we cannot secure such secrecy to the doctors in civil proceedings, I anticipate something approaching to a crisis.' In order to avoid Dawson's request for an investigation of medical privilege by a select committee, Mond proposed the passing of a short bill along the lines of the statutory medical privilege in New Zealand, but only extending to civil cases. If Birkenhead was in agreement then Mond would explain the situation to Dawson, otherwise a meeting the following week would be in order.

In stark contrast to the treatment his predecessor had received from Birkenhead, Mond received a reply from the LCO the following day. Apologising for not being able to write in person, Birkenhead welcomed Mond's stance against a medical privilege in criminal cases. However, he made clear that he was not wholly convinced of the Ministry's intentions:

> There has lately been a considerable disposition to obstruct criminal investigations in this way [claiming medical privilege], and … some of the communications made by the Ministry of Health to doctors in the country and to the Public Prosecutor and the Home Office have lent colour to the idea that the Ministry took a different view [to that now expressed by Mond]. (NA LCO2/624 Schuster to Mond 22 July 1921)

Birkenhead would respond to Dawson's motion that there would be 'no possibility that doctors can in criminal proceedings be allowed to escape from the ordinary obligations of citizenship'. Clearly, the Lord Chancellor had a very negative view of the motives and potential outcome of any medical privilege which had effect in criminal cases. As for civil cases, Birkenhead expressed his awareness of the excellent work the VD clinics were doing and the 'national importance which must be attached to their labours'. Despite this he found himself 'reluctantly unable to acquiesce' with Mond's proposal for a bill based on the New Zealand Evidence Act. His objection focused on the distinction between a doctor's behaviour when giving testimony in a civil case and their obligation outside the courtroom. Drawing on Hempson's speech to the BMA the previous year,[2] Birkenhead noted Hempson's belief that circumstances could leave a doctor in a position where, as citizen or friend, he felt it necessary to disclose information which had been gained in a professional capacity. As noted in Chapter 5, Hempson's example of the syphilitic fiancé produced a dichotomous response from the representative body at the BMA ARM in 1920. This, in Birkenhead's view, was evidence enough that public opinion would not support legislation which forbade disclosure of medical information within the context of a civil court case, but left disclosure outside the courtroom to the discretion of the individual doctor on a day-to-day basis. To emphasise the unanimity of legal thought on the matter Birkenhead cited the concurrence of his views with those of the previous Lord Chief Justice, the current

2 *BMJ* 3 July 1920. Supplement, 10.

Lord Chief Justice, the Master of the Rolls, the President of the Probate Divorce and Admiralty Division and, in his opinion, probably all of the high court judges.

However, although the judiciary was more unified in its opinion on medical confidentiality than the BMA members who had responded during Hempson's speech, they were aware that showing up inconsistencies in medical opinion would not be sufficient justification for opposing a select committee inquiry into the possibility of legislation on medical privilege. Certainly, judges were primed with examples in which doctors' reticence to provide the law with information had obstructed the ends of justice, but, by Birkenhead's own admission, the prevalence of VD, and the importance of secrecy to the efficacy of treatment programmes, made medical confidentiality the key to another public interest, the nation's health. The sanctity of the doctor–patient relationship was a foundation stone in the medical profession's code of ethics, and one which had already been shaken by government measures on notification and public health in the late nineteenth and early twentieth centuries. As medical officers working in the VD clinics had made clear, the limitations on the government guarantee of doctor–patient confidentiality were being highlighted in very public circumstances. If the law was to further undermine confidentiality by rejecting medical privilege, even in cases where treatment was received under the rules of secrecy for VD clinics issued by government, it had to do so in such a way as not to push the medical officers at the clinics into following through on their threat of resignation.

In a letter to Schuster, Bodkin suggested that the argument for privilege on the basis of the sanctity of the doctor–patient relationship could be undermined by drawing an analogy with another group of cases (NA LCO2/624 Bodkin to Schuster 21 July 1921). Under common law, a husband or wife was forbidden from giving evidence against a spouse because of the law's regard for the confidences between husband and wife. By section one of the Criminal Evidence Act, 1898 (section 1, proviso D) this rule was formalised in statute. However, in both forms of the law, exceptions were made in instances of criminal activity, such as violence on a spouse or incest. Bodkin suggested that if the confidentiality that existed in the more intimate relationship of a husband and wife was subject to limitations under criminal law, then there was less reason to insist that the doctor–patient relationship should be privileged. Certainly, this went some way to undermining the central argument of doctors with regard to the special nature of their relationship with clients, even in the sensitive context of VD treatment clinics. But by Bodkin's own admission, the analogy was for exceptions in criminal cases alone.

Davies, having acted on Birkenhead's request to examine the proposals for medical privilege and provide him with arguments as to how it differed from the established privilege of lawyers, produced a lengthy note on the subject. Citing many cases, he paid particular attention to the statement given by Lord Chancellor Brougham in the case of *Greenough v Gaskell* [1833]. He quoted at length Brougham's assertion that:

> The foundation of the privilege is not on account of any particular importance which the law attaches to the business of the legal profession or any particular desire to afford them protection. But it is out of regard to the interests of justice which cannot be upholden and to the administration of justice which cannot go on without the aid of men skilled in jurisprudence, in the practice of the courts and in those matters affecting the rights and obligations of which form the subject of all judicial proceedings. (NA LCO2/624 Davies to Birkenhead, undated)

Brougham's words, given during a case which revolved around the question of legal privilege, seemed to fit perfectly with the line of thought advocated by Birkenhead. The lawyer's privilege was not an effect of judicial favouritism to the legal profession, but rather a necessary element in the process of an equitable justice system. However, a closer look at the details reveals that Davies had been somewhat liberal with the truth in trying to manufacture continuity in legal opinion from the 1830s through to the 1920s. Without giving any indication that he had edited Brougham's statement, Davies removed the last section of Brougham's first sentence. In fact, having indicated that the law had no tendency to favour or protect the legal profession, Brougham actually went on to say: 'though certainly it may not be very easy to discover why a like privilege has been refused to others, and especially to medical advisers' (*Greenough v Gaskell* [1833] 1MY & K 38).

Clearly, the reintegration of these words into Brougham's statement gives an altogether different complexion to his thoughts, than the one presented by Davies. For a start, consensus on privilege between Brougham and Birkenhead only extended to the legal variety. On medical privilege, the more important issue for Birkenhead and Davies, the two Lord Chancellors had potentially conflicting ideas, so Davies had simply edited out that section of Brougham's statement. Considering that the judiciary's argument against medical privilege was rooted in the need for all relevant information to be made available to the law, it was more than a touch hypocritical for a member of the Lord Chief Justice's office to omit relevant information from the opinion of a past Lord Chancellor because it did not suit the argument which the current Lord Chancellor wished to make.

As already detailed in Chapter 4, Lord Dawson did not raise the question of medical secrecy in the House of Lords. In a printed memo Birkenhead indicated that at a Cabinet meeting on 25 July, where the Ministry of Health raised the question of Dawson's motion, it was agreed that 'no time would be available for the discussion of the question before the 27th', so Dawson would be asked to postpone it (NA LCO2/624 Birkenhead memo 28 July 1921). Evidently the Cabinet needed time to discuss the matter in detail and reach some form of consensus before a general discussion in the House of Lords, but the entrenched differences between the Ministry of Health and the Lord Chancellor would not make for a short discussion. However, Dawson, in complying with the Cabinet's wishes, indicated that he would seek to raise the motion again in the near future.

Before the Cabinet could have the chance to discuss the question at length, Birkenhead sent a copy of his views on the question to Cabinet members. He indicated that there was no disagreement between Mond and himself on the question of medical privilege with regard to criminal cases, neither supported a privilege. In other circumstances, however, there was greater division. Birkenhead was at pains to point out the unanimity of legal opinion against the granting of any form of medical privilege, suggesting that once Cabinet had assessed the merits of the legal and medical views it could announce a decision on the matter. Mond clearly did not wish to rule out the possibility of a select committee looking into medical privilege 'in view of the strength of medical feeling on this subject' (NA LCO2/624 Mond to Birkenhead 2 August 1921). The Ministry of Health was, by this stage, proposing that legislation on medical confidentiality should be along the lines of 'a physician etc. shall not without the consent of his patient be compellable to divulge in any civil proceeding, etc.' For Birkenhead this was proof that the privilege that was being sought was in fact the doctor's privilege to decide when he gave evidence. This being the case, all comparisons with legal privilege were forfeit for, as had been pointed out at length, legal privilege was the privilege of the client, not the lawyer. A medical privilege of the nature suggested by the Ministry of Health would give doctors the power to protect or injure their patient's case during hearings in court, based solely on their own judgement. Such a proposal was without precedent. Moreover, the LCO understood that doctors wanted a privilege that covered them in civil and criminal proceedings so, even if the Ministry of Health's proposal was agreed to, there was no indication that the medical profession would be content.

Should a Doctor Tell?

Even though Dawson's motion was edged off the Cabinet table, Birkenhead continued to be occupied with the medical profession's claims for privilege. He continued to receive letters presenting examples of medical incompetence obstructing the ends of justice, clarifying points of law on legal privilege and drawing analogy with the law's attitude to the confidentiality of information given to clergymen.[3] October 1921 was a particularly busy month in which Birkenhead's memorandum entitled 'Should a Doctor Tell?' was printed and copies circulated to all judges and Lords of Appeal. In it, Birkenhead collected together the morsels from which he had intended to produce his definitive speech in response to Dawson's motion in the House of Lords. He noted that the problem of medical privilege was exacerbated by the lack of clarity about what the medical profession was actually seeking, their claims and practice being 'discordant and loose' (Smith 1922). He dealt with the proposed analogy with legal privilege incorporating,

3 LCO 2/624 Bodkin to Schuster 27 July 1921; Davies to Schuster 4 August 1921; Davies to Schuster 10 October 1921; LCO 2/624 Schuster to Roche 29 June 1922.

unchanged, Davies' inaccurate version of Brougham's statement in *Greenough v Gaskell*. In ignorance of his misrepresentation of fact, Birkenhead went on to state, 'since the Duchess of Kingston's case it has never seriously been questioned that the law is as it was then stated to be by Lord Mansfield'.

He noted the statutory obligation on doctors to breach confidentiality imposed by the Infectious Disease (Notification) Act 1889 and the Notification of Births Acts of 1907 and 1915. Yet, unlike the impression which the Lord Chief Justice had conveyed to the BMA in 1915, Birkenhead was clear that the doctor was not to act as spy or detective. Nonetheless, in keeping with the impression conveyed to him by judiciary and police alike that, too often, medical men impede the law through lack of cooperation, Birkenhead was keen to stress the doctor's role in aiding the cause of justice. On notification of criminal abortion he went so far as to state, 'the attitude adopted by doctors in some of these cases almost makes one regret that the offence of "misprision of felony" has been allowed to become obsolete'. This statement provides a sharp contrast to the opinions expressed by Avory and Clarke during their consultation with the RCP in 1896. However, Birkenhead was aware that the key issue aggravating the early interwar debate was VD. He portrayed the reasonableness of legal demands on doctors by using emotive examples involving the abuse of women and children, and employing evocative phrases such as:

> The quarrel here, if there be a quarrel, is not between the law, on the one hand, and the medical profession on the other. It is between those who claim this privilege, and the parents of little children whose protection is the primary aim of the law. (Smith 1922, 62)

In his effort to provoke sympathy in the reader for the parents of little children, Birkenhead appears to have overlooked the contradiction in his argument. If the primary aim of the law was the protection of little children and the medical profession was, in the law's eyes at least, threatening to jeopardise that, then evidently the quarrel did exist and was indubitably between the law and the medical profession. In such points Birkenhead seemed more concerned with pulling at the heart strings of public opinion than giving an accurate account of the debate. Nonetheless, he claimed to recognise the importance of medical confidentiality, particularly with regard to the national problem of VD and the fact that 'the complexities of life in a civilised community such as our own produce a web of confidential relations and confidential communications round every citizen'. However, even in situations where confidentiality was central to a relationship there were always exceptions to the rule: be it in connection with an individual's finances at a bank; or, drawing on the example he had been furnished with by Bodkins, in the intimate relationship of a husband and wife. Save for the growing privilege of lawyers the tendency had been towards greater openness of testimony in court and Birkenhead, backed by 'most men of experience in every branch of the law', felt it would be a retrograde step to create an unprecedented level of privilege for doctors or indeed nurses and midwives, for he could not see why medical privilege would not extend to them.

The Very Pernicious Heresy About Medical Privilege

It seems that, in legal quarters at least, Birkenhead's essay was very well received. The Lord Chief Justice sent word that, at the meeting of judges, Birkenhead's stance against medical privilege had met with their approval. Again, the main reason appeared to have been the detrimental impact that such a privilege would have in impeding the ends of justice (NA LCO2/624 Lord Chief Justice to Birkenhead 13 October 1921). While outwardly the question of medical privilege was being referred to by high legal figures as 'a subject of great and pressing importance',[4] in their internal correspondence it did not receive such high praise. In complementing Birkenhead on his published memorandum, the President of the Probate, Divorce and Admiralty Division, Sir Henry Duke, wrote: 'I am delighted to find that you have made time to explode the very pernicious heresy about "medical privilege" which has spread in a remarkable way in the last few years.' (LCO2/624 Duke to Birkenhead 22 October 1921) It appears that in the opinion of the senior judiciary, Birkenhead had used his legal 'ammunition' to good effect.

4 NA LCO 2/624 Taken from printed note attached to 'Should a Doctor Tell?' memo printed for cabinet.

Chapter 7
The Attempts at Legislation

'A game of snakes and ladders' is how Roy Jenkins referred to the process of getting a private member's bill passed into legislation (Birch 1993, 184). Each year a small group of MPs, whose names are drawn from an open ballot, get the opportunity to propose and promote legislation of their choice. Since 1867, the government has dominated the legislative agenda and private bills have been limited to Fridays in the first twenty weeks of each parliamentary session. Success in the ballot allows an MP to give the bill its first reading in Parliament. This is a reading of the bill's title only and there is no detailed debate. Indeed, often the specific terms have not been drafted by the time of the first reading. Having been announced, a date and time is set for its second reading. At the allocated time, if there are no objections to its being read a second time then the bill moves to be considered in detail by a committee who make recommendations about its merits to the House, which then votes to accept or reject the proposal. In order to become law, the bill must go through these three stages in both the House of Commons and the House of Lords, making it a lengthy process. If a bill fails to make it through the committee stage before the end of the parliamentary session it lapses, along with all uncompleted legislation, and must begin the process all over again whenever someone chooses to reintroduce it. In such a process the threat posed by the 'snakes' must be minimised. As one authority on the British system of government observed: 'to get a bill enacted requires skill, patience, determination, a measure of support from more than one party, and the sympathy of the ministers most directly affected' (Birch 1993, 183). While private member bills are not nearly as numerous as governmental ones, they do at times lead to the passing of important legislation.

Chapters 4–6 examined the failed attempts to set a new common law precedent in the early interwar years. The current chapter analyses two subsequent attempts to pass legislation conferring a level of privilege to doctors in court: the first in 1927; the second in 1936. Both were private member bills and both were put forward by Ernest Gordon Graham-Little. Born in Bengal and educated in South Africa where he took a B.A. in literature and philosophy at the University of the Cape of Good Hope, Graham-Little won a Porter scholarship to study medicine at London University. After graduating he spent time in Dublin and Paris before specialising in dermatology. He was the Independent Member of Parliament for London University from 1924 until the abolition of the university franchise in 1950, and was knighted in 1931.[1] In 1931 he also changed his surname by deed

1 See entry for Ernest Gordon Graham-Little in *The Dictionary of National Biography* and *Who Was Who* Vol. 4 1941–50.

poll from Little to the hyphenated Graham-Little (*The Times* 12 February 1931, 9). While neither of his bills passed into law, they merit closer examination than they have hitherto received. Morrice mentions them in passing in his thesis, seeing them as nothing more than the reworking of old arguments (Morrice 1999, 279–80). While much of the debate associated with the bill was similar to previous discussions, this is indicative of the continued tension surrounding the issue of medical confidentiality throughout the interwar years, and the continued attempts to obtain medical privilege.

Medico-Legal Problems in Relation to VD

In November 1925, the Medical Society for the Study of Venereal Diseases held a discussion on 'Medico-Legal Problems in Relation to Venereal Disease'. Naturally, the meeting echoed earlier points on the merits of medical privilege in relation to the work of VD clinics. However, it is notable not only as evidence that the issue was continuing to provoke discussion, but also because one of the main speakers was Francis Crookshank, who had resigned from the BMA's PSC and CEC in 1922. His paper made clear his ongoing frustration at the confrontational position adopted by the BMA in earlier debates:

> Let us doctors, then, agree not to dispute the actual position of the law, as did the British Medical Association recently in one of its recurrent and rather ridiculous attempts to impose its temporary view upon the community … While a section clamour for permission to break the formal and quite unwritten seal of confidence when they think fit, others clamour for the right to refuse to do so when the State thinks fit that they should. Now the vast confusion at present existing is the outcome of the wholly ridiculous and thoughtless fuss made several years ago by that rather easily swayed organisation, the BMA. (Crookshank 1926, 38; 48)

Interestingly, Crookshank went on to note relevant changes that had taken place since the precedent on medical privilege had been set by Lord Mansfield in the Duchess of Kingston case. In particular, he noted that there were statute laws which now compelled the collection of personal information by the state, and that this information could subsequently be used against the expressed wishes of the individual concerned, as had recently happened in a case of disputed paternity in Ilford. Presumably this was a reference to *Devonshire v Devonshire and Eve* [1921], discussed in Chapter 5. Relating this general point to the issue of VD, Crookshank suggested that, if VD treatment was to remain voluntary, the pledge of secrecy associated with it should be withdrawn. Alternatively, if VD treatment was made compulsory then secrecy should be guaranteed to those forced to attend the clinics. A point of view that echoed that of Sir Henry Duke in his correspondence with the Lord Chancellor (see Chapter 6).

Mr Ewart Wort, a barrister who had been invited to present a legal perspective on the issue, stressed that there was not, as many doctors seemed to suspect, a conspiracy between judges and lawyers to deny professional privilege to doctors. He emphasised that legal privilege covered a class of communications that it was necessary to protect in order to facilitate the process of justice, rather than being a privilege attached to the legal profession itself. It is noteworthy that, like Birkenhead in his essay on medical privilege in 1922, Wort cited the authority of Lord Brougham on the point and, similarly, failed to mention that Brougham had questioned why a similar privilege had not been extended to medical practitioners (Wort 1926, 52). In the discussion that followed the two papers, Wort stated that if medical privilege was going to be given, it would have to be an absolute privilege, which, he feared, would bring the work of the courts to a 'standstill'. While he did not detail the reasons for this view, the subsequent attempts at a private member's bill certainly demonstrated the difficulties of seeking a qualified, or partial, privilege for doctors.

The Background to the 1927 Bill

It would be easy to interpret the 1927 attempt at legislation as a direct rerun of the early interwar years. It was triggered by the same factor as the earlier debate; a divorce hearing in which medical testimony was demanded on the presence of VD in one of the parties. Such cases were important both in terms of the issues they raised and, particularly, in the publicity and debate which they generated. Nonetheless, they were part of a broader underlying unease that surrounded the conflicting viewpoints on the boundaries of medical confidentiality, and also reflected questions about the relative powers of the executive and the judiciary. As previously detailed, Birkenhead's well-publicised and authoritative rhetoric, together with the consistency of his stance, had weakened support for medical privilege in the early 1920s. Yet, there were many areas of medical practice which were too ill-defined to permit of the type of definitive approach Birkenhead advocated. The CEC had come to this conclusion when they were asked to consider guidelines for BMA members in 1920 and Lord Riddell took a similar line in an address to the Medico-Legal Society in June 1927 (BMA CEC minutes 9 November 1920; for Riddell's address see *BMJ* 2 July 1927, 17). George Allardice Riddell was a talented lawyer who became legal adviser to the *News of the World*. In 1903 he decided to move from law into journalism. Being on good terms with Lloyd George he was often used as liaison officer between the press and British delegations to major international conferences such as the Paris Peace Conference of 1919. Despite no longer practising law, Riddell maintained a keen interest in medical jurisprudence.

Riddell had been among the audience at Dawson's controversial address on confidentiality at the Medico-Legal Society in 1922. In the prolonged discussion following that speech, Riddell disagreed with Dawson's belief in the sanctity of medical confidences, describing the latter's approach to privilege in civil cases as 'extraordinarily nebulous' (*BMJ* 25 March 1922, 495). Riddell had offered a simple solution to the problem of doctors testifying in court. Doctors, he suggested, could be in the habit of forgetting certain information before official proceedings, in which their evidence may be called, got underway, 'such a little lapse would not be visited with penalty on the day of judgement'. By 1927, Riddell was not so light-minded in his approach. The fact that the question was still the subject of discussion, coupled with the fact that Riddell changed his position, testifies to the persistence and complexity of the issue. The aim of the Medico-Legal Society was to discuss subjects of deep interest to lawyers, doctors and the public. In the opinion of some members, there was none more apt at fulfilling that criterion than medical confidentiality (Sir William Collins, *The Lancet* 2 July 1927, 14).

While Riddell had become more sympathetic to the case for the sanctity of secrecy, his address, entitled 'The Law and Ethics of Medical Confidences', was by no means revolutionary in content. In general, the doctor's duty to aid the law was clear in cases of crime, with abortion continuing to prove a moot point. There were, however, other areas where conscience was still put forward as the guiding light that determined whether a doctor should pass on information to a third party. These penumbral areas kept the question rumbling on, and the passage of time brought yet more examples to be added to the list of difficult scenarios. Riddell reeled off the familiar problems regarding doctors' duties to tell when they were employed by someone other than the patient or in cases where there was the potential of grievous harm being caused to a third party – the syphilitic fiancé again among the list of illustrations. More original was his querying of the ethics of selling doctors' case books containing information on their patients. A possible solution would be to insist on destroying such books when the doctor died but this 'might rob future generations of much interesting information' (*BMJ* 2 July 1927, 17). Duty and consequence seemed at loggerheads again.

Aside from the dilemma over case books, Riddell's address essentially summarised the main themes from earlier debates: Avory's remarks in 1914 and their heated aftermath were re-examined; the comparison with legal and spiritual privileges and the laws of other countries were rehearsed; arguments over public interest and the relative merits of public health vis-à-vis justice were all touched upon; and the pecuniary interest and advertising elements were not overlooked; martyrdom and the treatment of John Elliot of Chester came up in discussion; and the report of the address ended with Sir William Willcox's view that the 'fair and proper attitude' for a doctor to adopt when called as a witness, was to refuse to answer until ordered and then give evidence under protest – the line advocated, for many years now, by the Ministry of Health and the BMA. There were some signs that opinions on medical privilege were shifting as Riddell suggested that limited privilege was supported not just by medical men but by 'distinguished lawyers', assuming this held more weight than the support given by the *Solicitors Journal* in the aftermath of *Garner* in 1920. On the whole, however, the emphasis still lay on legal interests over medical.

As well as the report of Riddell's speech, *The Lancet* carried a leading article on professional secrecy in its early July edition. It noted that the old and honourable tradition of medical secrecy 'does not fit comfortably into legal theory' (*The Lancet* 2 July 1927, 23). This encapsulated a problem that had been frustrating participants in the debate since at least the time of the RCP consultation with Avory and Clarke in 1896, how to marry the interests of traditional medical ethics and legal procedure. The continued tension in the 1920s suggested that the solution imposed by Birkenhead would not last. However, if doctors wanted to change the arrangement, one essential ingredient was still missing: 'it is strange that the public has never insisted upon a change in the law and upon an absolute duty of medical secrecy in the law courts.' That the writer should have found the lack of public support strange, is itself intriguing. There had not been much cause for the public to make vocal protest.

Most of the discussions on privilege had taken place in private meetings between representatives of the judiciary, government and medical profession and had been predominantly reported in professional journals rather than newspapers. Indeed, keeping it out of the press had been one of the criteria stipulated by the Lord Chief Justice in 1915. The one exception had been the coverage of divorce cases like *Garner v Garner* and *Needham v Needham*. Yet, even in those instances the press coverage, though intense, had been short-lived. The general public was unlikely to be spurred into action by occasional cases involving doctors giving evidence about VD in a divorce hearing which had little relevance to them. If 'the public' meant those who were facing divorce proceedings from their spouse, who in turn was likely to cite VD as a principal ground for separation, then fear of guilt by association might well have discouraged the formation of a 'Keep my VD secret' campaign. All in all, the general discussion of the boundaries of medical confidentiality took place away from the general public. Important as the treatment of VD was, and significant as the rise in the number of divorce cases in the 1920s was (Phillips 1988), medical privilege – widely acknowledged to be a complex balancing act – was hardly the sort of bandwagon that the general public would be waiting to jump on in large numbers.

If public support was not likely to provide a useful basis to challenge the status quo, the power of government directives would have to be used again as the principle weapon. A fortnight after reports of his address, Riddell indicated that his attention had been drawn to the VD regulations issued by the Local Government Board in 1916 (*BMJ* 16 July 1927, 116). The terms of article II (2) had raised the possibility in Riddell's mind that statutory secrecy had been established in cases of doctors attending patients at the VD clinics. This was the argument that Elliot had attempted to make, with little success, in *Needham*, and in recounting the details during the Medico-Legal Society's discussion, Sir William Collins expressed his deep regret that Elliot had not gone further on the road to martyrdom (*BMJ* 2 July 1922, 18). An article in *The Lancet* (16 July 1927, 139), focusing specifically on secrecy and the VD clinics, followed Riddell's new line of thought by suggesting that government regulations might override judicial power to force medical disclosure, though it was unlikely that a judge would take this view. Citing McCardie's ruling in *Garner*, which stated the regulations were not authority to exempt a medical officer from giving evidence in court, *The Lancet* suggested that doctors should strive to claim the utmost degree of privilege possible, stressing the importance of secrecy to the success of schemes to tackle VD. A week later, the same journal was reporting that a medical witness had responded to the call.

Anything You Say Will Be Taken Down and Used in Evidence Against You[2]

Within a month of Riddell's address to the Medico-Legal Society the case which Graham-Little was to cite as the immediate trigger for his attempt at legislation was heard.[3] As well as involving a VD clinician refusing to give evidence in a divorce hearing on grounds of medical privilege, the case had two other similarities with previously significant trials. Firstly, it was heard at the Birmingham Assizes, the same court from which Avory had delivered his tirade against the medical profession's code of secrecy in the trial of Annie Hodgkiss in December 1914 (see Chapter 3). More importantly, it was heard before Justice McCardie, the judge involved in the *Garner* case which had sparked the Ministry of Health into action in 1920 (see Chapter 4). The *Solicitors Journal* at that time had suggested he should have had the courage to rule in favour of granting a measure of privilege to the doctor, but in the *1927 Birmingham case* it was clear that McCardie's position remained unchanged.

In *Garner* medical testimony on the presence of VD was sought by a patient who consented to the disclosure, but in the *1927 Birmingham case* a wife was seeking evidence of her husband's previous treatment for VD and had subpoenaed Dr Assinder, the medical head of the VD department at the Birmingham General Hospital. In the witness stand, Assinder explained that he had not treated the man in question in 1924, had not been head of department when the husband was alleged to have attended and that a number of doctors were engaged in the work at the clinic. Each doctor had his own papers which were personal property and could not be produced as evidence by the head of the department. While recognising the reasoning behind this position, McCardie emphasised that the doctor could not claim privilege and if he refused to comply with the request for evidence he would be imprisoned for contempt of court. McCardie further threatened that if the doctor did not give evidence:

> every medical man and a number of officials from the hospitals would have to be called to the court, and ultimately the documents must be made available.

---

2 *The Lancet*'s pessimistic assessment of patients' position during VD treatment after McCardie's ruling at Birmingham. *The Lancet* 23 July 1927, 178.

3 Although reported in *The Times*, the names of the parties involved in the case are not cited. The case will hereafter be referred to as the *1927 Birmingham Case*.

> If information were not given that should be given, and if documents were not produced which should be produced, the law … would be enforced. (*The Lancet* 23 July 1927, 178)

Not exactly the measured and sympathetic response doctors had been encouraged to expect from the judiciary, in response to their requests to protect confidentiality, during earlier debates. With the medical privilege debate on the rise again, McCardie seemed keen to nip it in the bud. Not only were government departmental regulations of inferior authority to judicial powers, but any doctor contemplating testing the strength of judicial opinion on the point would find himself in prison and his colleagues on the witness stand in his place. It is worth pausing to consider this further. If McCardie's antidote to medical martyrdom was to subpoena the rest of the hospital staff, the resultant disruption of services at the Birmingham General Hospital would likely awaken greater public interest in the issue. There would surely be public outcry at a judge who chose to disrupt hospital provision in order to get at medical evidence, covered by a government pledge of confidentiality, for use in a civil divorce suit. Presumably the local population would also be unhappy if the judge took to imprisoning the staff of the local hospital one by one until none were left. That would be a test case in which a new precedent for medical privilege could feasibly be set.

However, McCardie could always bank on the converse being true. The public, which had thus far failed to show interest in the medical privilege cause, might react against the doctor, who, having been warned of the consequences of his failure to give evidence, still maintained silence, leading to disruption at the hospital. McCardie, having addressed the question in the early 1920s, would be aware that the medical profession had a far more difficult task in making a persuasive case to change the status quo than the judiciary would have defending it. In a complex debate, the seemingly clear-cut ruling from the Duchess of Kingston's case gave the law the upper hand.

After an adjournment of five days while further evidence was produced, the surgeon to the hospital, B.T. Rose gave evidence under protest. It is noteworthy that while McCardie was clear that there was no medical privilege, he asked the counsel to the petitioner, 'if he had considered the question whether or not a doctor was bound to disclose to the court information obtained by him when acting confidentially in the special treatment of a particular disease' (*BMJ* Supplement 23 July 1927, 55). In other words, what weight should be put on the 1916 VD regulations that guaranteed confidentiality to patients attending VD clinics? Counsel did not think the regulations equated to privilege in court and, consistent with his own ruling in *Garner* and the line taken by Justice Horridge in *Needham*, McCardie agreed. The question that had been posed by Riddell and the medical journals only two days prior had already been answered in a test case. Regulations issued by a government department were clearly not sufficient to prevent breach of confidence when evidence was required in court, even when the case was a civil divorce suit. The *BMJ* concluded: 'the only way in which the Ministry of

Health can implement its promise of secrecy to patients attending VD centres will be by direct legislation stating in clear terms that communications by patients are protected from disclosure in a court of law.' Perhaps Graham-Little, a regular contributor to the *BMJ*, read this. Either way, it was this legislation that his private member's bill hoped to provide.

In Mr Neville Chamberlain's Hands the Matter Will Not be Allowed Again to be Forgotten[4]

Naturally the crescendo of interest in confidentiality had not passed by the Ministry of Health. Within days of McCardie's ruling memoranda started circulating on the subject. Many of the civil servants at the Ministry had been engaged in the early interwar debate. Given their experience of the difficulties involved in the question there was no repeat of Addison's approach to the judiciary with a request that they grant privilege to doctors. On the contrary, there was a palpable uneasiness in the air, particularly among three experienced figures: Machlachlan, Robinson and Newman. Machlachlan sent a memo to the others on 21 July indicating that McCardie's ruling in the *1927 Birmingham case* looked set to reopen the question. The Birmingham clinic was an important one and it was feared that the press coverage would deter patients. Moreover, just as the clinic advertisements, with their prominent pledge of secrecy, had been criticised in the aftermath of the early interwar rulings, VD doctors were again questioning their own position with regard to the guarantee of secrecy. The director of the Birmingham clinic who had originally been called before McCardie was reported to be saying that he would not issue any more pamphlets on which the government pledge of secrecy appeared. Having dissuaded Dawson from pursuing privilege in 1921, the Ministry would now have to return to a consideration of legislation. As Robinson put it, 'this is a most thorny subject and we must take it up where we left it in 1921' (NA MH55/184 Machlachlan memo 21 July 1927). For the time being they would have to prepare to field parliamentary questions on it. All three were agreed that a general statement, indicating an awareness of the *Birmingham case* and that it would require careful consideration, would suffice for the time being.

On 25 July, Dr Vernon Davies, Conservative MP for Royston, inquired in Parliament if McCardie's ruling at Birmingham had come to the attention of the Minister of Health (Neville Chamberlain). Furthermore, he wanted to know whether Chamberlain would consider introducing legislation that allowed doctors to refuse to give evidence about confidential information 'at least in the case of this disease' (*BMJ* 30 July 1927, 194). Sir Kingsley Wood, parliamentary secretary to Chamberlain, following the advice given by Machlachlan's memo stated that they were aware of the ruling and the difficulty of the questions involved and

4 *BMJ* 30 July 1927, 179.

would give it careful consideration. They were still giving it consideration in November when Vernon Davies repeated his question (*BMJ* 12 November 1927, 904). Meanwhile, the medical journals provided a measure of the difficulty to which Wood referred. On the same day Davies's question to the Ministry was reported, *The Lancet*'s correspondence pages contained three letters on the subject (*The Lancet* 30 July 1927, 253–4). The first, from W.P. Herringham, was clearly on the side of the judiciary and firmly pointed out that executive departments could not be lawmakers. Moreover, he was willing to state categorically that justice was more important than the dignity of medicine or any damage that may be done to public health.

H. Wansey Bayly of Harley Street took the opposite view, confidences should be kept at all costs. He indicated that, 'not infrequently a married patient has asked me whether all information that is given will be treated in absolute confidence even in the event of legal proceedings being instituted in the future'. This is an important example of the worry that lay behind the perceived need for privilege; that disclosure would undermine patients' confidence in the system and deter them from seeking proper treatment. Wansey Bayly was an advocate of martyrdom, 'willing to go to prison for conscience sake, as honourable men have so frequently been called upon to do in the past'. Such eloquence in describing the principled martyr is reminiscent of another Harley Street advocate of martyrdom, the Dr Baley who made similar claims in the *Daily Chronicle* at the time of the *Needham v Needham* case (see Chapter 4). Whether they were the same individual or not, their well-advertised, patient-enticing, willingness to sacrifice their liberty in order to maintain their honour seems never to have been put to the test.

The third letter came from Graham-Little. Beyond McCardie's ruling, Graham-Little had been aggrieved by what he saw as attempted encroachment by stealth into the boundaries of medical confidentiality. The House of Commons had recently considered a bill which contained a clause from the Corporation of the City of Liverpool that would have made it compulsory for doctors within the area to notify a public authority of patients suffering from VD. The clause, which would override the 1916 VD regulations, was part of a 136 page document and was only caught at the last moment. Graham-Little believed that public opinion was ripe for a change in the law in favour of medical privilege, indeed it would be like 'forcing an open door'.

On the same day as Graham-Little's letter was published in *The Lancet* the *BMJ* carried an article reciting the failed attempts to claim privilege in the early 1920s. It also extended the claim it had made a week earlier, stating that the only remedy left was special legislation which 'should deal not only with venereal clinics, but with other regulations under which the same or similar questions arise' (*BMJ* 30 July 1927, 179). This should have triggered warning bells. If they were to learn from the earlier debates, the pro-privilege lobby would have to establish a clear definition of the legislation they sought. But experience indicated that ring fencing an area where privilege would apply would be exceptionally difficult, and would be made harder by subsequently having to convince people that it merited overturning 150 years of case law which provided a simple and categorical rule that in the interests of public justice there was no medical privilege.

For the next three months the question lay beneath the surface both in the medical press and at the Ministry. Personnel at the latter were well aware that their first step had to be to address the case Birkenhead had advanced against medical privilege in 1922, and the lull in publicity on the issue masks the tactical thinking going on behind the scenes. A writer to the *BMJ* in mid-August, Alan Gemmell, suggested that legislation was the wrong route to take. Legislation was unlikely to provide the pro-privilege lobby with what they wanted and 'as the problem has nothing to do with votes, Parliament would never find time for it' (*BMJ* 20 August 1927, 329). Honour was the key element for Gemmell, and he joined those in favour of maintaining confidences, even if it entailed martyrdom. Raising, yet again, the analogy with penitent and priest. For R.M. Courtauld, however, the analogy was imperfect. Responding to Gemmell the following month, Courtauld provided reasons why the medical position was more contentious than the priest's. For instance, the priest only knew what he was told while the doctor had the knowledge gained by virtue of his observation and training. Thus the latter was the more valuable witness. Moreover, it was relatively easy to trace the doctor who had treated a particular patient when compared to the difficulties in establishing which priest had heard a penitent's confession.

> If the required doctor was as little discoverable as the required priest, and if his evidence was confined to relating verbal confidences that he had received from his patient, he would be as little troubled by subpoenas as is the priest. (*BMJ* 10 September 1927, 470)

The Ministry of Health were also looking at ways to avoid resorting to legislation to resolve the apparent conflict of interests. Writing in August, Slator summarised the position since the early interwar debate, noting in particular Birkenhead's essay. He summarised Riddell's address to the Medico-Legal Society and the details of McCardie's Birmingham ruling which had come just a month later. In light of all these, he foresaw no easy way to achieve the changes that had been sought in 1921. Rather than taking such a difficult route, Slator suggested a new solution which, 'while not solving the matter, would meet with less opposition and would minimise the harm done to the venereal disease campaign' (NA MH55/184 Slator memo 25 August 1927). In an attempt to steer a middle course through the extremes of new legislation or medical martyrdom, Slator suggested that the evidence of VD medical officers could be heard *in camera*. Recent legislation was noted to have extended the courts' facilities to hear evidence in private and Slator believed that private hearings would reduce the level of publicity such cases received and consequently there would be less of a deterrent for patients seeking treatment.

Naturally, Gemmell and others who saw the matter strictly in terms of honour would not have been mollified by such an approach as doctors would still be breaking their patients' confidences. A categorical approach would require the same action whether it was in public or private. From their view of ethics the fact that an action would not be widely seen did not affect its wrongness. However, just as Riddell had acknowledged that the law and ethics seemed at times irreconcilable, the Ministry were looking for a pragmatic approach. No scenario was likely to meet with universal approval. Rather than going down the difficult route of legislation, why not try to find the best angle on the status quo? The public had been most heavily involved in the subject when the newspapers had covered the divorce cases where doctors had unsuccessfully claimed privilege. Press articles had suggested that the whole philosophy underpinning the treatment schemes had been put under threat – comments which had forced the Ministry into action in 1920. If the negative publicity could be reduced, or even done away with, by having the evidence given in private, then the Ministry hoped to solve the problem without having to change the law.

A month later Coutts was pointing to deficiencies in Slator's proposed position (NA MH55/184 Coutts memo 20 September 1927). Giving evidence in private would presumably not prevent protest being made and, Coutts surmised, in all likelihood that protest would become public. While not questioning the undesirability of negative press, Coutts indicated that the history of the VD clinics showed little change in attendance despite the detrimental press coverage of cases like *Garner*. He suggested that the real problem was not sufferers being deterred from seeking treatment, but that VD medical officers were uncomfortable with their situation. The evidence certainly pointed towards more unrest among the VD doctors than the patients. The doctors involved in the high profile cases of forced disclosure – Elliot in *Needham v Needham* and Assinder in the *1927 Birmingham case* – had clearly been made uncomfortable in their position relative to their patients. Assinder was threatening to withdraw the clinic's advertisements. Elliot had threatened resignation. Coutts suggested that they had taken too literal an interpretation of the regulations as binding them to absolute secrecy. In his view the regulations were intended to provide no more than a general rule of confidentiality because of the sensitive nature of the complaint and the importance of secrecy to its treatment.

Having seemingly argued against the case for medical privilege, Coutts then suggested that the resolution was best found in establishing the right for VD doctors to refrain from breaking confidences without patient consent. Criminal cases would be exempt from such a rule and there would be provisos for consultations made on behalf of insurance companies, and for doctors to defend themselves in malpractice cases. Further exemptions might include a patient being examined at the request of a parent or employer, and communications with mentally deficient or unsound individuals. Special measures would also have to be considered for pathologists who had to examine specimens for VD clinics. Thus, Coutts had moved from a relatively simple position, educate the VD doctors that secrecy was a rule that could be broken when giving evidence in court, to one in which VD doctors should maintain secrecy, even in court, but with a number of other exceptions. Experience indicated that the latter approach was likely to be more complicated.

The following day, Colonel L.W. Harrison, the Ministry's adviser on VD, wrote to Coutts with his interpretation of the situation. In essence his argument was that VD treatment was an exceptional instance in which medical confidentiality was more important than medical testimony in court. In stressing the importance of encouraging sufferers to seek early treatment by guaranteeing confidentiality, he was speaking from a basis of knowledge:

> Some instances in my own experience of men concealing their venereal disease, or their suspicions of such, for years are almost unbelievable. Often enough in the meantime these persons have passed on their diseases to others, and frequently they have become mental wrecks. (NA MH55/184 Harrison memo 21 September 1927)

It was not enough to assess whether people turned up at the clinics for treatment. It was equally important to encourage *early* treatment. Consequently, anything which cast doubt in the sufferer's mind and may result in a delay in seeking treatment would be of detriment both to the individual and possibly the community as well. Therefore Harrison argued that, save in criminal cases, anything which implied that the guarantee of confidentiality was not as extensive as it had seemed, would be detrimental to the treatment schemes and the community. Clearly Harrison was making an argument based on personal knowledge and expertise rather than theory or conjecture and he claimed the support of 'all medical officers I know who are closely acquainted with the psychology of venereal patients'.

Doctors had previously presented the public interest case for allowing VD officers a level of privilege. Harrison would have known it would not in itself be enough. Rather than focusing solely on defending the medical position, he turned to attack the legal stance. Birkenhead and others had stressed the importance of medical evidence to the ends of justice. Treading carefully, Harrison ventured that medical evidence may not be helpful and indeed it could be 'positively harmful unless the judge and barristers possess the knowledge of a VD specialist'. On a number of occasions the opinion had been expressed that the judge was best placed to decide when medical testimony was important enough to override confidentiality. Harrison was implicitly attacking this assertion by querying the extent to which legal minds had a sufficient understanding of medicine to make an informed decision. Taking one of Birkenhead's hypothetical cases from 1922, Harrison outlined the difficulty of interpreting the medical evidence to prove with certainty which member of a couple had transmitted VD to the other. It is worth quoting at length his comments on the subject.

> In most cases of the kind assumed here it would be very difficult to prove either A.B. or his wife were guilty. Assuming that A.B. had taken the steps most

> favourable to a decision by seeking medical advice at once for an early primary sore and, on the diagnosis being pronounced, having his wife examined at once, the evidence would have to prove not only the earliness of the husband's syphilis and the greater age (by weeks) of the wife's but also the finding of a primary sore in the wife in a situation, such as the cervix uteri, where it could have been acquired only by illicit relations. I venture to say that such a combination would not be discovered once in a thousand times. The most usual event, even when the husband had been so prompt as supposed, would be failure to find any primary sore in the wife, and even if she were proved to have acquired syphilis, it would be unjust to conclude that she had done so other than accidentally. In most cases the story starts with the doctor at a much later date when nobody can say with certainty which party was infected first; the evidence is extorted but proves nothing to an informed mind. In Birkenhead's case A.B. might go to the doctor with a relapse of a primary sore having been infected two or three months before and been treated by another doctor but having in the meantime infected his wife. The doctor's 'simple sentence' might be to the effect that he found a primary sore on the husband and a syphilitic rash on the wife. The first conclusion, without careful cross-examination based on expert knowledge, could easily be that the wife had acquired the disease first and had infected her husband.

Medical evidence should not, therefore, be seen as an easy route to the truth, as it could not always establish with certainty the order of events which had led to the infection of either party. It is important to note that Harrison was not belittling medical expertise. Rather, in understanding the complexities of the disease, VD doctors were able to foresee the difficulty of using medical testimony to establish facts on which legal cases could be decided. It was their superior knowledge of the possible sequences of infection which led to their inability to provide strict factual evidence. The more they knew of the disease, the more they knew they could not be sure of its history of transmission.[5] Following this line of thought, if medical testimony did not serve the ends of justice in such cases and confidentiality was beneficial to the treatment of VD, then it was in the public interest for VD officers to have privilege.

As it turned out, the Ministry of Health did not opt to follow the line taken by Slator, Coutts or Harrison. At a Cabinet meeting on the morning of 11 September, Chamberlain spoke to the Lord Chancellor (Cave) about medical privilege. Contrary to Addison's approach to Birkenhead in 1920, Chamberlain did not believe that legislation was required. Rather, he suggested that the problem would be alleviated if the Lord Chancellor asked judges 'not to make a parade of their insistence of the evidence being given as was done by Mr Justice McCardie in the Birmingham case'

5 Michael Worboys (2004) gives an account of some of the significant changes that were taking place in the understanding, perception and treatment of VD in the late nineteenth and early twentieth century. For more on the changing balance of juridical power and biopower at the time, see Ferguson 2009.

(NA MH55/184 Memo 9 November 1927). Presumably this referred to McCardie's threat to subpoena the whole of the staff at the Birmingham hospital, which naturally attracted press attention. The Lord Chancellor agreed to talk to Lord Merrivale, the President of the Probate Divorce and Admiralty Division. This approach could help to solve two related problems: doctors' perception that they were being unfairly treated by judges; and the press interest in reporting confrontation between doctors and the judiciary in the public arena of the courtroom. However, Robinson saw two outstanding issues. It was unclear if the BMA were going to press the matter and Robinson suggested that in light of Birkenhead's well-known hostility to medical privilege, it was best to keep them quiet. Moreover, if there was to be no legislation, there was still a question of whether anything should be done regarding the pledge of confidentiality given at the VD clinics. This had been a sticking point for many of the VD officers and the Ministry's proposed action would do little to change that. Robinson's suggestion, endorsed by Chamberlain, was simple: 'I am for doing nothing and I do not think such passivity will do harm.' (NA MH55/184 Handwritten note by Robinson 14 November 1927) High profile cases were infrequent and if the judges tempered their demands for medical testimony they should receive even less publicity. There was, however, one key unknown factor, the likely impact of Graham-Little's proposed bill.

The Medical Practitioners' Communications Privilege Bill

Graham-Little announced his intention to introduce a bill on medical privilege in *The Times* on 14 November 1927. The following day he proposed to postpone the motion until 22 November, 'so as to give opportunity of further consideration of the measure by all concerned' (*The Times*, 15 November 1927, 12). On the same day he wrote to Kingsley Wood at the Ministry of Health enclosing a draft of his bill (NA MH55/184 Graham-Little to Wood 15 November 1927). Unlike the proposals Dawson had advocated in 1921, Graham-Little was proposing to limit the legislation to communications made under the 1916 VD regulations. He stressed the strength of feeling, evident in the medical press, that there was a need for change either in the law relating to evidence, or in the regulations which guaranteed secrecy. The former was the preferred option, and his bill had the support of several MPs. If the Ministry was to support it, he believed its success would be assured.

The Ministry drafted a response to Graham-Little indicating that despite its limited scope, the bill would raise the whole question of medical privilege 'as to which there are marked differences of opinion' (NA MH55/184). In the circumstances no guarantee of Ministerial support could be given. It is not clear whether this letter was sent, but Kingsley Wood did speak with Graham-Little before the date he was due to present his bill to the House of Commons. Noting that the question required careful consideration, Wood informed Graham-Little that parliamentary business would leave no time for his bill in the current session

(NA MH55/184 Wood to Chamberlain 21 November 1927). Clearly Wood was trying to dissuade Graham-Little from pursuing the matter in Parliament in the same way as Robinson had dissuaded Dawson in 1921. Graham-Little was not so willing to comply.

Graham-Little was not the only one still concerned with medical confidences. The day before his bill was due to be heard in the House of Commons, a joint meeting of the Bournemouth Legal Society and the Bournemouth Division of the BMA was held to discuss whether medical confidences should be privileged in civil and criminal legal procedure (*BMJ* Supplement 3 December 1927, 215–6). The discussion was opened by Dr E.K. Le Fleming, who put forward three arguments for medical privilege: honour; public demand for it; and the example of most European countries and some American states. These, along with the other views put forward at the meeting, were well-worn arguments. Marshall Harvey of the Legal Society stressed the importance of medical evidence to legal proceedings and the role played by a doctor's conscience. Dr L.A. Weatherley, asked to speak at short notice, pointed to a recognised medical privilege in Scotland. In this he was mistaken as the Scottish courts, while accepting that confidentiality was an integral part of the doctor–patient relationship, recognised that some circumstances justified breaching patient confidences. Disclosure at the demand of a judge in court was one such justification (Ferguson 2011). Weatherly also suggested, as Slator had done at the Ministry, that evidence could be heard *in camera*. Mr D'Angibau of the Legal Society pointed out that it would be extremely difficult to change a law which had been in force since 1776 – the Duchess of Kingston's continuing legacy. While there did not seem to be too much agreement between the lawyers and doctors – Le Fleming suggested that the Legal Society were unable to refute his arguments in favour of privilege – there was some. Mr Maud from the Legal Society supported privilege for both doctors and priests. But, with the usual broad arguments and divergence of opinions, Bournemouth did not provide a good omen for Graham-Little's bill entering Parliament the following day.

In the House of Commons on 22 November 1927, Graham-Little sought leave to introduce his bill. It was drafted in the following terms:

> Be it enacted by the King's most excellent Majesty, by and with the advice and consent of the Lords Spiritual and Temporal, and Commons, in this present Parliament assembled, and by the authority of the same, as follows:–
>
> 1. Any information obtained by a duly registered medical practitioner in regard to any person treated for VD under a scheme approved in pursuance of Article II (2) of the Public Health (Venereal Diseases) Regulations, 1916 shall be regarded as confidential, and shall be privileged from disclosure under the court of law.
>
> Provided that the information obtained shall have been obtained for the purpose of a cure or assisting in a cure, of a person so treated.

> And provided also that this privilege shall not extend to any communication made with the object of committing or aiding in the committing of any fraud or crime.
>
> 2. For the purpose of this Act 'Duly recognised medical practitioner' shall mean a person whose name is on the 'medical register'.
>
> 3. This Act shall be called the Medical Practitioners Communications Privilege Act, 1927.

Graham-Little declared that the bill was aimed at removing the deadlock between the authority of the VD regulations and the judiciary over the secrecy of treatment at VD clinics. Using information from the Royal Commission Report that had led to the adoption of the regulations in 1916, Graham-Little made clear the prevalence of VD in Britain. He noted that it was the third biggest killer, after cancer and tuberculosis, 'and probably ought to come first as it predisposes in very many cases to those diseases' (Hansard, House of Commons, 1927 (210), 1608). In strong rhetoric reminiscent of Birkenhead, he noted the extremely high mortality rates it caused among children. As well as 'slaying their tens of thousands,' VD topped the list of disabling diseases, were responsible for a large proportion of cases of insanity and caused many diseases of the nervous system, 'which make life a prolonged agony'. Again, quoting the figures from the Royal Commission, he estimated one in ten persons were infected, and that half of all cases of blindness in 'quite young children' were attributable to VD.

When the treatment clinics had been set up after the report of the Royal Commission in 1916, the regulations had made clear the prime importance of confidentiality to the success of the scheme. In Graham-Little's opinion, all information at the clinics was to be regarded as 'absolutely confidential'. A bold interpretation of article II (2), this was in keeping with the strong language he used to build the case for his bill. Modern treatment of VD had 'revolutionised' prognosis. Deterrence factors to treatment may cause 'irreparable' damage, presumably to patient and community. Two key factors were required for the success of the VD scheme: the enthusiastic cooperation of the doctors involved; and the complete confidence of patients. A ruling like that of McCardie in the *1927 Birmingham case* undermined both elements. Moreover, by implication any proposed remedy that did not guarantee complete confidence – a taming of the regulations for instance – would be detrimental. Graham-Little went further, suggesting that forcing VD doctors to disclose was not only a 'betrayal' of Hippocratic ethics, but was an affront to Parliament, 'because Parliament must be responsible in some measure for the acts of one of the most important Ministries under the Government'. Clearly, he was attempting to portray the situation as a stand-off between Parliament and the judiciary, rather than an inter-professional dispute between law and medicine. This argument would have had more force if it had come from, or been strongly supported by, the Ministry of Health.

Thus far in his speech, Graham-Little had adopted similar techniques to those Birkenhead had employed with such success in the early 1920s. His vocabulary and illustrations had evoked strong images of the need for absolute confidentiality: revolutionary treatment; irreparable damage; betrayal of trust; and children suffering the consequences. He even followed Birkenhead in being somewhat liberal in his interpretation of past events, claiming that his bill sought to legally sanction as privileged, 'communications which have been erroneously supposed during the past 12 years to be privileged'. In light of the legal rulings of the early interwar debate against medical privilege, this was a highly dubious claim.[6] For his finishing flourish, he presented a choice: either the law had to change or the regulations had to be scrapped. He had been assured by 'eminent' MPs that any legal difficulties could be 'readily overcome'. If, however, the House opted to scrap the regulations, 'the fate of a highly successful and important ministerial and medical effort is sealed'. A first reading of the bill was agreed to, and the second reading was scheduled for the following Monday.

An almost verbatim account of Graham-Little's speech in the House of Commons was published in the *BMJ* (26 November 1927, 1010). The correspondence pages of the same issue burgeoned with letters on the subject. Dr Pinkhof, from Amsterdam, while expressing appreciation of the line taken by Graham-Little was amazed that he had been advised to restrict the privilege to cases involving VD. If such a limited privilege were granted, then anyone claiming the privilege would be implicitly confirming the presence of VD. Pinkhof noted that the High Court of the Netherlands had recently granted doctors the right to refuse to give evidence in court after one practitioner had served as martyr for the cause and been imprisoned (see *BMJ* 3 December 1927, 1055). W.G. Aichison Robertson took a very different line. He thought far too much was made of claims to medical privilege and that it was right that judges, as accredited representatives of the Crown, had the power to demand medical evidence. The problem of negative publicity could be overcome by giving evidence in writing or *in camera*. Otherwise the law should be accepted as it stood.

A lengthy letter was received from one of the participants in the Bournemouth discussion. Lionel Weatherly, having been given insufficient time at the Bournemouth meeting, wanted to use the *BMJ* to voice his 'very definite views on this burning subject'. He suggested that judges had less respect for medical secrecy than they had forty years previously. Weatherly opposed the BMA's position that general rules could not be laid down and he was also against martyrdom as a route to privilege. Rather, he supported Graham-Little's bill because it resolved the inconsistency between the Ministry's pledge of secrecy and the judiciary's demand that the pledge be broken; and also because secrecy was so important to successfully combating VD. If evidence had to be heard, and each case where the question arose should be considered on its own merits, the evidence should be

6 Though, as noted in both Chapters 8 and 9, similar claims continued to be made in later decades.

given *in camera*. In other words, Weatherly advocated a privilege for VD doctors, but if it could not be granted then the judge in each case should consider whether medical evidence, received at the price of deterring sufferers from seeking treatment, was really necessary. If it was, then the damage should be limited by keeping the proceedings as private as possible.

The Lancet also carried a summary of Graham-Little's speech. In an article on medical confidences in the same issue, it was stressed that privilege would have to be consistently applied (*The Lancet* 3 December 1927, 1190). Obviously thinking along the same lines as Pinkhof, the *Lancet* quoted the *Solicitors Journal*'s belief that a privilege which applied only to VD treatment would be liable to provide evidence by implication whenever a doctor claimed privilege. Arguably, doctors should not even waive privilege at the request of the patient as it would have a negative reflection on defendants who chose not to consent to medical disclosure. The privilege would have to be sought on grounds of public interest, but, in the article's view, 'health is hardly a less urgent national need than justice'.

While the medical journals were assessing Graham-Little's bill, at the Ministry of Health Machlachlan instructed Slator to consult with the solicitors' branch and draw up a memo in response (NA MH55/184 Machlachlan to Slator 2 December 1927). Slator acted on this the following day, raising points for the solicitor to consider (MH55/184 Slator to solicitor 3 December 1927). Would the proposed privilege prevent evidence being given where the patient consented to disclosure? Which patients would be covered by the privilege? Under the strict terms of Graham-Little's bill, only information relating to individuals *treated* at the VD clinics would be privileged. Thirty percent of people turning up at the treatment centres were found not to be infected so would presumably not be covered by the law. Similarly, a number were diagnosed with VD who then abstained from treatment and so would also be denied privilege by the semantics of the bill. Slator also queried the purpose of the first proviso and the wording of the second proviso to the first clause.

On 8 December Slator wrote back to Machlachlan, indicating that the bill would need drastic redrafting and was therefore not worth devoting much time to. As an example of the inadequacy of the draft, Slator pointed out that the bill would only protect communications between the doctor and patient, not the information which the doctor obtained by his own observations or from laboratory reports. He suggested that the first clause would be better reworded as:

> A registered medical practitioner shall not, except at the request or with the consent of his patient, be compellable in any civil proceedings to disclose any information obtained by him in the course of attendance on the patient at an institution or centre for the treatment of VD established by or under arrangements made with the local authority. Nor shall he be compellable, for the purpose of disclosing any such information, to produce any books or documents kept at such institution or centre. (NA MH55/184 Slator to Machlachlan 8 December 1927)

This in itself would be insufficient if there were any documents in the custody of nurses or other staff that could be called as evidence in place of the doctor and his records. It was pointed out that at large treatment centres the register of patients was filled out by a clerk on behalf of the medical officer in charge. Therefore the clerk could be a valid witness. Other employees could also be liable to provide appropriate testimony: 'an orderly who prepared a solution of arsenobenzene and saw the medical officer administer it to a patient whom he could identify in Court might be a useful witness if privilege was extended only to medical officers of the centre.' (NA MH55/184 note to Slator 9 December 1927) Clearly the definition of the privilege would have to be more extensive than Graham-Little had envisaged, at the very least covering all staff and documents at the VD clinics.

At the bottom of the memo a handwritten note from Machlachlan suggested that the matter could be put on hold as there was no likelihood of the bill making progress in the current parliamentary session. He was right, the bill did not resurface until nearly a decade later. Talk of legislation did continue in the interim. Vernon Davies, a keen supporter of Graham-Little's bill, approached the Ministry to get a clause inserted into a National Health Insurance bill in early 1928. Frustrated that there was insufficient time to get a general bill enforcing article II (2) of the 1916 regulations, Davies was attempting to at least get a legislative guarantee of secrecy for insured persons undergoing VD treatment, by inserting a clause in a bill that was already going through Parliament. Coutts and Slator, who met with Davies, pointed out that such limited applicability was illogical. While agreeing that uninsured persons should also have a guarantee of secrecy, Davies argued that insurance patients were often afraid to seek official treatment for VD and in the long run this had a greater impact on insurance funds. Coutts and Slator suggested that Davies draft a clause and the Ministry could comment on whether they felt it worthwhile pursuing. Davies had a different plan. If the Ministry were to draft a clause along the lines they calculated would best deal with the problem of secrecy and it was then to fall into his hands, 'he would receive it confidentially and introduce the clause as his own without making any reference to the Ministry' (NA MH55/184 Coutts memo 27 April 1928). Having attempted a form of policy puppetry with Elliot in 1921, the Ministry gave the impression they were not too keen to go along with Davies's plan. Coutts summarised their response as follows:

> We mentioned the objections to such a procedure and did not encourage him to think that we should be able to do as he requested, but we promised that the matter should be considered in the department and that a communication should be sent to him.

Machlachlan asked Slator to contact Sir Walter Kinnear, controller of insurance and pensions at the Ministry of Health (NA MH55/184 Machlachlan to Slator 27 April 1928). Slator wrote back suggesting that any clause which sought to protect the secrecy of insured persons alone would be 'out of order' (NA MH55/184 Slator to Machlachlan 28 April 1928). Machlachlan passed this opinion on to Kinnear, who in turn persuaded Vernon Davies that 'we cannot deal with a general question of this magnitude in a NHI Bill' (NA MH 55/184 Machlachlan to Kinnear 30 April 1928; Kinnear to Machlachlan 3 May 1928). This negative response to Vernon Davies brought the question of medical privilege to a close as far as the Ministry of Health was concerned.

An additional reason for the Ministry's reluctance to support medical privilege was the simultaneous rise of interest in the benefits of notification of VD. This campaign was driven from Scotland where there was considerable interest in adopting legal coercion to get patients to undergo early and full treatment. The Edinburgh Corporation (Venereal Disease) Bill that sought to implement these measures on a trial basis in Edinburgh received its first reading in the House of Commons in February 1928 and forced the Ministry of Health to seriously consider its merits. The bill did not succeed, being defeated by 156 votes to 93 on its second reading in the House of Commons after a lively four hour debate on 19 April (Davidson 2000, 191). Its failure did not detract from the impact it had as a counterbalance to those lobbying the Ministry to support a bill aimed at medical privilege in cases of VD. It emphasised the fact that there were conflicting views on medical privilege, even when solely considered in connection with VD, and the Ministry would not solve its problems by supporting a bill like Graham-Little's.

However, while the Ministry had lost the desire to pursue the question of medical privilege, for others the question of legislation was still open. Speaking to the St Pancras members of the BMA in October 1928, Graham-Little announced his intention to reintroduce his bill, claiming he had 'received some encouragement from the Government Whips' (*The Times* 11 October 1928, 27). The fact that the Ministry of Health had closed their file on the question makes this unlikely but, if accurate, they were among other voices giving support for Graham-Little's bill.

At the Royal Institute of Public Health in January 1928, Lord Justice Atkin expressed support while presiding over a discussion on the position of medical witnesses. Roland Burrows, a lawyer, gave a speech entitled 'The Medical Practitioner in Relation to the Administration of Justice', in which he expressed the opinion that there was insufficient reason to grant doctors privilege. Drawing attention to the uneasy relationship between lawyers and medical witnesses, Burrows acknowledged that 'on occasions counsel did seem to have overstepped the limits of decorum', but often medical witnesses seemed, *a priori*, to object to cross-examination (*BMJ* 28 January 1928, 136). Cross-examination was important in establishing the strength of the evidence, and it was a key reason why medical evidence could not take the form of a written report. Burrows suggested that a doctor should understand the case before he took to the witness stand so that he could have clear in his own mind what information was relevant and could be stated as fact. He should also be conscious of not overstepping the mark with inference or hypothesis, making clear when he was simply expressing opinion. Burrows words were strongly reminiscent of the textbook writers on medical jurisprudence of the nineteenth century, echoing the idea that medical witnesses were uncomfortable in the witness stand, facing questions which probed how much they knew and could be sure of their subject.

Lord Justice Atkin stressed the importance of medical evidence to the justice system and suggested that, as a group, doctors received sympathetic treatment from the courts. Agreeing with Burrows that often cross-examination was difficult for medical witnesses, Atkin proffered his own golden rule, make clear when you are not sure of the evidence you are giving. Such an approach would leave the witness in a stronger position. As for medical privilege, Atkin placed the claims of justice on one side of the balance and those of public health on the other. In his opinion: 'in some cases, especially in connexion with venereal disease, he was of opinion that the claims of public health far outweighed the claims of justice, and he would be quite glad to see even the very small change in the law that was sought to be introduced by Dr Graham-Little's bill.' This was more than empathetic rhetoric. When Graham-Little made his second attempt at introducing medical privilege legislation in 1937, Atkin had drafted many of the bill's clauses.

One Hour and Forty Minutes on a 'Not Altogether Unusual'[7] Friday Afternoon

Given the voices calling for medical privilege in the months following the first reading of Graham-Little's bill in 1927 an explanation is needed as to why it took a decade to reappear. Certainly, the government had not made it a priority and judging by the memos at the Ministry of Health, they were hoping that the matter would fade away. However, in announcing his intention to make a new attempt at legislation in 1937, Sir Ernest Graham-Little, as he now was, gave his main reason for putting his bill on hold a decade earlier:

> I did not proceed further with the early Bill, as inquiries convinced me that even if the Bill passed the Commons, the Lords, led by Lord Birkenhead, would reject it. I believe there will be less opposition now from legal members of both houses, and this belief, as well as another consideration, has weighed with me in making my new Bill of wider application. (*BMJ* 6 February 1937, 302)

Clearly, in 1927 Birkenhead's shadow had loomed large in Graham-Little's mind. Birkenhead's death in 1930 lessened the obvious barriers to medical privilege. From the time of his early involvement in the debate as Lord Chancellor, Birkenhead had been the leader of opposition to medical privilege. His essay in *Points of View* had become a kind of talisman for the anti-privilege cause and a warning for those who sought to change the law. His presence in the House of Lords at the time of Graham-Little's first drive for legislation was clearly a disincentive to the bill's

7 Mr Dingle Foot's assessment of the situation at the time of Graham-Little's bill being discussed in Parliament (Hansard, House of Commons, 1936–7 (319), 1995).

supporters who chose rather to bide their time. The loss of Birkenhead's presence, debating skills and considerable influence, coupled with the support Graham-Little's bill was garnering from prominent lawyers, increased the chances of a new attempt at legislation being successful. Moreover, by 1937 Birkenhead was not the only key figure to have been lost from the anti-privilege lobby of previous debates. Henry McCardie, responsible for two important precedents against the concept of medical privilege, died in 1933.[8]

Of course Graham-Little was not simply waiting for the key opponents of his bill to die. Beaten by the demands on Parliament's time in 1927, he had taken stock of the measure he was proposing. His bill had been, by his own admission, a reactionary response to McCardie's ruling in the *1927 Birmingham case*. Seeing a public health problem arising from a conflict between the 1916 government regulations and the judicial ruling Graham-Little had, on the advice of legal friends, limited his proposal to cases involving VD treatment alone. On further consideration he realised that with such a limited definition, any plea for privilege would by default confirm an allegation of VD. Clearly this was unsatisfactory, and the privilege would have to be given a broader definition. Graham-Little was able to use his professional standing and expertise in dermatology to investigate what that broader definition should be.

In 1935, the Ninth International Congress on Dermatology was held in Budapest. Graham-Little presided over a committee appointed by the congress to consider medical problems affecting public interests. As one of the subjects for discussion, he asked members of the committee to indicate the degree of protection given to medical confidentiality in their home country. With most European countries represented, along with the United States, Graham-Little was able to gain further international perspective on the question. He felt the result of the discussion was quite clear. In a letter to the *BMJ*, he summed it up as follows: 'it became obvious that the protection given to the "professional secret" abroad was much more efficient than in our own courts, and no miscarriage of justice from this protection was recorded by the various speakers' (*BMJ* 1 February 1937).

In November 1936, Graham-Little's bill had been read for the first time. Its wording was almost identical to that of the long title of the 1927 bill: 'to provide that certain communications between medical practitioners and their patients shall be privileged from disclosure in evidence in courts of law.' Being no more than a formal notification of the bill, the first reading gave little indication of the extent and application of the privilege Graham-Little was going to propose. With the date of the second reading set for 5 February 1937, Graham-Little was using his letter to the *BMJ* to indicate his intention to push for a more extensive privilege than he had sought in 1927, and to reassure doubters that, given the experience of other countries, medical privilege would not be cataclysmic for the justice system. In fact, his letter was not published until the day after the debate took place in Parliament (*BMJ* 6 February 1937, 302).

8 *Garner v Garner* 1920; and the *1927 Birmingham case*.

At 1.40 p.m. on 5 February 1937 Graham-Little requested a second reading for his Medical Practitioners' Communications (Privilege) Bill in the, far from busy, House of Commons. At one point proceedings were interrupted while MPs were counted to confirm that the required number of forty were present (Hansard, House of Commons, 1936–7 (319), 1995). His introduction outlined the development of the debate throughout the 1920s, stressing the importance of secrecy to VD treatment. He cited the report of the London County Council which indicated that in one year there had been 1,050,000 attendances at VD clinics in the area, emphasising the scale of the public health question involved. While he cited other areas in which medical secrecy was needed, Graham-Little still based his bill largely on the circumstances which had arisen around McCardie's ruling in the *1927 Birmingham case*. This was where his problems in persuading the House, began.

He described his new attempt at legislation as 'very much the same' as his 1927 bill but without the restriction to VD cases only. However, while touching on the need for protecting medical information in other circumstances – young unmarried mothers afraid of stigmatisation; or national health insurance patients' medical records for example – the greatest time and detail was given to a reiteration of the arguments over VD. Familiar points came to the fore, a rise in the number of divorce proceedings and an extension of the ways in which medical evidence, particularly of VD, could be useful, led to a rise in the demand for medical testimony. Consequently, the guarantee of medical confidentiality was being broken on a regular basis and this was undermining confidence in the VD treatment scheme. Drawing on his investigations into the position in other countries, he cited examples in which secrecy was recognised by the law with little damage to justice. The Academy of Medicine had reaffirmed this as the French position in 1927. In order to emphasise international consensus over the protection of medical secrecy, Graham-Little indicated that the dermatology congress in Budapest had passed a resolution stating that medical confidences should be legally protected from disclosure except in cases of crime.

Having put forward the case as to why medical privilege should be recognised, he indicated that it could either be established in common law or by statute law. Attempts at the former had proven unsuccessful, judges had always ruled against medical privilege. There was the option of pursuing a common law precedent via the martyrdom route but he was not a strong advocate of this, favouring 'alteration by quiet, orderly Parliamentary procedure [rather] than in response to an explosion of public opinion which may or may not occur, but which is not the best way to reform abuse'. Reform not revolution was the way advocated by Graham-Little, but his words did seem to carry the implied threat that martyrdom was always a possibility, meaning anyone opposing his bill would have to consider a scenario of public outcry as judges sent doctors to prison because Parliament had refused to go down the peaceful route of legislation. Of course, after a decade and a half of such rhetoric, the threat may have seemed somewhat hollow.

Despite claiming to have had the bill vetted by 'one of our most eminent judges', Graham-Little rounded off with an offer of compromise. If MPs were unwilling to accept the bill's wider scope he would be willing, at the committee stage, to limit the application of privilege to VD cases alone. While on the face of it this demonstrated willingness to compromise and reach the best solution, in fact it illustrated the problem that constantly shrouded attempts to define the extent of medical privilege being sought. Graham-Little's arguments had stressed that his previous bill which focused on VD was not sufficient. He had ventured examples of other settings in which medical secrecy had to be protected in court and pointed to the fact that other countries benefited from medical privilege. Yet, he finished by saying his original bill would be available as a compromise, somewhat undermining his previous arguments. Unsurprisingly, the opponents of the bill noticed the inconsistency.

Graham-Little had taken 36 minutes to expound on the merits of his bill. Lovat-Fraser took seven minutes to second it. Searching for the earliest precedent on the question, he had found the Duchess of Kingston case. While citing Lord Mansfield as 'probably the greatest judge who ever administered justice in this country', Lovat-Fraser emphasised that the law as set down in that precedent had now to be altered. This was not because, having examined the details of Caesar Hawkins' plea, Lovat-Fraser had discovered the precedent was built on highly questionable foundations, rather he simply thought that there should be a medical privilege like that given to lawyers, spouses and public officers. He cited Justice Hawkins' endorsement of the concept of medical secrecy in 1896 as further support for privilege – a somewhat liberal interpretation of Hawkins' remarks. On the whole he kept his speech succinct, indicating that really all that needed to be said had been put forward by Graham-Little.

By contrast, Dingle Foot, MP for Dundee, was detailed and lengthy in proposing an amendment that the second reading of the bill should be delayed for six months:

> Those of us who have looked at this Bill find ourselves in a position which is not altogether unusual on a Friday when Private Members' Bills are introduced. We can, of course, sympathise with the objects … but it does seem to me and to some of my friends who have examined the Bill that those who are its sponsors have entirely failed to appreciate what the consequences would be if the Bill passed into law.

Foot was implying that despite having had almost a decade to clarify his original bill, Graham-Little and his cohort of supporters had presented an ill-thought-through proposal. In fact Foot suggested that it would have been better if they had stuck to the terms of their original bill, which had at least made clear when the privilege would be applicable. The new bill granted the possibility of privilege to safeguard information gained in a professional capacity, without specific guidelines on how the applicability of privilege would be determined in each case. This gave the impression that the privilege was more that of the doctor than of the patient, which clearly negated any analogy with lawyer–client privilege. This ambiguity was one of the key criticisms Foot had of the bill. In addition, he portrayed the situation vis-à-vis VD in a very different light. Quoting *The Lancet*, Graham-Little had painted a picture of significant growth of divorce cases in which medical evidence was required. By contrast Foot's characterisation of the situation was that VD only occasionally arose in divorce cases. Yet even if they accepted Graham-Little's compromise of limiting privilege to VD cases only, there would still be problems. If medical evidence was essential for a wife to prove her husband had knowingly infected her with VD then the narrower bill would prevent the requisite medical evidence being given. Thus: 'if you have the possibility of disclosure on the one side it is a hardship, and I agree with that statement, but in the instance which I have just put forward we have a hardship on the one side and a hardship and an injustice on the other.'

Arguably Foot was misrepresenting the factors involved in the equation. His analysis lumped together the personal detriment to the patient, the professional affront to the doctor's ethics and the potential damage to the VD treatment scheme (and by extension public health) into one 'hardship'. Correcting this misrepresentation should have been the pro-privilege lobby's response, but instead Vice-Admiral Taylor queried a semantic distinction as to whether the bill only prevented disclosure of what doctors had been told, not their own observations. If so, that would allow the doctor in Foot's example to recount what he had learnt on his examination of the patient, thereby allowing justice to be done, without disclosing anything the patient had said. Foot seized the opportunity to drive home his point:

> The hon. and gallant Member, whose name is on the back of the Bill, ought to have read the Bill … How ridiculous it would be for the doctor to be called, and say: 'Yes, this man was suffering from this disease, but I have found it out for myself and he did not tell me. Therefore, there is no privilege attaching to it'.

In attempting to defend it, the proponents of the bill were in fact demonstrating its protean nature, revealing the ambiguity and confusion which their opponents highlighted as its chief weakness. Having unsettled the pro-privilege lobby, Foot sought to add fear to their evident confusion and thereby seal the fate of the bill:

> I can only suggest that those who drafted the Bill did not appreciate the effect of what they were doing. If they did appreciate it, it appears to me that it would not merely be a case of righting a wrong, but it would almost amount to conspiracy to defeat the ends of justice.

Seconding Foot's amendment, Ernest Evans – MP for the Welsh universities – further emphasised the lack of public demand for medical privilege. In his view, public apathy meant there was no need to get bogged down in a debate over the relative demands of public health and justice. The bill sought privilege for the doctor not the patient, and this could prove detrimental to the latter as the bill did not make clear that patient consent would override the privilege of the doctor.

Thus, to agree the bill would be to give the medical profession 'a privilege to which they are not entitled, and what is much more serious, imposing upon them a responsibility which I should imagine very few of them would wish to have'. So, in addition to possible unfairness to the patient and interference with justice, the bill would give doctors an added burden of controversial responsibility they may not want.

Again, the pro-privilege lobby's response was less than robust. Sir J. Withers suggested that, just as in the case of solicitors, the court could decide when medical privilege applied. His response to the accusations that the privilege was more the doctor's than the patient's was tentative at best: 'if the Bill goes to Committee and is dealt with sympathetically, I am sure this question of privilege, whether it is of the doctor or the patient, could be cleared up.' Seeming to play on the sympathy which had been expressed at the difficulty of the doctor's position by opponents of the bill, its supporters pointed to the committee stage as the area where the complexities could be ironed out. The unease demonstrated by the pro-privilege lobby when the bill's foundations were questioned, gives the impression that, Graham-Little's lengthy introduction aside, they had assumed the bill would get to committee stage where the real debate would take place.

The penultimate speaker was Sir Terence O'Connor, the Solicitor General. Speaking with the authority of his office, his arguments again pointed to problems interpreting the bill. Imperfect as the current situation was, it would not benefit from new difficulties likely to arise under the proposed legislation. That, in short, was the key problem: finding a definition of privilege which would overcome the perceived shortcomings in the current situation, without creating a whole new set of problems of equal or greater consequence. 'I think the promoters of the Bill, when they came to describe what privilege was, found themselves in the same difficulty as I should be in if I attempted to put into statutory form any of the safeguards of justice.' This was the crux. Since 1914, those in favour of medical privilege had struggled to encapsulate with exactitude the privilege they sought. Legal privilege was recognised in common law and had not needed to go through the complex procedure of defining itself in a way specific enough to satisfy Parliament that it should be written into statute. By contrast, common law precedent recognised no privilege for medical practitioners, the position established by Mansfield's ruling in the Duchess of Kingston's case.

Being the first attempt at getting statutory privilege for a profession, O'Connor suggested that an already complex bill would be further complicated by amendments at the committee stage, which added clauses dealing with the secrecy of communications to members of the clergy. The analogous comparisons used to bolster the cause of privilege in the past were coming back to haunt it. The clergy would complicate the bill and may prevent it getting through committee stage, and a prominent member of the judiciary was openly stating that he did not think legal privilege could be sufficiently defined to pass as statute law – though, of course, it did not need to be. O'Connor's position was clear: 'I venture to think that I am not overstating the matter when I say that there is hardly any branch of the law, civil or criminal, in which the passage of this Bill in anything like its present form would not impede the administration of justice.'

An hour and a half after it began H.G. Williams became the final speaker in the debate. He stressed that he understood Graham-Little's intentions were connected with the difficulty arising from the demands on medical information, rather than professional self-interest. Nonetheless, the proposed bill was ambiguous. Did it entail that doctors were bound to absolute secrecy or that a court could not compel disclosure? If a doctor could choose when to disclose information, this would open up the possibility of a doctor blackmailing his patient. Doctors demanding money in order to provide their patients with the evidence relevant to their cause would be a rare occurrence in what was perceived as an honourable profession. Yet, even the possibility of such a position was intolerable. If a doctor felt he had strong justification not to give evidence, he could give his reasons, in private, and let the judge decide whether evidence should be heard. This was a more desirable outcome and there was no need of legislation to achieve it. Echoing earlier debates of the issue, Williams finished by presenting a positive slant on rejecting the bill, suggesting that a solution should be sought in an improved version of the status quo: 'I have no doubt that those eminent in the law will take notice of the discussion, and, possibly, where the practice has been defective it may be improved as a result of the debate.'

Williams's opinions had been expressed without interruption or objection from the bill's supporters. The House voted against an immediate second reading and in favour of the amended time of six months. Effectively, this was a rejection of the bill as it would fail to reach conclusion by the end of the parliamentary session and thus would have to be introduced afresh. That Graham-Little asked leave to withdraw his bill is an indication that he had been persuaded of its inadequacy. After an hour and forty minutes deciding the fate of medical privilege, the House turned its attention to the abolition of the tipping system for waiters, chambermaids and porters in hotels and restaurants.[9]

Conclusion

Graham-Little's 1927 attempt to get Parliament debating the merits of medical privilege got further than Dawson's in 1922. While the Ministry of Health had dissuaded Dawson from introducing the question in the House of Lords, they did not manage to convince Graham-Little to keep it out of the House of Commons. His determination to proceed with his private member's bill is testimony to the strength of feeling that the issue of medical confidentiality still provoked. The relative powers of the judiciary vis-à-vis ministerial regulations were continuing to cause tension, and discussions like that of the Medico-Legal Society in early 1927 emphasised the lack of a satisfactory resolution to the question in 1922.

9 Hotels and Restaurants (Gratuities) Bill.

Birkenhead's essay had been a key factor in blocking the promoters of a stronger definition of medical confidentiality at that time, but it had not resolved the underlying difficulties or tensions between competing interests. McCardie's ruling at Birmingham brought press attention to bear on the discrepancy between article II (2) of the VD regulations and judicial demands for medical evidence of VD in divorce cases, thereby making more public an issue that had continued to be debated in professional circles. While there were marked differences of opinion over medical privilege, there was also evidence of a higher level of cross-professional support. Riddell certainly thought there was a case to be made for a limited privilege, and Atkin lent the weight of his support to the 1937 bill. Both bills received the support of some lawyers in the House of Commons. An important step considering that a greater number of MPs came from legal than medical backgrounds.

While Graham-Little cited the lack of time on the parliamentary agenda, and the threat of a hostile House of Lords led by Birkenhead, as the reasons why his first attempt failed, the lack of ministerial support was also a key factor. As the 1927 bill specifically focused on giving statutory protection to government regulations, the lack of visible support from the Ministry of Health was a conspicuous shortcoming. It seems that the memory of the difficulties the Ministry had experienced in trying to extend the boundaries of confidentiality in the early interwar years was still too fresh in their mind. In contrast to Addison, a quiet word to the Lord Chancellor, requesting that judges tone down their demands for medical evidence, was as much as Chamberlain was willing to do.

By contrast, advocates of medical privilege resorted to more extreme measures to get statutory support for doctors, Vernon Davies' attempt to get a clause inserted into a National Health Insurance bill, being a notable example. But it was not until late 1936 that Graham-Little got another chance to promote the cause in the House of Commons. Having used the intervening time to further investigate the international dimension of the question, at a medical conference in Budapest the previous year, his new bill sought to emulate the concept of medical secrecy in Europe and certain states in America. Making it a stage further than he had done in 1927, Graham-Little's request for a second reading of his 1937 bill was met, not unjustly, by queries about its scope, applicability and intent. Avoiding the minutiae of the problems that needed to be addressed, presumably because of the difficulty of the task, the bill had been framed in broad terms in the hope that it would receive a second reading and could have its finer points defined at the committee stage. But broad, in this case, meant vague and the critics of the bill had little difficulty in demonstrating that even the signatories of the proposal had conflicting views of what it would mean in practice. Graham-Little's offer to confine the terms of his bill to VD alone, only compounded the confusion, coming as it did after arguments about why the broader privilege was needed. By the end of the debate, it was apparent that Graham-Little had himself been persuaded of the inadequacies of his proposal. Hope for legislation had become hope that the process of seeking legislation might itself have caused a change in judicial perception of the problem, with positive consequences for medical witnesses in the future. However, the boundaries of medical confidentiality were no nearer to being defined in a wholly satisfactory way. Having familiarised themselves with the 'snakes' of statutory change, future promoters of medical privilege in Parliament would have to focus much more attention on the 'ladders' of skilled legislative craftsmanship and ministerial support.

Chapter 8
The Nature and Extent of Crown Privilege

Common and Statute Law

The interwar debate highlighted two fundamental difficulties in achieving any change on the position of medical privilege in court. Firstly, provoking a test case to challenge the common law required a doctor willing to go to prison as a martyr. Despite some strong candidates, no one had been willing to turn the confrontational rhetoric into decisive action. Secondly, Graham-Little's attempts to gain statutory recognition of medical privilege had underlined the two problems of defining its boundaries in detail, and justifying them in the face of stiff opposition. Few were in favour of a blanket privilege for all communications to a doctor. Rather, advocates of medical privilege sought to strike a new balance between the need to guarantee confidentiality as an integral element of medical treatment while recognising the need to disclose information in a variety of circumstances. However, the complexity of finding this delicate equilibrium was further underlined in the post-war decades, a period that witnessed the Lord Chancellor advocating a change in practice on privilege and a common law test case involving journalists as martyrs.

One issue that generated considerable debate was the practice of claiming Crown privilege for certain classes of documents held by, or on behalf of, the state. Under the terms of the Crown Proceedings Act 1947, the Crown could be cited as a party in legal proceedings. Subsection 28 of the Act made provision for the discovery and disclosure of documents relevant to a case, or for a representative of the Crown to appear and give evidence in person. However, this requirement was qualified by continued recognition of the need to exempt any documents or evidence that 'it would be injurious to the public interest to disclose', as determined by the relevant head of department.[1] The Crown was involved in numerous cases in the years after the legislation was passed. Sometimes the Crown was the defendant, for example in cases of industrial accidents at state-run factories. At other times, information held by the Crown, such as medical records of prisoners or of military personnel, was sought in litigation between private parties. Growing numbers of both types of case meant increasing demands for state-held documents. Frequently, requests for discovery or disclosure of documents were met by a claim of privilege, a pattern that led to mounting frustration among the legal profession that evidence was often being unnecessarily excluded. Before long, the extent of Crown privilege was being questioned, prompting examination and review

1 Crown Proceedings Act 1947 c.44 ss.28.

of practice and guidelines. While the privilege covered a range of information and a variety of types of document, medical records and reports were often the subject of debate. As the examples discussed below demonstrate, the discussion encompassed elements of military and civilian medical practice.

Military and Civilian Medicine

In the House of Commons on 3 May 1949, Lieutenant Colonel Lipton asked the Secretary of State for War (Shinwell) why, in a case that had been brought to his attention, the legal advisers of an ex-soldier were denied a copy of his medical history sheet.

> Mr Shinwell: A soldier's medical history sheet is maintained for strictly Service purposes, and copies are not furnished to individuals or their legal advisers. The disclosure of medical history sheets would be detrimental to the public interest, as tending to deter Service personnel from seeking medical treatment, and to impair the frankness of Service medical officers in reporting on them. It is the invariable practice to plead privilege for Service medical documents, a fact which is, I think, widely known.
>
> Lipton: Is the Minister aware that this particular ex-soldier was, in the course of matrimonial proceedings, seeking to disprove a serious allegation that he had contracted venereal disease while in the Army? In those circumstances, why would not the War Office help in a matter affecting the private, personal and moral character of an individual, where it could not possibly affect any question of privilege or security?
>
> Shinwell: This case has now been settled, and I think we had better leave it alone. (Hansard, House of Commons, 3 May 1949 (464), 811–2)

The focus of the analysis thus far has been confined largely to the boundaries of medical confidentiality in civilian medicine. This encompassed a diverse range of settings in which doctor–patient relations arose: from private practitioner to medical officer of health, ship surgeon to panel doctor. Certainly, legal and public health policy demands had placed new emphasis on the value of medical information beyond its immediate function in the doctor–patient relationship, reflecting growing state interest in a healthy population as a key resource for the economic and military competitiveness of Britain. The shift, from the relative freedom of the individual in the private medical marketplace to greater emphasis on the collective, pulled doctors between competing agendas: individual and state; medical and legal. However, there were ways in which civilian medical practice was thought to differ from military medicine in relation to medical confidentiality.

Although doctors frequently had to mediate competing demands in both civilian and military practice, the public debates and controversies over the confidentiality of VD treatment and the lack of medical privilege had been largely limited to the former. While the sharp rise in divorce cases, and the associated demand for medical testimony in court, had triggered confrontation in the interwar years, Crown privilege for service medical records meant that military doctors were comparatively insulated from the battle between the judiciary, the Ministry of Health and the medical profession described in Chapters 4–6. The government guarantee that treatment at VD clinics was confidential had been undermined by judicial insistence that patient records and doctors' testimonies be disclosed in the divorce courts. Conversely, doctors in military service were regularly expected to override patient confidentiality in pursuit of military efficacy, but service medical records were privileged from disclosure in civilian courts.

In the divorce case of *Anthony v Anthony* ([1919] 35 T.L.R. 559), the judge was forced to accept the Secretary of State for War's insistence that the husband's service medical records could not be used as evidence – a stark contrast to the outcome in contemporary cases involving civilians. Although military doctors sometimes expressed concern about being called on to breach patient confidentiality during courts martial, these generally took place away from the media gaze and were unlikely to involve breaching a government pledge of patient confidentiality. However, the blurring of the boundaries of civilian and military medicine during the Second World War, and the imminent prospect of a national health service in the early post-war years, provoked questions about the distinction between allowing disclosure of civilian medical records in court while applying a class privilege that denied similar access to service medical records. In the case of the latter, the Lord Advocate (John Wheatley) – the UK government's adviser on, and representative within, the Scottish legal system – questioned 'whether the detriment to the public service adduced as the reason for withholding these documents really is sufficiently great to outweigh the detriment to the interests of justice which is clearly caused thereby'. In other words, questions were being asked about the scope of Crown privilege.

Crown Privilege

In *Duncan v Cammell Laird & Co.* ([1942] A.C. 624), the House of Lords established that Crown privilege was based on the determination by the head of the political department involved that disclosure would be detrimental to the public interest. This was either because the particular document itself contained sensitive information or because it belonged to a class of documents withheld from production on grounds of public interest. The War Office (WO) believed that service medical reports fell within the second justification, as 'if the communications were liable to be produced in a Court of Justice, the effect would be to restrain the freedom of the communications and to render the reports more cautious, guarded and reserved' [NA WO 32/12406]. However, the Lord Advocate questioned the validity of exempting medical records of service hospitals as a class, especially when the medical records of the wartime Emergency Medical Service hospitals, run by the Department of Health, were not privileged from disclosure in Scottish courts, and he felt there was little difference in principle between the two. While acknowledging that the threat of subsequent disclosure in court might deter a serviceman with VD from reporting sick, Wheatley observed that the importance of ensuring treatment was as much a public interest in civilian, as in military, medicine. He advocated that, except in cases where there was 'some special reason' for non-disclosure in the public interest, service hospital records should be made available to the courts.

This proposal triggered alarm bells at the War Office, as it threatened to undermine the established practice of claiming class privilege for all such documents. However, it was felt that a defence of current practice could be made on the basis that there were cogent distinctions to be drawn between civilian and service medical practice.

> The difference in status between the service doctor on the one hand and the private practitioner or a publicly employed doctor on the other is clearly brought out in the Service regulations, which show that the relations between doctor and patient within the Services and without are totally different on account of Service discipline. (NA WO 32/12406)

In effect, doctors in civilian life were concerned only with their patients' well-being; whereas service doctors had additional obligations related to military discipline: 'the doctor being an officer as well as a doctor, is under a duty, in making his medical report, to pass any comment which might bear on discipline e.g. that a soldier is malingering.' [NA WO 32/12406] In other words, two arguments were put forward for maintaining a distinction between military and civilian approaches to confidentiality. The first was consequentialist. If doctors were concerned that their medical reports were liable to be produced and scrutinised in court it was less likely they would be open and frank in the opinions they expressed within them. This would have detrimental consequences for the communication of information within the military. Similarly, concern that medical records could subsequently be produced in court might deter servicemen from seeking early medical treatment for a disease such as VD, despite being subject to disciplinary action for failure to do so. The second defence focused on dual loyalties. Doctors not only had obligations towards the well-being of servicemen, as officers they also had a duty to maintain service discipline.

Of course, both defences also applied in civilian practice. As discussed in Chapters 4–7, the revelation that the judiciary were prepared to override the Ministry of Health's publicised pledge on the confidentiality of VD clinics led some doctors to consider resigning from their posts and likely led others to review the information they recorded on patient files. Equally, as noted in Chapter 3, concerns about malingering were not confined to the military, and civilian doctors were under pressure to consider the discipline of the insured labour force in a similar fashion to their military counterparts. Expansion of welfare provision in the 1940s – as proposed by the Beveridge Report and implemented in legislation including the 1946 National Health Service Act – meant civilian doctors were frequently tasked with certifying, and thereby validating, claims for sickness benefit. While doctors actively resisted becoming incorporated as a specialist branch of the civil service, their surveillance and investigative duties when assessing claims for sickness benefit was seen, by some, as a step on their road to becoming a 'medical Gestapo' ('Lords and Medical Services' in *The Times*, 22 March 1944, 8).

Despite an obvious hostility among senior personnel at the Ministry of Defence, War Office, Admiralty and Air Ministry towards the suggestion that service hospital records should be made available to the courts, the Lord Advocate persisted.

> I think it would be invidious in a normal case if a distinction were drawn, for instance, between medical reports in a military hospital and medical reports in an ordinary hospital which will soon become a state hospital. I should state here that, so far as hospitals run by the Department of Health for Scotland are concerned, I have advised the Department to make such reports available in the ordinary case. (Lord Advocate to MoD, 14 January 1948, WO32/12406)

Further internal correspondence at Whitehall confirmed the opposition to Wheatley's stancc, and a reply detailing this was sent to the Lord Advocate in late February 1948. In light of the interwar attempts at legislation on medical privilege, it is interesting to note that the correspondence highlighted a strong preference for maintaining privilege on a class basis – not least because it avoided the difficult task of trying to define in detail any exceptions to the rule. The reply sent to the Lord Advocate therefore stressed the difference between service and civilian medicine and removed references to civilian doctors treating serving soldiers in the Emergency Medical Service Hospitals. This last example had been included in an earlier draft, but was edited out of the final version of the letter on the basis that 'it would be better not to enter into details of this slightly more complicated situation'. While the War Office was evidently keen to avoid discussion of the implications, there was little doubt that the distinction between the principles underpinning approaches to medical confidentiality in civilian and military medicine was increasingly blurred.

Although the Lord Advocate's suggestion was opposed by the military service departments in Whitehall, it served to illustrate how the changing legal context and reorganisation of medical services had increased scrutiny of the whole question of medical confidentiality and privilege in a broader sense than previously. Emphasising a distinction between the role of the doctor and the medical record in military and civilian settings may have bought some time, but the argument would not stand up to sustained examination. Pressure continued to be applied as questions about the extent of Crown privilege arose in both the military and civilian contexts.[2]

Personal Injury Cases

A key area of recurrent debate was the demand for medical evidence and documents in litigation involving claims for compensation for personal injury and accidents. In part, the increase in such cases reflected the frequency of serious accidents in an 'age of scientific discovery and mechanical progress'. Although injury had been a feature of working life for many in industrialised Britain for a long time, in the second half of the twentieth century victims had greater opportunity to seek compensation through the courts. According to Dix and Todd (1961), following on from the establishment of the legal aid scheme in 1949 around '14 per cent of certificates issued to assisted persons were to enable them to take proceedings for damages for personal injuries'. Medical evidence had great significance in such cases, and could assist the petitioner's legal team in determining the strength of their client's case, as well as the defendant's lawyers to refute or limit their client's liability. Medical evidence was also vital in helping the judge to assess the merits of the case and the extent of any damages awarded. In addition to requiring a doctor to attend and give evidence in court, there was also a demand for copies of medical reports made at the time of the accident or medical certificates completed by the doctor in connection with a claim for insurance benefits.

The requirement that doctors must give evidence when called to do so in court was rehearsed along similar lines as before, with reference to Mansfield's ruling in the Duchess of Kingston's case denying privilege to medical practitioners (Dix and Todd 1961, 198). However, requests for medical information in advance of legal proceedings caused concern among doctors and many were unsure how best to respond.

In terms of the Scottish courts, the case of *Watson v McEwan* (1905) had determined that such information could be given to a lawyer during a precognition in advance of legal proceedings. While it was always possible that the case would not subsequently come to trial, it was felt that disclosure in such circumstances posed a minimal threat to the efficacy of doctor–patient relations and the perception of confidentiality within them (Ferguson 2011). A related point was raised in the English courts in the case of *C v C* at the Birmingham Assizes ([1946], 1 A.E.R. 562). As a divorce case in which medical evidence was sought from a VD doctor with the consent of the patient involved, there were obvious similarities to *Garner* (1920). In *C v C* the petition was made under the terms of the Matrimonial Causes Act 1937, which provided grounds for divorce in cases where, at the time of marriage, either party was of unsound mind, a mental defect, subject to recurring

2 For more detail on the gradual convergence of approaches in civilian and military medicine over the course of the twentieth century see Ferguson 2013.

fits of insanity or epilepsy, suffering from VD in a communicable form, or was pregnant by a third party. The petitioner (husband) sought divorce on grounds that, shortly after marriage, his wife (the respondent) showed symptoms of VD. She attended a VD clinic where she was diagnosed as suffering from syphilis. On discovering this, the husband attended the same clinic and was examined by the same doctor, but no evidence of syphilis was found in any form.

Divorce proceedings were instigated and, in order to facilitate her defence, the wife sought further details of her illness, including whether it was in a communicable form and approximately when it was likely to have been contracted. Other than stating that the disease was secondary syphilis, the doctor refused to disclose any further information. Approximately six months later, the doctor received a questionnaire signed personally by both the petitioner and respondent and approved by their legal teams requesting further information considered vital to the presentation of their respective cases. The doctor refused to answer the questions, indicating that, if subpoenaed, he would give the information in court.

Both parties in *C v C* were clearly hindered in preparation of their respective cases by the doctor's refusal to answer questions in advance of appearing as a witness in court. Consequently, the judge (J. Lewis) issued a direction on the point which the President of the Probate, Divorce and Admiralty Division (Lord Merriman) had approved. This acknowledged the importance of confidentiality to the treatment of VD and the obligation on doctors to ensure that patients had continued confidence in the system. However, when disclosure was sought at the patient's own request and with signed consent, the doctor could disclose the relevant information without fear of breaching confidentiality.

Textbooks of medical jurisprudence offered general advice on disclosure of medical information in advance, or preparation, of a legal case. The doctor should always ensure that the patient had consented to disclosure, rather than assume that a request from a solicitor's firm claiming to act on behalf of the patient was sufficient. Even when there was firm evidence of patient consent, it was important for doctors to make sure that only the minimum amount of information necessary for the specific purpose was disclosed, a point still emphasised in current guidance on the topic.

While doctors considered the propriety of releasing information in advance of legal proceedings, lawyers continued to be concerned about medical information being unnecessarily withheld from court.

Background to Committees and Reports on Privilege

At the time of *Duncan v Cammell Laird* [1942], discovery of documents could not be ordered against the Crown in English courts. Crown privilege was claimed in response to a subpoena, typically in litigation between third parties. Where the Crown was a party in the case, documents were usually:

> produced as a matter of grace, and there was no need for the Crown to set out in an affidavit of documents those which were not being produced. In fact it was the invariable rule to withhold all minutes and most other documents passing between Government servants, and this was accepted as a matter of course. (Report of the Committee on Crown Privilege, NA PCOM9 1825)

Following the Crown Proceedings Act 1947, regular orders for discovery against the Crown often met with a claim of class privilege, provoking concern that the scope of the privilege was being extended, and the class exemption element of it was being more readily applied than previously.

Growing unrest over the application of class privilege was evident in *Ellis v The Home Office* ([1953], 2 QB 135). While accepting that government departments were entitled to claim privilege and that the minister's decision to do so was final, the judge emphasised the need to ensure that each individual document was properly examined before the claim was made. While privilege was claimed in the public interest, it was noted that denying relevant information to a court might hinder justice, which was also an important facet of the public interest. A similar point was made in *Broome v Broome* (1955, A.E.R 201), where the report of the case noted:

> It is of obvious importance to ensure generally that claims of Crown privilege are not used unnecessarily to the detriment of the vital need of the courts to have the truth put before them; and the courts would consider carefully before conceding to the Crown a general power wholly to suppress evidence from every source upon the unexaminable opinion of a Minister as to what that Minister regarded as the public interest.

The Lord Advocate's earlier query regarding service hospital medical records had been an indication that Scottish legal opinion was in favour of pushing for greater disclosure. The Scottish courts had traditionally retained power to overrule a ministerial claim of privilege and order production of documents by the Crown. However, in *Duncan v Cammell Laird*, Lord Simon had suggested that a claim of Crown privilege was as conclusive in Scots Law as it was in English Law. Lord Guthrie felt obliged to follow this line when privilege was claimed for an accident report made by a War Office driver in *Smith v Lord Advocate* ([1953] S.L.T. Notes 74). However, the subsequent House of Lords decision in *Glasgow Corporation v Central Land Board* ([1956] S.C. (H.L.) 1) determined that a claim of Crown privilege made by the relevant minister of state was not definitive in Scottish courts. The latter could choose to overrule the decision and demand that the evidence be produced. Lord Radcliffe's insistence that such a power should not become 'a mere ghost of theory' raised the possibility that Scottish courts might make more frequent use of their discretion to override ministerial decisions on disclosure.

> The phrase 'necessary for the proper functioning of the public service' is a familiar one and I have a misgiving that it may become all too familiar in the future, if the cases to which our attention is directed, *Ellis* v *Home Office*, *Smith* v *Lord Advocate*, *Broome* v *Broome*, are symptomatic of the kind of situation which the formula is supposed to cover. I take it that it is lifted direct from the last paragraph of Lord Simon's speech in the *Duncan* case: but if it is to become accepted doctrine that this very general phrase covers everything, however commonplace, that has passed between one civil servant and another behind the departmental screen on the special ground that the possibility of its disclosure in a legal action would impair freedom and candour of official reports or minutes, I do not think that it will be a matter of surprise if some future Judge in Scotland finds himself obliged to disregard the Crown's objection and to hold that disclosure can do much less injury to the interests of the public than non-production of a particular document may do to that other public interest which is represented by the cause of justice.

The decision that Scottish courts retained the right to overrule a minister's claim of Crown privilege, in effect confined *Duncan v Cammell Laird* to no more than obiter dicta in Scotland. This revision combined with, and probably added to, growing discontent in the English courts that the privilege was too broadly defined and too readily applied.

Official Committee on Crown Privilege

In February 1955, an Official Committee on Crown Privilege was set up in recognition of the fact that 'judicial and public opinion has grown restive' (NA PCOM9/1825). Tasked with examining the circumstances in which privilege was claimed, together with the principles involved and the procedure that was followed, the committee were to advise on whether any modification to current practice was necessary.

The resultant report, produced in April 1956, suggested two possible approaches. The first was to encourage a more flexible application of Crown privilege. However, this posed obvious problems. While some decisions might be tackled in this way, claims of privilege based on the class of document, as opposed to its specific content, depended on consistently claiming privilege for certain types of documents, such as service medical records. If, instead of a class privilege, the decision to disclose a particular record was made on an ad hoc basis, this would generate uncertainty in the system, undermining confidence and inhibiting the candid communication of information. Candour and open communication, within and between government departments and institutions, was necessary for their efficient running and would be adversely affected by any possibility that the documents might later be made public.

A more suitable alternative was to review the range of documents currently covered by Crown privilege and agree to exclude certain types of documents that no longer merited blanket protection, based on their nature or subject matter. To this end, the committee chairman, Harold Kent[3], sought the views of government departments[4] 'about the kinds of documents for which privilege is claimed and the kinds of circumstances in which the question of claiming privilege arises' (NA PCOM9/1825).

Paragraphs 22–27 of the report dealt with the issue of medical records and reports that came into the custody of Government departments. These fell into six categories:

1. Medical records and reports in the fighting services.
2. Medical records and reports relating to persons detained in prisons.
3. Medical records and reports relating to industrial injuries and accidents giving rise to claims for benefit under the National Insurance (Industrial Injuries) Act 1946.
4. Medical records and reports kept by doctors employed at Government factories.
5. Medical records and reports kept at nationalised hospitals, and special medical reports made to the Minister of Health, or in Scotland, to the Secretary of State.
6. Other departmental medical records and reports about the health of government employees.

Medical records and reports relating to industrial injuries and accidents (point 3) were already made available in any legal proceedings. Similarly, privilege was not claimed for medical records and reports kept at nationalised hospitals, although the special medical reports, also referred to in point 5, were privileged. The committee proposed that there should be no change in this regard, however, they advocated that privilege should not be claimed for the records kept by doctors at government factories (point 4). Privilege should not be claimed for records covered by point 6, with the exception of confidential reports made by doctors for the purpose of

---

3 Sir Harold Kent was a trained Barrister who had previously served as Parliamentary Counsel to the Treasury 1940–53, before becoming Procurator General and Treasury Solicitor 1953–63. See his entry in *Who Was Who* for further details.

4 A questionnaire was issued to all departments and evidence was heard from the following: Admiralty; Ministry of Agriculture, Fisheries and Food; Air Ministry; Board of Customs and Excise; Ministry of Fuel and Power; Ministry of Health; Home Office; Board of Inland Revenue; Ministry of Labour and National Service; National Assistance Board; Ministry of Pensions and National Insurance; Post Office; Director of Public Prosecutions; Ministry of Supply; Board of Trade; Ministry of Transport and Civil Aviation; War Office; Ministry of Works. Informal advice was also received from 'two big commercial companies', the British Transport Commission and a prominent firm of Scottish solicitors.

administering the superannuation and sick leave arrangements of the civil service and 'other establishment purposes'. While the right to claim privilege was retained for the latter documents, it was noted that there had never been a need to make the claim in practice.

The medical records and reports of the fighting services and of persons detained in prison had clearly posed the greatest challenge for the committee. Its recommendation was that privilege should be maintained for such records except:

a. Where the Crown was being sued for negligence – although even then, some 'specially confidential reports' prepared for prison governors might still need to be excluded.
b. Where the documents were required by the defence in any criminal proceedings.

The justification for treating these medical records and reports in a different way to the others was the belief that there was a substantive difference in the position of doctors and the function of the medical report in prisons and the fighting services. In essence this argument echoed the line previously taken by the War Office in correspondence with the Lord Advocate. Emphasis was put on both the overt dual loyalty demands on doctors in military and prison settings, and the negative impact on necessary communications that would follow any removal or dilution of privilege.

Comments within the Prison Commission file on the issue point to the difficulty of the position in which the commissioners found themselves. On the one hand, they felt under considerable pressure to facilitate the legal process by making information available to a greater extent than previously. Moreover, 'the willingness of the Ministry of Health and NHS doctors and consultants to disclose these documents is a formidable argument against the Commissioners declining to do so'. On the other hand, removal of Crown privilege protection was likely to inhibit doctors, making them less open, frank, and detailed in the information they included in communications and medical reports made to prison governors. Similarly, the information recorded within departmental minutes would also be constrained if correspondents always had to consider the possibility that it might become public. Evidently, they felt squeezed.

> I am pretty sure we are not going to get much sympathy or support unless we show some willingness to meet so far as we can a point of view strongly held by Bar and Bench alike. Indeed I think even a refusal to disclose medical reports from an outside consultant or hospital will be hard to defend in view of the NHS capitulation. And while I am personally satisfied that the disclosure of departmental minutes in this and other fields might well have disastrous results I am also conscious that this view is based on mere expediency and owes little if anything to logic or equity. (NA PCOM9/1825)

This gives a clear sense of the legal pressure that was being applied in an attempt to reduce the boundaries of Crown privilege and ensure greater disclosure. Two other elements of the statement are striking. Firstly, the characterisation of the lack of desire to claim privilege for NHS records as a 'capitulation'. Certainly, the fact that such records were in public ownership had raised the possibility that, in principle, they could be covered by Crown privilege. However, in practice, civilian medical records had always been made available to the courts. While the Ministry of Health had argued in favour of privilege in relation to VD doctors in the early 1920s, this had been an atypical example of a communicable disease in which, from the government's point of view, the public interest seemed to be better served by guaranteeing the confidentiality of diagnosis and treatment.

The second striking element of the statement is its similarity in tone to the view expressed by Cox after compiling the BMA PSC's defence of confidentiality, and its package of support for anyone willing to become a medical martyr (see Chapter 5). Considered in isolation, confidentiality was an integral element of the efficacy of the system, and any threat to it could cause significant damage to internal communication. However, the fact that government departments could now be sued, and legal aid was available to provide financial assistance, meant that the benefits of open communication within government institutions and departments could no longer be considered in isolation. Just as demands for medical evidence in the growing numbers of divorce petitions had challenged the guarantee of confidentiality at VD clinics in the interwar years, so now the benefit to the public of unbridled communication within government departments had to be weighed against the public interest in facilitating justice. While an instinctive urge to defend the status quo and protect the previous boundaries of privilege remained, it was increasingly difficult to maintain in the face of a changing legal context and growing disquiet among the judiciary.

The Prison Commissioners certainly mounted a strong defence of Crown privilege. At the request of the Chairman of the Prison Commission, representatives met with Sir Leslie Brass, a member of the Committee on Crown Privilege, at the Home Office at the end of July 1955. The hope was that Brass could be persuaded of the continued need to protect 'certain very confidential papers such as psychiatrist's notes and examinations, which could not strictly be called department minutes'. Brass pointed out that the Armed Services' medical authorities had maintained a less cooperative policy than the Ministry of Health on this, but they had only been able to do so because in law the military authorities could not be sued by soldiers in the kind of case which was mainly under consideration, such as damages by an individual against the Department for negligence. Unfortunately, the same did not hold true for the Prison Commissioners. Moreover, their position was made more difficult by the fact that the Ministry of Health had no reservations about the production of NHS medical records. The NHS produced all of theirs, 'no matter how confidential the document, or whatever the disclosures made in it'. If the Home Office wished to defend the position desired by the Prison Commission, they would have to convince the committee that there were material differences between prison medical records and the records of the Ministry of Health and NHS, sufficient to entail that they should be treated differently.

Representatives of the Prison Commission had attempted to do this, putting forward four points:

1. The Prison medical officer is not simply a doctor but is also part of the general disciplinary machinery of the prison and his advice and opinion are of great value to the Governor and the Commissioners not only as regards the health of his patients but also as regards the general disciplinary treatment of prisoners.
2. The establishment of a satisfactory doctor–patient relationship in prison is peculiarly difficult and yet must be established if the Commissioners are to fulfil their duty to look after the health of their prisoners. The prisoner has no choice about his medical adviser. He has to accept the prison medical officer available; he cannot change his doctor if he does not like him and, in practice, he cannot refuse to be medically examined by him.
3. Prison doctors are dealing, particularly in recidivist prisons, with often quite unscrupulous, malicious and untruthful prisoners and the prison doctor is at special risk as a result in anything he says or does. It is necessary for him to be able to comment freely otherwise his use to the Governor and the Commissioners is impaired and he would be unable to do so if he knew of the likelihood that what he said on the record was going to be produced in Court.
4. A doctor's position vis-à-vis his prisoner patient would be seriously affected if it were known to prisoners generally that he had made the kind of comment which it may be his duty to make for the information of the Governor or the Commissioners, and the prison doctor has to live in close and continuous contact with his patients.

While sympathetic to the arguments presented, Brass was unconvinced that the current position could be maintained, given that 'the temperature of judicial comment about the claiming of Crown privilege was much hotter than it had been in the past and it might be necessary to concede something in order not to lose still more'. He suggested that the Home Office might concede that, in cases where the Prison Commissioners were being sued, they would agree to disclose any records except for departmental minutes. However, he also noted that there was no firm definition of what was included in the latter, but assumed it meant 'anything written by one official to another in the nature of a report or a comment or a minute'. As another comment in the file highlighted 'the root of the difficulty seems to me to lie in the impossibility of defining precisely the type of "Departmental Minute" we would wish to withhold'.

In essence, under pressure from the committee as well as the judiciary, the Prison Commissioners found themselves trying to defend the need for privilege while demonstrating willingness to cooperate with judicial demand for greater information to facilitate the justice system. As with service medical records, it was much easier to base the claim for privilege on a class basis, in this case departmental minutes, provided that it was broad enough to encapsulate all the types of documents they desired to keep away from public scrutiny.

Ministerial Committee to Consider the Report on Crown Privilege

The Working Party Report sought to balance greater disclosure of information, in order to facilitate the legal process and quell judicial discontent, with recognition of the continued benefits of claiming class privilege for certain types of documents. A committee of ministers was appointed to consider the report and to advise the Cabinet on which of the recommendations should be followed.[5] Growing legal pressure on the issue was coming to a point, with the Bar Council's Law Reform Committee likely to recommend that the courts, rather than a Minister of the Crown, should have power to decide whether non-disclosure of specific documents was in the public interest in each case. Mr Simon,[6] MP for Middlesbrough West, had already tabled an amendment to the Restrictive Trade Practices Bill which, if passed, would give the Restrictive Trade Practices Court the power to decide whether Crown privilege was merited for particular documents in relevant cases not directly involving national security.

A note prepared in advance of the meeting suggested that the committee's first consideration was the desirability and possible effects of making any change to Crown privilege. As already noted, the Kent report recommended that departmental papers including reports, memoranda and minutes, should continue to be protected by privilege as their non-disclosure was considered essential for the proper functioning of the relevant public service. Indeed, of the fourteen recommendations summarised in paragraph 61 of the report, eight recommended that there should be no change to existing practice; three suggested minor concessions; two recommended concessions; and on one issue – the non-disclosure of addresses and personal information held by government departments concerned with social services – there was no recommendation. If

5 This was composed of the Lord Chancellor as Chairman, Home Secretary, Secretary of State for Scotland, Secretary of State for War, Minister of Health, Postmaster General, Attorney General, Lord Advocate, Solicitor General, and the Treasury's Financial Secretary.

6 Jocelyn Edward Salis Simon (from 1971, Baron Simon of Glaisdale) was a trained barrister. After military service during WWII, he resumed practice at the Bar. His political career as an MP from 1951–65, included time as Joint Parliamentary Under Secretary of State, Home Office 1957–8; Financial Secretary to the Treasury 1958–59 and Solicitor General 1959–62. He subsequently became President of the Probate, Divorce and Admiralty Division of the High Court 1962–71; and then a Lord of Appeal in Ordinary 1971–77. See entry in *Who Was Who*. See also his article on Crown privilege in *The Observer* 13 November 1955. (NA PCOM9 1010077).

the committee agreed with this approach, then related questions arose. Firstly, if the recommendations left such a broadly defined class of 'departmental papers' protected, were the recommendations likely to be sufficient to appease judicial discontent? Following on from this, if the recommended concessions were likely to be considered insufficient, were they worth making at all? As Critchley[7], the note's author, queried: 'is there a case for defending resolutely the line formerly taken rather than advancing a few paces and, in doing so, possibly exposing the whole front to attack?' For example, the suggestion that departmental minutes should be disclosed in cases of road accidents was an issue of particular concern as it seemed 'likely to endanger a considerable section of the line. Is it not the thin end of a very large wedge?'

Critchley's note is therefore revealing of the attitudes underpinning policy discussions and decisions on Crown privilege at the time. Most obviously, the language is very defensive and militaristic. As so often before, it also pointed to the difficulties of defining in greater detail, and justifying in the face of legal demands for greater information, what should or should not be covered by privilege. Pointing to the terms of Simon's proposed amendment to the Restrictive Trade Practices Bill, Critchley suggested that the committee would likely agree that a backbench amendment to a bill with limited application was the wrong way to set up a new pattern of policy with much broader implications. His note ended by posing a general question to the committee:

> Are the Government prepared to announce, in advance of the Report Stage of the Bill, a policy in this matter so liberal that this amendment could be accepted within the letter and spirit of that policy; or alternatively, should the Government announce that subject to minor changes the existing policy regarding Crown privilege must be maintained and that Mr Simon's amendment is consequently unacceptable? (NA LCO2/5123 Critchley Note 15 May 1956)

When the committee met, it largely endorsed the view that departmental papers should remain protected, but that other classes of documents, specified in the Working Party report, could be disclosed or should be considered on a case by case basis.[8] However, echoing the concern expressed in Critchley's note, the Committee rejected the Report's recommendation that official minutes and reports

7 Thomas Alan Critchley was a civil servant in the Cabinet Office 1954–6, before becoming Principal Private Secretary to the Home Secretary (Butler) 1957–60. See entry in *Who Was Who*.

8 These included: documents kept by doctors employed at government factories, and, in some cases, departmental medical records about the health of government employees; medical reports by service and prison doctors in cases where the Crown was sued for negligence or the documents were required by the defence in criminal proceedings. While communications made in confidence by members of the public (such as income tax returns or economic information given to the Board of Trade) would remain protected,

relating to road accident cases should be disclosed. 'The apparently anomalous effect would be produced that minutes were disclosed in one type of accident case and not in another; and there would be a dangerous and significant inroad into the principle that Departmental minutes should be protected.'

Additionally, the committee came to no final decision on the issue of claiming privilege for the documents and records of welfare officers employed by the Soldiers, Sailors and Airmen's Families Association (SSAFA). It recognised a clear argument in favour of ensuring that service personnel and their spouses could seek advice, 'particularly with matrimonial difficulties', in the knowledge that their confidences would be respected, and therefore the work of the SSAFA was important to the morale of Forces deployed overseas. However, it was difficult to argue that non-disclosure of these records was essential to the proper working of a public service, and it was noted that privilege had never been claimed for the documents of welfare officers employed under the aegis of the Ministry of Health. The committee therefore referred the issue on to the Cabinet to decide.

The committee believed that the proposals did not merit the publication of a White Paper, 'particularly as these limited changes are unlikely to appease critics of the Government's policy on this question'. Instead, they agreed that the Attorney General be authorised to announce the changes during the debate of the Restrictive Trade Practices bill in connection with Simon's proposed amendment. Evidently, there was a belief that a statement of the government's new policy in this context was likely to 'have the effect of restraining opposition to the Government's policy in this matter by the recognition that a major departure of policy could scarcely be initiated in reference to the Restrictive Practices Court alone'.

As the committee chairman, the Lord Chancellor (Kilmuir)[9] prepared a summary of the committee's view and circulated it to members of the Cabinet. Another paper was also circulated by the Minister for Pensions and National Insurance. The latter's concern was that any official statement regarding Crown privilege should not prejudice the findings of a paper, currently in preparation, which considered Crown privilege in relation to social security records. A note, summarising the content of this paper for the Lord Chancellor, ended by suggesting that the importance of the subject of Crown privilege to the administration of justice was such that, while the Attorney General might give a limited statement during debate of the Restrictive Trade Practices Bill, 'the Bench and the Profession would hope and expect to see a comprehensive statement made by the Lord Chancellor'. This view was endorsed by the Cabinet when it met on 29 May 1956, suggesting that the Lord Chancellor should make a comprehensive statement in

---

other statements made in confidence by the public (such as minor complaints), would be 'examined critically' to determine whether privilege was required.

9 David Patrick Maxwell Fyfe, Viscount Kilmuir (subsequently Baron Fyfe of Dornoch) held numerous positions during his career. He served as Solicitor General 1942–45, Attorney General in 1945, and Lord Chancellor 1954–62. See his entry in *Who Was Who*.

the House of Lords the following week, prior to the debate of the Bill in the House of Commons. Steps would be taken to ensure that the statement did not prejudice the proposals being developed at the Ministry of Pensions and National Insurance relating to private requests for disclosure of confidential information contained in social security records. With regard to the reports of welfare officers of the SSAFA, the Cabinet advocated that privilege should still be claimed.

Lord Chancellor Statement, 1956

Over the following days, a draft statement was drawn up for the Lord Chancellor and circulated for comment. Arrangements were also made for a suitable question to be tabled, in the name of former Lord Chancellor, the Earl Jowitt[10], in the House of Lords (NA LCO2/5122). While there were numerous comments on, and alterations to, the draft statement, two elements are worth noting in particular. Firstly, Simon – the MP who had tabled an amendment to the Restrictive Trade Practices Bill – was evidently not satisfied that the contents of the Lord Chancellor's statement were 'in any way adequate to meet the evils that all now agree arise in the present system'. As Simon's amendment had already made clear, the crux of the issue was judicial determination of whether privilege applied, which he considered was 'essential to prevent Departments deciding where the balance of public interest lies in cases where their own departmental convenience is necessarily one of the relevant circumstances'. Pointing to the fact that judicial determination did not appear to impede the work of government departments in other countries – including Scotland, America or 'the Dominions' – Simon suggested that the government's insistence that Ministers should retain the decision seemed 'a quite unjustified slur on our judiciary'. This appeared confirmation that, as predicted in discussions over previous weeks, the proposals did not go far enough towards meeting demands for change.

A second point of note is the letter sent on Monday 4 June from the LCO to Jowitt, thanking him 'for having agreed to ask a question on this subject, which he thinks the Judiciary and the legal profession as a whole would prefer to see dealt with in the Lords between the present Lord Chancellor and an ex-Lord Chancellor'. It was hoped that Jowitt would be available to meet the Lord Chancellor to discuss the statement on the morning of 6 June, prior to presenting it in the House of Lords that afternoon. With strong opinions held on all sides of the debate over Crown privilege, the process of raising the issue and providing the statement was carefully managed to ensure that everyone understood their part.

When Jowitt asked the question in the House of Lords on the afternoon of Wednesday 6 June 1956, the Lord Chancellor set out the agreed statement outlining

10 William Allen Jowitt, had served in a number of senior roles, including Attorney General 1929–32, Solicitor General 1940–42, and Lord Chancellor 1945–51. See his entry in *Who Was Who*.

changes in the application of Crown privilege. In relation to medical records and reports, privilege would no longer be claimed for the medical records of civilian employees, or in cases where the Crown, or a doctor employed by the Crown, was being sued for negligence. However, privilege would still be claimed for service and prison medical records in proceedings between private litigants.

With regard to who should make the decision as to whether a claim of Crown privilege was justified, he stressed that, where privilege was claimed on the basis that the open communication facilitated by the guarantee of confidentiality was necessary for the proper functioning of a public service, the decision had to be taken by the relevant Minister.

> A judge assesses the importance of a particular document in the case that he is hearing, and his inclination would be to allow or to disallow a claim for privilege according to the contents and the relevance of the document, rather than to consider the effect on the public service of the disclosure of the class of documents to which it belongs. (Hansard, House of Lords, 1956 (197), 743)

Given the earlier debate over disclosure of VD records in the early interwar years, this is an important statement. As noted in Chapters 4–6, judicial overruling of the government pledge of confidential VD treatment was seen by some as primarily motivated by the convenience of using medical evidence of VD to process a mounting backlog of divorce cases. The advice given by both the Ministry of Health and BMA during debates of the issue, was that doctors should always make an appeal for privilege and that the judge was best placed to determine the balance between protecting confidentiality and the public interest in disclosure. This idea was, in part, based on the assumption that judges would take into consideration the broader implications of each decision. In other words, the judge would consider the effects of forcing disclosure on the public service. By contrast, the Lord Chancellor's statement in 1956 made clear that judges were likely only to consider the relevance of the document to the case before them, and therefore should not be given responsibility for determining when Crown privilege applied.

It is noteworthy that, when questioned, the Lord Chancellor stressed that the changes would not require legislation. This was, no doubt, a thinly veiled reference to Simon's amendment to the Restrictive Trade Practices Bill, but it also negated the need to justify the details of the new arrangements amidst further parliamentary scrutiny and debate. The Lord Chancellor had, however, received the views of the Bar Council and the Law Society[11]:

> I do not pretend that my proposals meet their views in toto. The Bar Council were anxious for a judicial decision on the matter, and it was in deference to

11 As discussed in Chapter 9, these two legal organisations subsequently formed a joint committee with the BMA and issued a couple of reports on the broader question of medical evidence in court.

> these views that I dealt somewhat fully with that aspect of the matter. I should like to assure the noble Lord that they have been taken into account fully by all who have examined this problem before we came to our decision. (Hansard, House of Lords, 1956 (197), 748)

While the Lord Chancellor's statement was intended to alleviate the growing frustration at the frequent application of Crown privilege, the class exemption of service and prison medical records from use in private litigation continued to provoke problems. For example, although the Lord Advocate had been unsuccessful in his earlier attempt to persuade Whitehall that Crown privilege was, at times, unnecessarily claimed, he had evidently not lost confidence in the merits of his argument. In light of the decision in *Glasgow Corporation* [1956], the Lord Advocate resumed debate about the scope of Crown privilege when the case of *McLeod v Walker* arose as an example of ongoing difficulties.

Continued Unrest in the Courts

A memorandum prepared for him outlined the case of *McLeod v Walker* in the Scottish Court of Session (NA LCO2/5132). McLeod, an able seaman, went out 'first footing'[12] in Glasgow, in the early hours of 1 January 1956. He was very drunk. He was later admitted to the Victoria Infirmary suffering from extensive injuries that left him hospitalised for seven-and-a-half months, until 18 August 1956. He subsequently brought an action against a police constable who, McLeod alleged, had inflicted the injuries while attacking him with his truncheon. The constable maintained that the injuries had been sustained as a result of McLeod falling against cars and pavements while inebriated.

In addition to requiring the evidence contained in the books of the Victoria Infirmary, an NHS hospital, McLeod also sought documents from the Cowglen Military Hospital, to which he had been transferred on 18 August for three days while being assessed before returning to his unit on sick leave. While the documents requested from Cowglen were unlikely to contain material that would be harmful if disclosed, they formed a part of his service medical records which were, as a class, covered by Crown privilege. Not to claim privilege for them would go against War Office policy and the recent statement by the Lord Chancellor in the House of Lords, and would weaken future claims to class privilege. However, in light of the *Glasgow Corporation* [1956] decision, the case seemed to be an example where the justification for claiming Crown privilege was exceptionally weak.

A memorandum on the issue, prepared for the Lord Chancellor in late September 1957, acknowledged that disclosure of the information requested in the case would pose no real threat. Nonetheless, as the information was contained

12 A Scottish tradition where friends call on their neighbours carrying a small gift, traditionally a lump of coal for the fire, after the bells ring in a new year.

in McLeod's service medical record, privilege would still have to be claimed. However, the use of privilege on this class basis carried significant risks, as the Scottish courts retained the discretion to override ministerial claims to Crown privilege 'and it is known that they are now very ready to do so' – presumably a reference to Lord Radcliffe's statement in *Glasgow Corporation* [1956] as quoted earlier. However, Kent, Treasury Solicitor and chairman of the Working Party on Crown Privilege, regarded this as a risk that simply had to be taken.

Perhaps most interestingly, the memo referred to the fact that the Lord Chancellor had previously expressed the view that he 'should not be asked to give advice about the detailed application to individual cases of the statement [he] had made in the House of Lords as this might lead to [him] being placed in an embarrassing situation'. Rather than agreeing to a meeting with the Lord Advocate, which would also be attended by the Attorney General and might require the Lord Chancellor to adjudicate between conflicting claims of the public interest, a simpler solution was suggested. 'Tomorrow's breakfast might provide a convenient opportunity for you to tell the Lord Advocate that, having read the Treasury Solicitor's memorandum, you think there is no alternative to claiming privilege, unpalatable though that may be.' A note indicated that the Lord Chancellor entirely agreed with this line. Evidently, his statement in the House of Lords had done little to ease the pressure on the class application of Crown privilege. While service guidelines for doctors followed the terms of the Lord Chancellor's statement, solicitors continued to subpoena service medical officers and documents in divorce proceedings.

In *Gain v Gain* ([1961] 1 W.L.R. 1469), a naval officer was subpoenaed as a witness and asked to testify regarding the previous medical condition of one of the parties in a divorce case. He was invited to refresh his memory from the relevant service medical records before answering, but objection was raised on grounds that the records were subject to a claim of Crown privilege. The court upheld the objection, determining that if the documents were privileged and could not be admitted as evidence in court then oral testimony following examination of their contents must also be excluded. In effect, the case picked up on the paradox that had been highlighted by the Working Party in 1956, and naturally it caught the attention of its former chairman, Harold Kent, the Treasury Solicitor. A letter from his office to the Admiralty, in November 1961, drew attention to reports of the case in *The Times*, and suggested that 'the implications behind this case seem to us to make the existing practice in relation to the production of medical evidence difficult, if not impossible' (NA ADM1 27936). If medical officers were unable to refresh their memory from records prior to giving evidence, it was difficult to see how reliable medical evidence could effectively be given. Consequently, service policy on medical records and medical evidence might have to be redrafted.

In February 1962 Kent again wrote to the Admiralty. He was concerned that, if the ruling in *Gain* was accepted, the lack of oral or written medical evidence from the Armed Services would make the Crown 'appear very unreasonable'. In order to avoid such difficulties, he suggested distinguishing between documents that had to be treated as confidential and those which might be produced. In the former category, Kent placed records relating to psychiatric or mental illness or VD – the types of record usually sought in matrimonial proceedings. In the non-confidential category he placed records relating to physical injury or illness (other than VD), which were likely to be sought in claims for damages resulting from accidents. 'Fishing' enquiries could be countered by requiring the solicitor to specify the particular matter on which evidence was required. In Kent's opinion, evidence of malingering would fall under the confidential class. While classification of information as confidential or non-confidential could, in Kent's view, be made to be consistent with the class-based justification of Crown privilege as defined in *Duncan v Cammell Laird*, it was obvious that a single document might contain elements from both classes. He suggested recording information separately in future, as 'the business of "blacking out" parts of a document is always awkward'.

The replies Kent received did not favour his suggested course of action, echoing earlier concerns that keeping two separate records for each person would be too complex. Recognising that the removal of all medical evidence from matrimonial proceedings would not go down well with the courts, it was suggested that the Attorney General might be approached with a view to maintaining the pre-*Gain* practice. It was acknowledged that:

> The practice of allowing a service doctor to refresh his memory from the actual records before testifying in civil proceedings has always been recognised as somewhat illogical and open to challenge, but it served its purpose, so long as the doctor was not required to admit that he had had access to privileged documents. (NA ADM1 27936)

In effect, previous practice had been based on a charade but, as long as everyone played along, the system functioned. The decision in *Gain* had thrown this into jeopardy. The Admiralty suggested that an interdepartmental committee might be established to consider the situation and make recommendations.

The case of *Devilez v Boots Pure Drug Co.* ([1962] 106 SJ 552) had arisen during the course of this correspondence and had been an ongoing concern in it. Devilez, a serviceman in the Navy, was suing Boots, as manufacturers and vendors of a corn solvent he had purchased, for negligence. After bathing and then applying the solvent, which contained salicylic acid, Devilez had dropped the bottle while replacing it on the window sill. The cork had come out, spilling the contents over his abdomen and genitals. Devilez cleaned himself, but, having found nothing on the label indicating he should seek medical advice, he took no further action. Over the next few days a painful reaction developed that eventually required him to be admitted to hospital, receiving plastic surgery, and subsequent treatment for thrombo-phlebitis. During the court case, evidence was sought from a naval medical officer. The officer requested an opportunity to refresh his memory with reference to Devilez's service medical record. On several occasions he was permitted to leave the court in order to consult the notes before returning to give evidence. This happened so frequently, that the judge decided to allow him to keep the records by the witness box. Obviously, this went against the ruling in *Gain* and could easily have been interpreted as going so far as to waive the class privilege exempting disclosure of the records in court. It certainly made a mockery of the previous policy of allowing oral testimony while denying direct access to written records. The court held that Boots had a duty to make sure that the bottle carried a warning that the contents were dangerous, and to secure them using something more reliable than a cork. Devilez was held one-third responsible for not appreciating the need for careful handling of the bottle and not calling a doctor soon enough. Damages were therefore reduced from £1800 to £1200. However, much to the surprise of those watching closely in Whitehall, Mr Justice Elwes made no reference to Crown privilege during his judgement.

Having avoided a potentially embarrassing situation, Kent noted 'we may not be so fortunate another time'. He therefore took up the Admiralty's suggestion to establish another Working Party in the hope of clarifying the position in advance of any new case.

Working Party on Crown Privilege for Service Medical Records

In August 1962 the Working Party on Crown Privilege for Service Medical Records was established.[13] Its terms of reference asked the group to consider whether it was practicable to make documentary or oral testimony available in proceedings between private litigants without imperilling the maintenance of Crown privilege in areas where the public interest required that there should be no disclosure outside the service. The Working Party produced two reports, circulated in May 1963. The first outlined current practice and the principles underpinning it; the second presented recommendations for the future.

First Report

Paragraph 18 of the first report explained that there were two reasons for seeking Crown privilege for service medical records. Firstly, it helped to ensure that servicemen were not deterred from seeking treatment. Secondly, it facilitated the necessarily frank reporting of information by medical officers. These had been publicly stated on two previous occasions: the Secretary of State for War's statement in the House of Commons on 3 May 1949; and the Lord Chancellor's statement in the House of Lords in 1956. The working party ascertained that nearly all requests for medical information in litigation came from servicemen,

13 Chairman was Mr B.B. Hall and Secretary was Mr A.W. Baker (both from the Treasury Solicitor's Department). Additional members came from the following: Admiralty, War Office, Air Ministry, Home Office, Lord Advocate's Department, Treasury Solicitor's Department.

and disclosure in such cases was therefore unlikely to prove a significant deterrent to service personnel seeking treatment. However, privilege was usually claimed on a class basis for medical records. In the few cases where the application for disclosure came from someone other than the service patient:

> The existing practice is not entirely consistent with Crown privilege being founded on the need for confidentiality between service doctor and service patient so that servicemen should not be deterred from seeking treatment in Service medical establishments. If there were any class of case in which a serviceman might be deterred from seeking treatment by fear of disclosure, it is where the condition treated is of a kind which an ordinary person would wish to conceal. Instances are venereal disease, alcoholism, illegitimate pregnancy, illness after abortion, attempts at suicide, sexual aberration, and mental disorder … In these instances, if the public interest requires that records of such conditions of servicemen should not be disclosed for the purposes of private litigation, because fear of disclosure might deter them from seeking treatment, it would appear to follow that information in other forms about such conditions should not be volunteered for those purposes. (NA ADM1 27936)

However, it was noted that Crown privilege was never claimed for oral medical evidence. It was accepted that this inconsistency to some extent invalidated a claim for privilege founded on the necessity for confidentiality between service doctor and patient. The policy on written records was based on a concern that allowing solicitors to access service medical records might encourage them to fish for evidence of VD relevant to matrimonial proceedings. This could be avoided by only making the records available at the time of a hearing, but it was feared that such a policy, entailing that the existence and extent of evidence would be unavailable prior to the hearing, would be unpopular with the courts. It was therefore easier simply to claim Crown privilege for all medical records. However, the Working Party understood that Crown privilege was not claimed for NHS medical records and that inspection of records by the other party without the patient's consent for the purpose of civil proceedings was refused. Except where the other party was the hospital or body holding the records, or a member of its staff, in which case records were disclosed on discovery. On the order of a court, all records could be produced but without an opportunity for previous inspection being given to the person calling for them, unless it was the patient or the patient had consented, and the record did not relate to VD. This procedure had received general acceptance and had not been criticised by the courts.

In Scotland, requests to inspect NHS records were refused, regardless of whether the information was sought by the patient or a third party. If disclosure was ordered by a competent court, the records were made available to parties before the hearing and Crown privilege was never claimed. It was also noted that the number of applications for production of service medical records was much smaller in Scotland than in England.

In summary, it was evident that service medical information was disclosed for a variety of purposes, but requests for the production of medical records for use in litigation were refused. If necessary, the name of a medical officer was put forward so that a statement could be taken with a view to giving evidence. Traditionally, the medical officer could look at the medical records before making the statement. However, *Gain* [1961] had determined that a medical officer could no longer be asked to refresh his memory in court by referring to medical reports. This ruling was not binding in the Scottish courts.

The Working Party also noted respects in which the current system appeared to work unfairly, making it difficult for servicemen to obtain redress from third parties who had injured them. Similarly, the fact that the name of a medical officer able to give oral evidence of a serviceman's health could be given to a third party, was viewed as 'not wholly consistent with confidentiality', particularly when evidence was sought of VD 'or other conditions which the average person would wish to conceal'.

The practice of claiming Crown privilege for medical records but not for oral medical evidence was recognised as illogical, as comments critical of a serviceman could still be disclosed in oral evidence. In light of NHS practice, it appeared that fears that courts would be against the withholding of medical records prior to the start of a hearing were unfounded. Therefore, the major reason for claiming class privilege for service medical records no longer applied.

The fact that it was predominantly service personnel who sought their own medical records for use in litigation undermined the argument that absence of Crown privilege would deter personnel from seeking medical treatment. The second major justification for claiming class privilege was also questioned. The report noted that comments in reports by medical officers were typically made for clinical and not administrative reasons. Therefore there was little reason to think that freedom of clinical comment would be inhibited by the knowledge that the records might subsequently be disclosed in civil proceedings. However, it was noted that special considerations would apply to psychiatric reports.

Second Report

The second report of the Working Party set out recommendations for the future, in particular with regard to avoiding the inconsistency of claiming privilege for written records while permitting oral evidence 'of matters to which the records relate'. The Working Party did not favour the simple solution of claiming Crown privilege for oral testimony, as this would add further obstacles to the administration of justice, and make it considerably more difficult for a serviceman to obtain medical information for the purposes of private litigation in comparison to a patient treated privately or in an NHS hospital. While they recommended further exploration of the idea of using a summary sheet, which would include relevant medical facts but exclude medical officers' comments, it was noted that such a change in the law of evidence might not be readily acceptable and would likely require legislation in Scotland. They therefore considered other options, making recommendations based on three general principles.

The first recognised that where the state interest required non-disclosure, this was paramount. Second, in cases where there was no specific overriding state interest and a serviceman required medical evidence that was only contained in service records, he should be given assistance. Third, a serviceman was entitled to expect at least the same degree of confidentiality between doctor and patient as obtained in civilian life, a position that probably had more rhetorical than practical recognition at the time (Ferguson 2013).

The recommendations included furnishing servicemen, on request, with summaries of the relevant sections of their medical records for use in claims for compensation stemming from accidents. No limit would be imposed on the extent of their use in such cases. Similarly, the service departments should permit special medical examinations of injured servicemen with the reports being made available for use in any claim. With regard to the third general principle, it was recommended that the current practice of providing the name of a medical officer who might give a statement with a view to giving evidence in court should be dependent on the explicit consent of the patient involved. The Service departments' administrative instructions should be altered to make this clear. While it was hoped that these recommendations would reduce the demand for medical evidence in court, the Working Party recognised the need to consider a possible relaxation in the application of Crown privilege.

The first recommendation in relation to privilege was that service departments and their legal advisers should consider whether factual clinical reports relating solely to physical injuries or disease 'of a kind which the average man would not wish to conceal' should cease to be protected. The Working Party felt that disclosure of such reports in civil proceedings was unlikely to inhibit frank reporting by medical officers, 'disclosure is already made in so many fields that this addition would be without practical significance'. However, they recommended that privilege should continue to apply to records relating to mental disorders, including drug addiction and alcoholism, and 'sexual aberrations'. With regard to diseases which the average person would wish to conceal (like VD, attempted suicide and illegitimate pregnancy), the Working Party recommended that privilege should continue 'for the time being at all events', and protection of written records in such cases should logically extend to oral evidence as well. However, it was clear that few such cases arose, and the blanket application of privilege to such records could work against service personnel who required, but could not be furnished with, evidence of their own condition. 'Nonetheless, the majority of the Working Party felt that it would be premature to waive Crown privilege in respect of diseases and conditions of this kind until the effect of the other measures suggested in this report had been felt.'

After consideration of the reports, and discussion with Hall, Kent indicated that he thought the recommendations should be adopted. While largely agreeing, the Admiralty expressed concern that by subdividing service medical records into two classes – privileged records relating to diseases that most would want to conceal; and non-privileged records relating to other forms of illness and injury – any claim of privilege might be interpreted as providing implied confirmation that there was evidence of, for example, VD or a mental disorder. Kent considered this issue along with Hall, concluding that the proposal would present no more problems than currently existed. If such records were protected by a class privilege, then claiming this in response to a request for such records did not necessarily imply that the records existed. Only that, whether they existed or not, they could not be produced.

> I do not think that the courts will view our behaviour, in the cases in which we claim Crown privilege, with any greater disfavour than heretofore. The great advantage, from our point of view, is that in most of the cases where the service medical documents have real evidential value and cannot be distinguished from similar documents in civil life, we shall no longer have to claim Crown privilege. That is the kind of case that causes the most difficulty, e.g. the recent corn cure case, where we claimed privilege for the case notes relating to the plaintiff's treatment in a service hospital. Of course, as you know, my own conviction is that we ought not to claim Crown privilege at all for service medical documents and that no great harm would be done if we abandoned it altogether. (NA ADM1 27936)

Evidently Kent was not concerned about the proposed reduction in the scope of Crown privilege for medical records. In fact, perhaps in recognition of how problematic the issue had remained since the changes following the recommendations of his own working party in 1956, he was now in favour of making all service medical records available to the courts. However the War Office was not at all keen on the proposal to reduce the scope of class protection for Crown privilege. In its view, the proposed changes would bring little benefit, but would add significantly to the administrative burden.

> Solicitors who now accept the position when it is pointed out, or, knowing our practice, do not apply for disclosure at all, will tend to argue every case with us. This will doubtless lead to a large increase in correspondence, and, as solicitors will probably be more inclined to press cases to the limit, an increase in certificates formally claiming Crown privilege. (NA ADM1 27936)

Kent found this reply, with its attempt to defend the status quo, 'rather depressing'. While recognising that the traditional approach might be more convenient in terms of administration, 'neither the courts nor Parliament regard it as a valid ground for withholding relevant evidence'. Emphasising that the Law Officers of the Crown in both England and Scotland wished to go a good deal further, Kent suggested 'the issue will be whether you can hold the line suggested by the Report, or will be driven to make further concessions', in effect the same choice presented to the

Prison Commissioners by Brass a decade earlier. After further consideration, the War Office wrote to Kent in April 1964 indicating that, provided that the proposal to allow greater disclosure was limited to requests received from a solicitor for information in connection with litigation, the change was agreeable.

However, further developments in the Court of Appeal held up action on the issue, by insisting that a claim of privilege must be specific. Hall indicated that it was difficult to find a form of words that distinguished between '"disgraceful" and other diseases', and therefore it was proposed that the relaxation of privilege should be limited to medical reports on accidents. A point agreed after discussion with the Lord Chancellor, Attorney General and Solicitor General. It was also decided that the Attorney General would make a statement in response to a question on the issue on 21 December 1964.

> Mr Silkin asked the Attorney General what changes he proposes to make in regard to the disclosure in civil proceedings of medical records of members of the Armed Forces.
>
> The Attorney General: The current practice is to claim privilege for these records in proceedings between private litigants on the ground that they belong to a class which the public interest requires to be withheld from production. Privilege is not claimed on this ground where proceedings are brought against the Crown, or a doctor employed by the Crown, for negligence. It is proposed to modify the practice in proceedings between private litigants and in future a claim of privilege will not be made on this ground in such proceedings for clinical reports made by doctors treating Service men for injuries sustained in accidents. (Hansard, House of Commons, 1964, 198, Written Answer. NA ADM1 27396)

The previous month, the government had announced that it had referred the whole issue to the Law Reform Committee.

Law Reform Committee Report on Privilege

In December 1967, the Law Reform Committee presented its sixteenth report, examining the extent of privilege in civil proceedings, to Parliament (Law Reform Committee 1967). In Paragraph 7, the report indicated that Crown privilege had been excluded from consideration and would be the subject of a separate report. With this important qualification, the early sections suggested that privilege was not a controversial issue, or one that caused much difficulty in civil proceedings, 'although we recognise that the exercise by the judge of his discretion is potentially controversial in those rare cases where communications made pursuant to confidential relationships which are not entitled to absolute privilege are involved'. Such confidential relationships included that between doctor and patient, though, as detailed in earlier chapters of this book, the controversies that had arisen over medical privilege tended to arise out of the failure of the judge to accept non-disclosure. Certainly, Sections 48–51 of the report, dealing with communications between doctor and patient, give the impression that the Committee had an incomplete awareness of the controversy which the lack of privilege had caused in the interwar years, a point reflected in other publications on medical testimony which suggested that judges were typically sympathetic to requests for privilege made by medical witnesses (see, for example, Pearce 1979, 81).

The report indicated that it would be 'impracticable to define in statute' any privilege for communications between doctor and patient. This resonates with the difficulties highlighted by Graham-Little's attempts at a private member's bill in 1927 and 1936. However, it also claimed that judicial discretion to demand a medical witness disclose confidential communications had, in the past, 'given little ground for complaint from the medical profession'. Moreover, it was stressed that any claim for privilege were far more likely to arise in criminal rather than civil cases, indicating that earlier controversies over testimony in divorce cases had been banished from memory, probably as a result of changes to both the law relating to divorce and the VD regulations.[14] The final recommendations indicated that there was no need to confer a statutory privilege on communications made to doctors; judicial discretion to determine whether disclosure was necessary, was sufficient. While the decision to consider the application of privilege in civil and criminal cases in separate reports received some criticism, the Law Reform Committee's rejection of a privilege to protect confidential relationships was generally welcomed, despite being 'slightly weakened by the emphasis on the judges' discretion to allow a refusal to disclose in certain unspecified circumstances' (Tapper 1968, 202), a point that split opinion and drew comment in later cases.[15] While the committee avoided the controversy over Crown privilege, its report was an indication that, while much of the focus in the post-war decades was on increasing the information available to the courts, earlier demands for some form of medical privilege had not entirely gone away.

Section 11 of the Winn Committee's report on *Personal Injuries Litigation* (1968 Cmnd 3691) sought to clarify the position on medical examinations, reports and evidence. It recognised that medical concerns over disclosure of medical reports and evidence often entailed unnecessary and expensive delays. The report therefore sought to improve on the prevailing procedures regarding exchange of medical reports and the process of undertaking medical examinations. It advocated that legislation should be drawn up confirming that patients who chose to pursue damages for personal injury:

> Should be deemed thereby to request and authorise any doctor and the authorities of any hospital by whom or in which the person to whom or to whose death such

14 See Chapter 9.

15 For example see *D v NSPCC* [1978] A.C. 171, discussed in Chapter 9.

> a claim relates has been treated for or in respect of any such injuries, to supply upon the request of solicitors or a Trade Union acting for any such claimant or for any defendant or for insurers concerned with any such claim … photocopies of all hospital notes or entries on a National Health Attendance Card which are relevant to treatment afforded for such injuries or to any physical state of the injured person since the date of the said accident which may be attributable to those injuries. (1968 Cmnd 3691, Paragraph 301(a))

The Committee had considered whether the claimant's full medical record should be made available, as this would be likely to assist in determining the full extent of the impact of the injuries. However, the proposal was rejected on the basis that 'such an extended provision would involve a greater infringement of personal liberty than seems in present circumstances necessary' (Paragraph 302). Drawing on a recent article (Bernfeld 1967, discussed in Chapter 9), the report noted that the law had 'progressively encroached upon medical secrecy in the public interest', citing the Duchess of Kingston's trial in relation to common law and Infectious Disease Notification Acts in relation to statute. In its recommendations, the report indicated that consideration should be given to whether further protection by legislation was required to facilitate disclosure of a doctors' report prior to its being given in evidence in court, where it was covered by privilege (Recommendation 14). However, no change was envisioned in terms of the existing practice in relation to Crown privilege.

Conway v Rimmer

After two decades in which mounting legal frustration led to a sequence of committee reviews that produced limited change, a decisive moment came in the case of *Conway v Rimmer* ([1968] A.C. 910; 2 W.L.R. 1535). The case stemmed from an accusation that Conway, a probationary police constable in the Cheshire Constabulary, had stolen a colleague's electric torch. The matter was investigated by Rimmer, a Superintendent of the police in the Cheshire Constabulary. Rimmer spoke to Conway, indicating that his probationary reports were not good and he should consider resigning, but Conway refused. Rimmer subsequently prepared a report for the Chief Constable, with a view to it being sent to the Director of Public Prosecutions, and was 'instrumental in bringing a charge of larceny' against Conway. However, despite Rimmer giving evidence in court, the jury stopped the case after hearing the prosecution and returned a verdict of not guilty. Soon afterwards, another probationary report about Conway was produced and he was dismissed from the police without opportunity to appeal.

Unable to obtain suitable employment, Conway sued Rimmer for damages resulting from malicious prosecution. At the discovery stage of evidence it was revealed that five documents existed: two probationary reports from January and July 1964; a report on Conway by a district police training centre; the report prepared by Rimmer to his Chief Constable for submission to the DPP; and the final probationary report on Conway from April 1965. However, the Home Secretary (Roy Jenkins) submitted a sworn affidavit claiming these five documents were covered by Crown privilege and could not be disclosed.

> I personally examined and carefully considered all the said documents and I formed the view that … (four of them) … fell within a class of documents comprising confidential reports by police officers to chief officers of police relating to the conduct, efficiency and fitness for employment of individual police officers under their command and that … (the fifth document) … fell within a class of documents comprising reports by police officers to their superiors concerning investigations into the commission of a crime. In my opinion the production of documents of each such class would be injurious to the public interest. (Conway v Rimmer [1968] A.C. 913)

While the Home Secretary claimed to have personally examined each document before concluding they could not be disclosed, Conway's legal team stressed the reports' importance to the case. They therefore posed a series of questions, focused on whether a claim of Crown privilege expressed in such broad terms was sufficient to be conclusive, or whether the courts had power to give the matter further consideration, including requesting judicial examination of the documents. In short, the court was encouraged to re-examine the weight of *Duncan v Cammell Laird* in light of continued questions about courts passively accepting ministerial affidavits claiming Crown privilege on either a class or contents basis. Following the example of recent Scottish and Commonwealth cases, the court was asked to consider balancing the weight of competing public interests in the information against any adverse effect that disclosure might have on departmental interests. It was also stressed that the grounds of claiming Crown privilege for these police records was symptomatic of the misinterpretation of a series of cases leading to a false idea that Crown privilege could be claimed for police reports.

> There has been a blurring of the distinction between state and military documents, on the one hand, and departmental documents on the other. In the case of Crown papers involving the security of the nation, authority is clear, but when the interests are not those of high state policy or national defence, all is confusion … The police came wrongly to be regarded as if they were the military or a high and secret department of state. The military deal with the Queen's enemies, while the police are local bodies concerned with the general public; they are not secret police. (Conway v Rimmer [1968] A.C. 919–920)

This is an interesting point, as it suggested that a misinterpretation of legal precedent had wrongly influenced the recognition of privilege for certain police reports and therefore should be reviewed. As an aside, it is worth noting that a similar type of argument was never made in the many debates over medical privilege.

Proponents of medical privilege stressed traditional principles, professional ethics, government regulations, and legislative approaches in other countries and jurisdictions. However, at no point did anyone consider detailed examination of the strength of existing precedent, starting with the Duchess of Kingston's trial.

Returning to *Conway v Rimmer*, the defence argued that the basis of Crown privilege had been firmly established. *Duncan v Cammell Laird* was said to be binding, in accordance with earlier authority, and a ministerial claim of privilege in the public interest should be regarded as definitive. This was partly based on a somewhat blinkered view of *Duncan* and subsequent cases. For example, the later qualification of *Duncan* by the Scottish courts[16] was regarded as 'a theoretical sanction designed to restrain the power of the executive rather than a practical principle to be put to effective use' (Conway v Rimmer [1968] A.C. 926). By this view, the right of Scottish courts to overrule a ministerial claim of privilege was the 'mere ghost of theory' that Lord Radcliffe had warned against during *Glasgow Corporation* [1956]. However, the argument went beyond precedent, emphasising that it was appropriate that the executive, rather than the judiciary, should have the final word on disclosure whenever there was a conflict between the public interest in good government and the administration of justice; and that the relevant Secretary of State was best placed to evaluate the relative importance of restricting disclosure of documents from a public service, bearing in mind the importance of free and open communication necessary for the effective working of public services. A position that would be jeopardised if such departmental documents were no longer privileged.

Having reviewed the arguments and case law, the House of Lords decided that the documents should be produced for their own inspection, and 'if it was then found that disclosure would not be prejudicial to the public interest or that any possibility of such prejudice was insufficient to justify their being withheld, disclosure should be ordered' (Conway v Rimmer [1968] A.C. 911). As stated by Lord Reid, their initial reasoning was twofold. Firstly, decisions since *Duncan v Cammell Laird* had produced differing positions in the Scottish and English courts, which was undesirable on a matter of public policy relating to the balance of power between the executive and the courts. Secondly, Reid noted the considerable discontent that rules on Crown privilege had produced in recent years. Having reviewed Lord Simon's views in the *Duncan* case, it seemed evident that the emphasis on ministerial discretion to deny documents to the courts was based on consideration of matters that involved genuine danger to the national interest, not the disclosure of routine reports about a probationary police officer.

Drawing on the accumulation of cases since *Duncan*, it seemed that while courts were highly unlikely to overrule a minister's claim of privilege for documents directly connected to national security, there appeared to be grounds for judicial consideration of the balance of public interests in cases involving routine administrative documents. Therefore, while a claim of Crown privilege

---

16 *Glasgow Corporation v Central Land Board* ([1956] S.C. (H.L.) 1).

could still be based on either the content of the specific document or the fact that it belonged to a class of documents that required protection, the basis would have to be specified and, if necessary, the judge could review the document(s) in question. While the Attorney General had intervened to support the case for the final decision residing with the executive, Lord Morris rejected the idea. He stressed that an independent court was better placed to assess the competing elements of public interest in controversial cases, giving full weight to consideration of any argument from the executive's representative as part of the process (*Conway v Rimmer* [1968] A.C. 957). He also gave detailed consideration to case law on the point – paying particular attention to cases in Scotland and Commonwealth countries in which the courts retained power to override executive claims to non-disclosure – and concluded that there were strong grounds for following a similar practice in England.

Lord Hodson pointed to the fact that Lord Chancellor Kilmuir's statement to the House of Lords in 1956 had pointed to the difficulty and undesirability of maintaining the position established in *Duncan*. He also noted that *Duncan* had presented an inaccurate account of Scottish law on the issue and had been revised by later cases (977–8). Lord Pearce echoed the opinions expressed by Lord Reid, and found in favour of the appeal by Conway. Lord Upjohn also found in favour of the appeal, agreeing that in cases where the claim of privilege was based on a non-specific appeal to the importance of candour in communications, the judge should have power to consider the document and the accompanying claim of privilege with a view to making a final judgement on its disclosure in court. With the ruling unanimously in favour of the appeal, the five documents in question were produced in order that the judges could review their content and decide the balance of public interests in their disclosure. When the hearing reconvened on 2 May 1968, Lord Reid stated:

> I have examined the five documents with which this case is concerned. I can find nothing in any of them the disclosure of which would, in my view, be in any way prejudicial to the proper administration of the Cheshire Constabulary or to the general public interest. I am therefore of opinion that they must be made available in this litigation.

The original order of the District Registrar that the five documents be produced for inspection by Conway's legal team was restored. So, after numerous committees, reports, parliamentary statements, decisions and obiter dicta, it was a case stemming from the alleged theft of an electric torch and its aftermath which led the House of Lords to follow its own lead – the decision in *Glasgow Corporation* in relation to the Scottish courts – and recognise the authority of English courts to scrutinise, and if necessary overrule, claims for Crown privilege.

Conclusion

The interwar debates focused on securing some form of limited privilege for medical practitioners. In the decades following the Second World War, the focus shifted towards the nature and scope of Crown privilege. Both periods of intense debate were symptomatic of the extending reach of the law into areas previously considered confidential, demanding increasing amounts of information be made available to the courts in response to a changing socio-legal context. Both debates also revealed that privilege was far easier to claim and defend on a class basis, rather than attempting to define and justify increasingly limited subgroups of information and records to be protected.

Another common factor was the focus on who should decide on the need for disclosure. In this regard, initially at least, there was a difference. In the earlier debates, the standard advice given by the Ministry of Health and the BMA was that, if called on to give evidence, a doctor could appeal to the judge to be exempted on grounds that the information was confidential. While questions were raised about the extent to which a judge would, or could, take full account of the medical argument, the absence of medical privilege entailed that the judge had power to decide. By contrast, much of the controversy over Crown privilege surrounded the fact that the decision to exclude information from the courts on grounds of public interest was taken by the relevant Secretary of State. Growing numbers of claims of Crown privilege provoked concern that it was being applied too broadly, and raised questions about the propriety of allowing the political heads of government departments to make the decision on an issue in which they had a direct interest. Yet, as the Lord Chancellor's statement in 1956 confirmed, judges were just as liable to limit their consideration to the relative utility of the information in the case before them.

While numerous committees considered the issues involved, it was the courts which finally decided the matter. In *Conway v Rimmer* ([1968] A.C. 910), the House of Lords decided that a Minister's declaration that disclosure would not be in the public interest, was no longer conclusive. Under the terms of the Administration of Justice Act 1970, the power of the courts to determine disclosure was formally recognised in statute. The numerous reports and statements resulted in a reduction in the scope and extent of Crown privilege, although public interest immunity, as Crown privilege came to be known post-*Conway*, continues to be recognised as valid grounds for excluding evidence from court. Where dispute arises, the court has the power to decide (McHale and Fox 1997, 496).

Given that the judiciary was handed the ultimate responsibility of determining the balance of public interests in disclosure of public service records, minutes and reports, it would be interesting to analyse the extent to which this made a substantial difference to practice, especially in relation to disclosure decisions involving issues that had proven controversial in the past. As a contemporary textbook noted, while a claim of privilege relating to ordinary hospital records was unlikely to be made, or upheld,

> one can speculate whether Crown privilege could successfully be claimed for, say, records relating to the treatment of a patient for venereal disease, this having regard to the Secretary of State's express intention that records of such treatment in his hospitals should be treated as confidential, hospital authorities being required by regulation to see that such records are so treated. (Speller 1971, 351)

As the quote suggests, and as Chapter 9 details, familiar issues – including VD and medical privilege – continued to be discussed. However, administrative and technological change also raised new questions about data protection and the need for greater recognition of a right to personal privacy.

Chapter 9
Old Issues and New Challenges: Confidentiality and Privacy

> The doctor's consulting room should be as sacrosanct as the priest's confessional. The whole of the art and science of medicine is based on the intimate personal relationship between patient and doctor, and to this it always returns, however scientific medicine becomes and whatever the great and undeniable benefits society receives from the application of social and preventive medicine. That I believe is why we should examine with profound scepticism any special pleading that professional secrecy is becoming outmoded. (Clegg 1957, 44)

Over the course of two centuries following the Duchess of Kingston trial, common and statute law exceptions to the traditional ideal of medical confidentiality were defined in more detail; and changes in medical practice and medical employment focused greater attention on dual loyalty obligations for doctors. By the second half of the twentieth century, individual patient–doctor relationships were subsumed within an increasingly complex health and welfare system. Approaches to medical confidentiality had to be reconciled with the fact that information gathered in the patient–doctor relationship was used by a number of healthcare workers who might be involved in a patient's care within a state-run service, and could be of additional value in non-therapeutic contexts, including medical research and the administration of public services as well as the legal justice system.

The debate over confidentiality reflected significant changes in medical practice, employment and administration; the consequences of centralised information gathering in a socio-political context shaped by total warfare and centralised welfare; and the implications of technological innovation, particularly the possibilities for electronic data storage and record linkage using computers. The traditional principle of confidentiality appeared to diminish as the scope of officially acknowledged exceptions extended. However, at the same time, medical confidentiality became one aspect of a broader discussion about privacy and the storage, use and control of personal data in an age of rapid developments in information technology. The number of people to whom confidential information could legitimately be given was extended to cover healthcare and administrative teams. Combined with an acknowledged list of broad exceptions to the general rule of medical confidentiality, this led to questions about whether the concept retained anything beyond rhetorical value as a moral principle. Detailed analysis of these developments over recent decades requires its own book. What follows is an outline of key themes, illustrating how old issues continued to evolve and were joined by new challenges and topics of debate.

Information Sharing Within Medicine and Access to Medical Records

As a central pillar of the post-war welfare state, the implementation of the NHS was viewed with suspicion by some sections of the medical profession. A significant concern was that decisions would be taken by those at the top of the bureaucratic hierarchy, with loss of autonomy for doctors in regular contact with patients. While a top-down chain of command might have been accepted in other state services, such as the military, 'very many doctors feel that such a service is not applicable to a free community of civilians of all ages and scores of different avocations, and that it contains inherent dangers both to patients and doctors – dangers to access, confidential relations, initiative and personality' ('Hospitals and General Practice', *The Times* 19 November 1946, 5). Yet the pressure on the traditional model of doctor–patient confidentiality was not just a product of the central organisation of medical care and the shifting balance between personal, professional and policy agendas. Medicine itself continued to develop, 'becoming a more complicated art based upon a large number of sciences' ('The Beveridge Report', *The Times*, 25 February 1943, 8). More detailed scientific knowledge produced further medical specialisation. Diagnosis and therapy were evolving to become more dependent on technology which, in turn, often required specialised environments and equipment – diagnostic machines, laboratories, aseptic operating theatres – as well as trained staff. As a result medicine became increasingly institutional, involving teamwork to a greater degree than ever before. Healthcare efficiency required that patients experienced a relationship with, or had input to their healthcare from, a number of individuals across the NHS. The traditional model of medical confidentiality, based on a one-to-one relationship, had to be extended to cover an undefined number, and broad variety, of staff. Unsurprisingly, this was often interpreted as a gradual erosion of patient confidentiality.

> Medical confidentiality has become increasingly diluted by the development of the principle of 'extended confidence': medical records may be seen not only by the patient's doctors but also by the health care team, secretaries, administrators and in some cases by social workers. Whatever limits are placed on the boundaries of extended confidence, it is ironic that amongst the interested parties it is only the patient himself who is regarded as incompetent to see his own confidential record. (Dworkin 1979, 90)

Patients' right to access their own records was given consideration during the debate over privacy and data protection, and was subsequently included in legislation, including the Access to Health Records Act 1990 and Data Protection Act 1998. However, in the early years of the NHS, the issue of ownership and access to medical records was the focus of some debate. At the same time as the protection of Crown privilege for service medical records as a class was being questioned, an article on professional privilege (Nokes 1950) raised the possibility that, since the medical records of NHS patients were now in public ownership, they might become eligible for Crown privilege protection. Drawing attention to the 'radical alteration' in the medical relationship that was taking place, Nokes stated that:

> the nationalisation of medical practice may produce the anomalous situations that disclosure in court is dependent upon the will of the Minister; that even if the Ministry does claim privilege, the previous liability to disclose in court is merely exchanged for disclosure to officials; and that if the Ministry does not claim privilege, there may be disclosure both to officials and to the court.

Under the terms of the National Health Service Act 1946, while a regional hospital board, the board of governors of a teaching hospital or a hospital management committee carried out their duties on behalf of the Minister for Health, and were responsible in all legal actions, they did not have any scope to claim Crown privilege for medical records (Speller 1948, 41).[1] In 1948 the Minister for Health issued Statutory Instrument 507, which included rules for the compilation of medical records of NHS patients by doctors in state service, and for their inspection by a supervisory committee (Speller 1948, 406). The latter included several lay members, raising concerns, such as those expressed by Nokes, that medical records were increasingly accessible to non-medical officials. This raised the hackles of many doctors, including the champion of attempts to gain legislation on medical privilege in the interwar years, Graham-Little (see Chapter 7). He added his voice to medical concerns over the 'serious threat to professional secrecy foreshadowed in the increasing tendency to disclosure to lay persons by Government departments of professional confidences contained in medical certificates' (*BMJ Supplement* 31 July 1948, 70). As an MP, he also took an opportunity to raise the issue directly with the Minister of Health, but Bevan rejected calls for the requirement to be withdrawn (*BMJ* 24 July 1948, 230). Pressure to share information with bureaucrats and lay persons seemed to confirm concerns, expressed in the run-up to the NHS, that further state interference in medical care would fundamentally alter the doctor–patient relationship.

> There is something personal in medicine, something in the doctor–patient relationship, something private and confidential which is essential to good medicine. Break into that, make the doctor not your doctor but the State's doctor; no longer your friend, your advocate, and you will have done some damage to medicine that it will be impossible to repair. (NA CP48/23)

With changes to medical employment and practice, combined with growing demands for medical certificates and reports, the question of ownership of medical records became ever more important. The medical notes made by a doctor in

1 Though Crown privilege could still be claimed by the Secretary of State for Health if disclosure of information was contrary to the public interest.

consultation with a private patient, remained the property of the doctor. They could still be disclosed under compulsion in legal proceedings, and where there was a need for information to be communicated between doctors, for example a specialist passing on test results to the patient's GP, consent was taken to be implied (Speller 1971, 359).

By contrast, the records of general ward patients remained the property of the hospital. Under the Schedule to the Public Records Act 1958, NHS hospital records became publicly held records, with the exception of private patients who entered into a contract with the doctor treating them. Nursing records and X-ray films were not so clear cut. Speller believed these belonged to the hospital authority, but were not public records. In the case of non-paying patients, this made little difference as the additional notes and X-ray films simply constituted part of the patient's medical record. If, however, the patient had paid for the X-ray, the question of ownership of the film arose. There was some debate over whether payment was for the physical slide, or for the medical expertise used to interpret it and, while noting that the position was not without significant shortcomings, Speller was inclined to favour the latter interpretation (1971, 360–1). Although state ownership of medical records for NHS patients had raised the possibility that they may be covered by Crown privilege, in practice they were made available to the courts when required (see Chapter 8).

The Growing Information State

The middle decades of the twentieth century were those of 'total warfare and total welfare' and both played a significant role in the transition to the modern information state (Higgs 2004). However, it is important to emphasise that these were steps in a broader process of centralised information gathering dating back to the nineteenth-century Registration Acts, which, over time, produced a symbiotic relationship based on the flow of information between doctors and the state. From the mid-nineteenth century, the central state's collection of vital statistics complemented the decennial census, allowing a general overview of the national population. Over time, the collection of information on births and deaths helped to identify specific areas of specialised medical interest, such as the problem of high infant mortality in the late nineteenth and early twentieth century. The medical and social response included attempts to gain contact with newborn infants, in order to assess, monitor and support them through locally organised infant welfare schemes. These aims were facilitated in the early decades of the twentieth century by legislation requiring the early notification of births.[2] As the value of detailed statistics on the population increased, so too did the pressure on doctors to ensure that accurate information was provided on death registration certificates in order

2 Notification of Births Acts 1907 and 1915.

that problematic trends could be identified and, where possible, protective or remedial measures be taken.

Davis and Elliot (2011) argue that, at least for a time in Scotland, the General Registrars' Office sought to strike a balance between the benefits of increased data collection for the state and the importance of recognising and respecting the privacy of citizens. While the political and administrative state was interested in the utility of information in facilitating systems of central taxation, conscription and public service provision, the agenda was increasingly shaped by medical interest in epidemiology and statistical analyses of trends and patterns of disease. Where a death from VD, or some other stigmatic cause, might previously have been recorded under a more neutral or ill-defined heading in order to save the reputation of the deceased and protect the sentiments of the remaining relatives, the benefits of accurate reporting to medical research and health service provision placed pressure on doctors to prioritise the collective interest in full and accurate disclosure for medical, as well as administrative, reasons.

As a result, doctors were a key source of information for the state. The utility of information gained in doctor–patient relationships went beyond its immediate, or direct, diagnostic and therapeutic role. Information about citizens was the staple fuel of an expanding centralised bureaucracy. Concerns about the implications of this for individual privacy were magnified by the growing use of computers and the potential impact of information technology on the storage and linkage of personal information.

Early Attempts at Privacy Legislation

There were a number of parliamentary debates, motions and attempts at private member bills focused on personal privacy during the 1960s. Those raising the issue included Lord Mancroft in 1961, Alexander Lyon (MP for York) in 1967 and 1968, Lord Wade in 1969 and Brian Walden in 1970. Their main focus was a perceived problem of press intrusion, including invasion of personal privacy in medical settings. Mancroft noted recent cases in point, including 'the most unhappy situation in the German hospital which attended upon the sick beds of Mr Matt Busby and his colleagues of the Manchester football team' following the Munich air crash; and also 'the shocking case of the late Mr Aneurin Bevan, where photographers and newspapermen sought to invade the privacy of the hospital and obtain interviews and photographs of him lying on a bed of sickness' (Hansard, House of Lords, 1961, 607–8). Noting that there had been growing interest in establishing a right to privacy in recent decades, and citing growing international action on the issue, in 1967 Lyon also cited the example of the press intrusion into the privacy of Bevan while recovering from illness in hospital. Similarly, he drew attention to a case of two Vietnamese children brought to East Grinstead Hospital for plastic surgery, where 'some members of the press tried to get into the hospital to try to photograph them, although the children were disfigured' (Hansard, House of Commons Debates, 8 February 1967).

In 1969, Lord Wade moved a motion, drawing on the European Convention on Human Rights and calling attention 'to the need for protection of human right and fundamental freedoms … to the increasing power of the State in relation to the individual, to the threat to personal privacy resulting from technological advance; and to possible measures, including the enactment of a Bill of Rights' (Hansard, House of Lords, 18 June 1969). In Wade's view, the new kinds of threats and complexity of modern society were such that personal privacy required statutory protection, rather than relying on the piecemeal development of common law. As in earlier debates, while the discussion covered a range of topics, medical information was a recurring example. The Lord Chancellor suggested that there were obvious benefits to having a patient's medical history collected together on a computer: 'you can see how convenient it would be if you were injured in an accident, and became unconscious. Your entire health record can be obtained at once or in a few seconds from the computer for the benefit of the doctor.' This view was endorsed by Lord Ritchie-Calder, who thought it would be 'eminently satisfactory if the doctors could get an instant talk-back of your medical history' (Hansard, House of Lords, 18 June 1969).

Momentum on the question continued with the second reading of the Right to Privacy Bill in the House of Commons on 23 January 1970, introduced by Brian Walden (MP for Birmingham, All Saints). Again the discussion ranged across topics, including personal health information, highlighting in the process the difficulty of sharply defining information that could or could not be shared. As Eric Lubbock (MP for Orpington) suggested:

> An example of information not generally available is a person's medical history or his financial status or political background, all of which are sensitive to some degree. But even here the line that has to be drawn cannot be drawn absolutely sharply. A man's medical history is contained in the records of his own GP, but parts of it are quite legitimately available to other people. The Department of Health and Social Security will have a record of his absences from work because of illness, because on those occasions it will have paid him sickness benefit, and a record has to be kept in its files. A man's employer … will need to know something about the man's health. He will be aware of periods of sickness while the man is in his employment, but even before he engages the man he may want to be satisfied that his health will enable him to take up the work involved. That is why many employers ask that a man should first undergo a medical examination. This is an example of the way in which information which at first sight one would say was highly personal and confidential may sometimes need to be made available to others than those one first has in mind, such as, in this case, one's doctor. (Hansard, House of Commons, 23 January 1970, 930–31)

While the need to balance the protection of sensitive personal information against the potential benefits of disclosure or linking of information was not new, computers undoubtedly added a new dimension to the debate. As Lubbock noted, it would take someone a great deal of time and effort to locate and collate the disparate pieces of information about an individual held in separate manual records in a variety of locations. By contrast, computers presented the possibility that information could be collected together and stored in a single electronic file, or separate electronic files could be easily linked together. While there were potential benefits to computerised records, there needed to be appropriate security for personal data, for 'once it is on an inch or two of magnetic tape it would be possible without very strict safeguards for a person to gain access to the whole of such information and use it for unauthorised purposes'. During the course of debate in the House of Commons on 23 January 1970, Callaghan indicated that Kenneth Younger had agreed to act as chairman of a committee on privacy.

Younger Committee on Privacy

Chapter 13 of the Younger Committee Report dealt with the issue of privacy in relation to medicine. The committee had received written evidence from a range of medical bodies[3], as well as comment and help from the GMC. All had stressed the importance of medical confidentiality to the doctor–patient relationship and its long-standing recognition in codes of ethics.

> Modern life, however, in the medical sphere as in others, calls for the availability of information outside the sphere in which it was gathered and it is this tendency and the techniques – such as computerised data banks – which are devised to serve it which, in view of the medical world, threatens or could threaten the privacy of the relationship between doctor and patient.

Excerpts of the evidence given to the committee by the BMA illustrate how changes in the format and structure of medical practice had implications for the traditional model of medical confidentiality, while continuing to recognise the functional, and symbolic, significance of confidentiality to effective medicine.

> It is no longer practicable to look upon the single physician as the patient's sole confidant in any serious illness, and it is assumed by public and profession alike

---

3 The British Medical and Dental Associations; the British Psychological Association; the British Sociological Association; the Medical Research Council; the National Institute of Industrial Psychology; the Patients Association; the Royal College of Midwives; the Royal College of Nursing and National Council of Nurses of the United Kingdom; the Scottish Association of Executive Councils of the NHS; the Society of Occupational Medicine and the Teaching Hospitals Association.

> that any contact with the complex machinery of today implies acquiescence in some degree in extended confidence.
>
> The fact that the definition of confidence is changing does not mean that the concept itself has less significance than heretofore. On the contrary we must accept that issues of confidentiality and confidence are of the greatest importance to the whole art and practice of medicine, for the individual doctor and patient in confrontation is the basis of medical practice. We must therefore maintain as great a degree of confidentiality over all forms of medical record as lies within our power without compromising the complex medical machine within which we work. Not only must we do so, but we must be seen to do so. (BMA evidence to Younger)

This encapsulated the tension between the basic importance of confidentiality in the doctor–patient relationship as the basis of medical practice, and the fact that healthcare had become a 'complex medical machine' dependent on information sharing. Focusing on the private sector, the committee's terms of reference excluded hospital practices under the NHS and medical records of the DHSS, though it was hoped that 'the medical profession as a whole will note what we say where they think it concerns them'.

While highlighting a number of concerns – including the use of identifiable data in research, and the assessment of employees by occupational physicians – the report also indicated that the problem should not be blown out of proportion. In Paragraph 381, it stated that 'the evidence given to us indicated that the public are not much exercised about invasion of privacy in the practice of medicine and our survey of public attitudes seemed to confirm this'. The survey had indicated that while the majority of respondents would object to details of their medical history being made available to anyone who wanted to know, less than 1% said that their medical privacy had been breached. Nonetheless, echoing the concerns raised by Nokes (1950), the committee recognised that:

> there are dangers to privacy presented by the growing tendency for people outside the strictly medical field – social workers, researchers, demographers, administrators and others in, for example, hospitals and group practices – to acquire medical information about individuals. We have noted this tendency and also the growing use of computers in information storage and retrieval and we would therefore draw attention to the principles which we believe should govern the handling of personal information set out in Chapter 20.

The committee concluded that there was no obvious need for legislation, believing that the answer instead lay within professional ethics – drawing attention to the Medical Research Council's decision to draw up a code of practice and guidelines on 'the practical and ethical aspects of undertaking research involving access to personal medical information and the maintenance of confidentiality'. However, in addition to setting out core principles for handling personal information, the report also indicated that the Law Commissions of England and Wales, and of Scotland, should give further consideration to the existing legal protections available. This recommendation was acted upon, as outlined in the relevant section below.

Government White Papers on Computers and Privacy

In parallel to the Younger Committee's analysis of the private sector, an interdepartmental working party carried out a review of the categories of information held in the computer systems of government departments, and the rules governing its storage and use (White Paper: 'Computers: Safeguards for Privacy'. Cmnd. 6354, December 1975). The investigation had finished in 1972, but before publication in late 1975 the findings were updated to include comparable information about computers in parts of the public sector that did not form part of the central government – and were therefore not included in the original study. Giving a sense of the speed of development, Table 4 of the paper estimated that the number of computers in the private sector had more than doubled from 4,036 in April 1971 to 10,008 in April 1975. Unsurprisingly, the largest number (4,499) was in the 'Insurance, Banking, Finance and Business Services'. Table 5 indicated that computers in the public sector had grown from 1,870 to 3,255 in the same period.

The paper included the results of a British Computer Society questionnaire which had been sent to 56 large organisations between August 1972 and January 1973. Analysis of the 44 replies received showed that 'the amount of personal information held about people is increasing and that computers have made it easier to hold such information. But it also showed that much of the information thought by respondents to be sensitive was still held manually and there was little evidence of the exchange or transfer of such information between organisations' (Paragraph 66). This echoed the Younger Committee's assessment of the issue as more of a potential, than an actual, problem at the time. However, with this in mind, it also noted that 'organisations varied a good deal in the amount of attention which they devoted to privacy (as distinct from security) questions, and the Committee thought that there was a need for greater awareness in this area'. As a result of both this finding and those of a further National Computing Centre (NCC) survey of over 150 organisations, the NCC initiated a series of projects designed to increase knowledge and understanding of security. It also established a central reference body to provide computer users and manufacturers with information and guidance.

Chapter 3 dealt with computers in the NHS. Medical records, while still largely manual, were recognised as containing personal information about 'nearly everyone in the country'. GPs held their own patients' records and each Health Board or Authority or Agency held records about the services it administered. Information from these records was collected together, either regionally or nationally, for management and research purposes, using a combination of manual and computer systems. Three large NHS Central Register manual record systems were in place, one for each of England, Scotland and Northern Ireland. These contained limited amounts of non-medical information about all infants, as well as everyone registered with an NHS GP. They were used to issue NHS numbers, and to disseminate information about deceased patients or those who chose to emigrate or join the armed forces. Family Practitioner Committees used them to maintain the accuracy of doctors' lists, which were important in defining each doctor's obligations to the NHS, and provided the basis for a substantial part of their remuneration. When patients changed doctor, the registers acted as a clearing house for communication of information between Family Practitioner Committees. A pilot scheme had pointed to the administrative benefits of using computers to store the relevant records, as a result of which a second localised scheme was planned with a view to extending the approach to the system in general.

While most Health Authorities and Boards and a number of hospitals had their own computers, these were predominantly used for statistical and administrative purposes. However, it was evident that the potential scale and scope of uses to which the new technology could be put was being explored with favourable results. Specific guidance on confidentiality in relation to the use of computers in the NHS stressed that the same rules applied to electronic records as manual records. Paragraph 35 of the White Paper echoed the Younger Committee in emphasising the primary role of professional ethics and the 'old-established tradition of maintaining the confidentiality of information'. Evidently, confidence in the traditional importance of confidentiality in medical ethics remained high.

The Younger Committee had recommended that the techniques of gathering and processing personal information should be kept under review in both private and public sectors. A second White Paper, on 'Computers and Privacy' (Cmnd. 6353, December 1975), indicated that the government believed legislation was necessary 'to set up machinery, not only to keep the situation under review, but also to seek to secure that all existing and future computer systems in which personal information is held, in both private and public sectors, are operated with appropriate safeguards for the privacy of the subject of that information' (Paragraph 4).

The benefits of using computers to store and process personal information included 'saving in routine clerical work; in the economy, accuracy and speed with which information can be processed; in forecasting, planning or matching supply to demand; and, in the service of central and local government, in making public administration more responsive to the needs of the individual citizen and his family'. However three principal dangers to privacy were also noted as stemming from:

1. Inaccurate, incomplete or irrelevant information;
2. the possibility of access to information by people who should not or need not have it;

3. the use of information in a context or for a purpose other than that for which it was collected.

In order to minimise these difficulties, it was suggested that individuals should have an opportunity to check and correct records held about them. This required that people knew about each system and what information it held about them. It also required safeguards to ensure that information was only given to the individual concerned and could not be accessed by others. In terms of the third highlighted danger, access to information would be limited by ensuring only authorised personnel could process it in authorised ways. Even authorised personnel would be restricted to accessing only necessary information, and would be under an obligation to ensure it remained confidential.

Data Protection (Lindop) Report, 1978

Momentum on the issue of personal privacy and data protection continued to build with the establishment of a further committee under the chairmanship of Norman Lindop. Chapter 7 of the Lindop Report examined data in the NHS, considering how it was collected, stored and the use to which it was put. In terms of collection, while some details came direct from patients themselves or were supplied on their behalf and with their knowledge, NHS records also contained clinical notes and observations made by professional staff. There were three major categories of NHS records:

1. Personal health records used for diagnosis, treatment and care and maintained by professional staff including doctors, nurses and physiotherapists.
2. Patient administrative records, which were used to manage and administer services in support of health care delivery. These included registers of patients on GP lists; payments to pharmacists and dentists; and records used to call patients for immunisation, screening and hospital appointments.
3. Records used for statistical or research purposes. Many of these were relatively small-scale local research projects drawing information from personal health or administrative records. However, there were a few much larger projects using centrally-held records that were compiled specifically for statistical and research purposes, such as Cancer Registration Scheme; Hospital Activity Analysis; Mental Health Enquiry.

It was noted that these three categories of records often interconnected. For example, personal health records might be used administratively. While most records were still kept in manual format, it was deemed likely that there would be a move towards using computers, and there was growing concern that the combination of technological and administrative changes posed a threat to confidentiality, meaning safeguards were required. As an example, the report outlined concerns raised by the Health Visitors Association regarding the working of the Community Health Register and Recall System operated under the NHS.

> Through the notification of birth procedure (under section 203 of the Public Health Act 1936, as amended) health authorities collect information about births in order to provide a means of alerting those responsible for the subsequent care of the mother and baby, and also to provide the basis for various health records used to ensure periodic recall for screening and immunisation. The storage and retrieval of some of those records is done on computer and attention has recently turned to the standardisation of the computer systems (the National Standard Register and Recall System) to achieve economies. In its evidence to us the Health Visitors' Association (HVA), representing those largely responsible for ensuring that infants receive proper medical care, expressed strong concern that the introduction of the National Standard Register presented a threat to privacy, in that information about each child could be placed on computer without its parents' knowledge and that there was no guarantee that government could not use the information for other purposes. (Paragraph 7.05)

Some of the data recorded referred to sensitive matters, including the conditions of the home and whether the child was illegitimate. The report recognised that extremely careful safeguards were needed to preserve confidentiality. It endorsed the concerns expressed by the Health Visitors Association, advocating that the Data Protection Authority should investigate the uses made of such information. The example provides an excellent illustration of how the debate over medical confidentiality had evolved. While confidentiality remained a valuable component of the medical relationship, statute legislation required disclosure of certain information, such as notification of birth. This information was then centrally stored and used to provide public services, including medical, which required sharing of information with a range of staff. However, information gained for one purpose, or in one context, might be used for another. Information given to a health visitor, or ascertained during a domestic visit, could be stored centrally and used for other purposes; potentially undermining not only the privacy of families but also the relationship of trust on which a Health Visitor's contact was based.

Echoing earlier reports, the committee had been assured by the DHSS that the confidentiality of information in patient records was ensured by professional ethics, enforced by the relevant regulatory bodies, including the GMC and General Nursing Council.

> We were told that administrative staff who have access to medical records (e.g. medical records officers, medical secretaries) are 'expected to conform' with the ethics of the medical profession on confidentiality. DHSS said that the confidentiality of patients' records is also safeguarded by the liability of all staff to NHS or Civil Service disciplinary procedures. (Paragraph 7.09)

Ownership of NHS medical records was also discussed, indicating that as the doctor's time, the premises and the paper were all paid for by the Secretary of State, this entailed a legal right of ownership of the records, though not necessarily of the information they contained.

> We mention this because there may be occasions when the Secretary of State has a legitimate need to see records, and it can in general affect a practitioner's obligations to supply data to central government. The Department issues guidance to Regional and Area Health Authorities on the supply of information about patients, particularly in connection with legal proceedings. Although the general policy is to assist the courts as far as possible, care is taken to protect the legitimate interest of the medical practitioner, especially where other legal proceedings may arise or have arisen. (Paragraph 7.11)

As noted in earlier sections of this chapter, following the National Health Service Act 1946 concerns had been expressed about the growing tendency to require disclosure of medical records and information to non-medical officials and personnel. Lindop indicated the legal position and attempted to address medical apprehension that disclosure might put a doctor at risk of legal proceedings. Paragraph 7.12 confirmed that information gained in the course of a medical examination for employment or insurance purposes could be communicated to a third party, provided both the doctor and patient had knowledge of, and consented to, the disclosure.

The sections of the Lindop report that focused on medicine therefore echoed issues that had sparked or stoked debates over medical confidentiality in the early post-war years. However, they also pointed to the new challenges connected to the growing use of computers. For example, the Hospital Activity Analysis was understood to hold about five million records on NHS computers summarising facts about individual inpatients. This data included 'a great deal of identifying information, and further data of a highly sensitive nature such as religion, number of abortions … and medical diagnoses', it was collected and held in 'partially identifiable form' and analysed 'for local, regional and national use' (Paragraph 7.13). In terms of safeguarding privacy there was 'no rigid practice, but the DHSS lays down rules which require high standards of confidentiality, privacy and security to be applied to all "in-house" computer projects. It also requires that there shall be an officer clearly answerable for maintaining those safeguards'. Recognising the importance and scale of the issue, the Lindop report advocated the need for legislation to protect privacy and safeguard personal data.

The Hospital Activity Analysis, record linkage projects in Exeter and Oxford, and the Child Health Computing Committee's standardised system for recording information on preschool children (scheduling immunisations and developmental examinations), were discussed at length in articles and by specialist committees on data protection. While the potential of computerised records to have a positive impact on administration, resource allocation, service efficiency and medical research were obvious, there was no doubt that, without appropriate safeguards, they posed a threat to patient privacy. However, those involved in medical research emphasised that a balance was needed. While anonymous information could facilitate some work, other studies required patient-identifiable information.

> Some epidemiologists are worried that any restriction in information as a result of fears about confidentiality could make their job impossible. E.D. Acheson, the architect of the Oxford Record Linkage Study, has argued that just as infectious diseases of the 19th century demanded a breach of confidence to overcome them – statutory notification – so the major diseases of the 20th century – non-infectious chronic diseases – demand a different sort of breach: the causes of many of these conditions may lie in family or childhood history and might be elucidated only by following episodes of illness in individuals – and this needs identifiable data. ('Confidentiality, Records and Computers' *BMJ* 10 March 1979, 699)

In addition to this *BMJ* briefing paper, a number of articles at the time also pointed to the ongoing challenge of balancing the traditional, functional, importance of respecting patient confidentiality with the demands for information in modern healthcare systems, administration and research (see for example: Vuori 1977; Dworkin 1979; Appleyard and Maden 1979; Kenny 1982).

Evidently, during the course of the 1970s there was increasing interest in the issue of privacy. It is important to recognise that this supplemented, rather than replaced, interest in medical confidentiality. As discussed below, there was continued discussion of the boundaries of confidentiality and further consideration of the issue of medical privilege. The Younger Committee report had advocated that the Law Commissions should give detailed consideration to the existing law on breach of confidence, and, during the course of the 1960s and 1970s the common and statute law understanding of privilege continued to evolve.

Law Commission Reports and Continued Interest in Medical Privilege

Chapter 21 of the Younger Committee report advocated that the Law Commissions in England and Wales, and in Scotland, should seek to clarify the law relating to breach of confidence. Younger had concluded that: 'the action for breach of confidence afforded, or at least was potentially capable of affording, much greater protection of privacy than was generally realised; and second, that it would not be satisfactory simply to leave this branch of the law, with its many uncertainties, to await further development and clarification by the courts.' Acting upon the Younger Committee's recommendation, on 6 June 1973 the Secretary of State for Scotland requested that the Scottish Law Commission:

> With a view to the protection of privacy –
>
> 1. To consider the law of Scotland relating to breach of confidence and to advise what statutory provisions, if any, are required to clarify or improve it;
>
> 2. To consider and advise what remedies, if any, should be provided in the law of Scotland for persons who have suffered loss or damage in consequence of the disclosure or use of information unlawfully obtained, and in what circumstances such remedies should be available.
>
> (Scottish Law Commission Memorandum No. 40 'Confidential Information' 14 April 1977)

Paragraphs 5 and 6 of the Scottish report indicated that breach of confidence was not recognised as a separate category in Scotland, as it was in England. Rather, legal protection was found in a variety of sources, principally in the law of contract, with associated delicts of breach of contract and interference with contractual relations. To illustrate the point, Paragraph 25 cited *AB v CD* [1851] as precedent on the fact that confidentiality was an implied condition of doctors' employment, though *Watson v McEwan* [1904–5] was also cited as evidence that the obligation of confidentiality was not absolute. However, Paragraph 85 recognised that the law relating to implied confidence was 'not very fully developed' and the decisions cited were 'now rather old'.

Unsure about the extent to which the issue raised problems in practice, the report suggested that any difficulties could be minimised if both parties to a contract agreed any terms of disclosure in advance. If there were significant problems in practice, then legislation could provide guidelines on the circumstances in which an implied restriction on disclosure, or use of information, would apply. 'Obligations could be implied by statute in the relationship between a doctor and his patient, a clergyman and his parishioner, a lawyer and his client, a student and his teacher, school, college or university, and so on.' In other words, if needed, a new statute could add further weight to the common law recognition of confidentiality as an important element of the implied contract between doctor and patient. However, it was also acknowledged that 'the individual circumstances in which such obligations are likely to be required are so varied that no good purpose is likely to be served by providing by statute pro forma terms in particular cases' (Paragraph 86). As had been illustrated in earlier debates, it was easier to consider the protean issue of medical confidentiality in broad terms, rather than attempt to define it in detail in statute law. The report noted that there were public interest exceptions to the obligation of confidence, including disclosure in a court of law. However,

> The public interest is a concept which courts have always found somewhat difficult to apply in practice. It would be possible to enlarge that concept in the present context, so that courts would not be entitled to require a person

> to disclose information acquired under an agreement of confidence even in connection with proceedings in a court of law. We understand that this is the position with regard to professional secrets in most legal systems in the EEC, where it is also a crime for a professional person to disclose information which has been confided in him in his professional capacity by a client. We would welcome comment on this question, particularly in relation to the position of doctors in the National Health Service. At present their reports and notes of their examination of patients contained in the hospital records may well be subject to disclosure in a court of law. We would welcome comment upon whether disclosure in a court of law should be restricted, and if so how such a restriction might operate in practice. (Paragraph 88)

A footnote to the paragraph cited *D v NSPCC* ([1977] 2 W.L.R. 201), in which the House of Lords recognised that the public interest in protecting the effective functioning of an organisation could outweigh the law's demand for disclosure of information in court. The circumstances of the case, discussed in detail later in this chapter, may have been considered exceptional, as the NSPCC was authorised by Act of Parliament to bring legal proceedings for the protection of children; and, in its ruling, the court had emphasised that confidentiality alone was not sufficient grounds to refuse disclosure in court. However, it is also worth noting that the test cases over medical privilege, which had generated so much controversy within medico-legal circles and the Ministry of Health in earlier decades, had all arisen in English courts. While obiter dicta of Scottish judges and jurists had often endorsed English precedent, there was very little Scottish case law on the issue (see Ferguson 2011).

Therefore, the summary of provisional proposals, put forward by the Commission for consideration and comment, recognised that the law on confidence was not fully developed. Proposal 6 raised the possibility that the doctor–patient relationship might be covered by future legislative guidelines restricting disclosure of information obtained in circumstances where confidentiality was implied. While this had the potential to add legislative force to existing common law, Point 8 of the proposals invited comment on whether 'a person, in particular a doctor employed in the NHS, who has acquired information under an agreement of confidence', should 'be obliged to disclose it in connection with proceedings in a court of law?' This is significant for a number of reasons. Firstly, it shows that the issue of medical privilege was still sparking interest. Secondly, it was a reminder that the foundation of the common law denial of medical privilege, the Duchess of Kingston's trial, was not binding as a precedent on the Scottish courts. Thirdly, the absence of recent, specifically Scottish, case law presented obvious opportunity for fresh consideration. Finally, since the proposal was explicitly related to Paragraph 88 of the report (quoted above), it suggested that serious consideration should be given to the much stronger definition of medical confidentiality in many European countries. Taken together, there was evident potential for medical privilege in Scotland.

On 16 March 1974, the Lord Chancellor asked the Law Commission for England and Wales to undertake a review of existing law on breach of confidence. Although, in contrast to its Scottish counterpart, its terms did not include the opening sentence: 'with a view to the protection of privacy.' The Commission published a provisional working paper at the end of 1974. This was followed by prolonged consultation, including a seminar held at All Souls College, Oxford in January 1975. The final report was published in October 1981 (Law Commission of England and Wales. Report on 'Breach of Confidence'. October 1981).

The debate regarding the need for legislation to protect privacy was recognised as the impetus for the report. However, as noted above, its terms of reference were limited to the disclosure or use of information in breach of confidence and information unlawfully obtained, and did not explicitly mention privacy. With regard to breach of confidence, the report sought to clarify and improve the existing right of legal action for breach of confidence. An individual who received information in circumstances giving rise to an obligation of confidence was under a duty not to disclose it. Selected legal cases[4] pointed to the 'readiness of the courts to recognize relationships involving the transfer of information and giving rise to an obligation of confidence in respect of that information' (Paragraph 3.9). Doctors were listed in the examples of professional relationships that typically carried an obligation of confidence, but it was emphasised that the extent of the obligation varied according to the exact nature and precise circumstances of each relationship (Paragraph 4.2). The report quoted Lord Wilberforce in *British Steel Corporation v Granada Television Ltd.* (1980, 3 W.L.R. 774), noting the emphasis placed on the discretionary nature of a court's ability to order discovery of information:

> Courts have an inherent wish to respect confidence whether it arises between doctor and patient, priest and penitent, banker and customer, between persons giving testimonials to employees, or in other relationships … But in all these cases the court may have to decide, in particular circumstances, that the interest in preserving confidence is outweighed by other interests to which the law attaches importance. (Paragraph 4.64)

The Law Commission for England and Wales was therefore reflecting the status quo. The doctor–patient relationship was based on an obligation of confidence, breach of which was actionable. But the courts retained power to override this when necessary, including demanding disclosure in court.

However, elsewhere, there was evidence of more radical views on privilege. In 1960, representatives of the General Council of the Bar of England and Wales, The Law Society and the BMA were appointed to a joint committee to examine, and report on, the presentation of medical evidence in courts of law. Their remit included consideration of the question of professional confidence, and the views

---

4 *Prince Albert v Strange* ([1849] 47 E.R. 1302); *Morison v Moat* ([1851] 68 E.R. 492); and *Tournier v National Provincial and Union Bank of England* ([1924] 1 K.B. 461).

they expressed on the topic in the final report are noteworthy (BMA 1965). Having outlined the difference between the legal and medical position on privilege, the report suggested that the absence of privilege for the doctor–patient relationship 'can tend to defeat the ends of justice' and, in some situations, 'must act as a discouragement to complete frankness' (Paragraph 44).

The Committee therefore advocated urgent consideration of 'whether means can be devised that would enable a medical witness to claim some limited privilege'. In part their concern was prompted by the recent case of *Nuttall v Nuttall and Twyman* ([1964] 108 SJ 605), in which a psychiatrist was called to give evidence in a divorce case. The husband's lawyers sought evidence from consultations the psychiatrist had had with the wife and co-respondent. The psychiatrist protested that the information had been obtained under professional confidence, and he did not wish to give evidence.

> The Judge: I am sorry. The law is that you must.
>
> The Witness: These parties consulted me professionally in my consulting room. They entrusted their confidence to me. I accepted their confidence on the basis that everything said between us was privileged.
>
> The Judge: It is not privileged.
>
> The Witness: If you order me to give this evidence it will really strike at the roots of my profession. How can people consult a psychiatrist if they cannot feel sure their confidence will be protected from disclosure?
>
> The Judge: I cannot alter the law. You must go to your MP to do that. I have this very often. The alternative before you is either to give the evidence or to go to prison. (*Lancet*, 18 July 1964, 2, 145)

A report of the case in the *BMJ* (15 August 1964, 2, 455) referred to an article published the previous year that had summarised the common law position with reference to both the Duchess of Kingston trial [1776] and *Garner* [1920] (*BMJ* 15 June 1963, 1, 1616). While acknowledging that there had been some judicial criticism of the position, 'in England (and indeed in most Common Law jurisdictions throughout the world) the courts would hold that the rule was too well established to be changed by the revelation of some fresh wisdom in the breasts of the judges'. It seemed that the denial of medical privilege was too engrained in judicial minds and any change would have to come through statute.

The debates of the 1920s had often included consideration of the possibility of a medical martyr, a doctor who refused to disclose professional confidences in court and was willing to go to prison in order to provoke a reconsideration of the common law's denial of medical privilege. As discussed in Chapters 4–6, while both the Ministry of Health and BMA had independently considered the merits of the strategy, and John Elliot had come close to turning *Needham v Needham* [1921] into a test case, the confrontational rhetoric had not been matched with action. By contrast, in the 1960s two journalists were willing to go to prison rather than reveal the source(s) of information contained in articles they had published.

Mulholland and Foster – Journalist Martyrs

Mulholland and Foster were journalists who had written stories about an employee at the Ministry of Defence who was believed to have been spying for the Russians. When summoned to reveal the sources of quotes in their articles, both journalists refused, pleading that journalists had a privilege not to disclose the source of information which had been published in the public interest. In an oft-cited opinion, Lord Denning emphasised that lawyers were the only profession to have a privilege of non-disclosure in court, noting that other professions, including medicine, did not (*Attorney General v Mulholland* and *Attorney General v Foster* [1963] (2 Q.B. 477)). Counsel for the journalists set out the reasons why their clients should be exempt from forced disclosure in the following terms:

> 1. A journalist is under an obligation of confidence and it would be dishonourable for him to disclose the source of his information.
> 2. A journalist owes a duty to other journalists not to imperil their future prospects of obtaining information. If it is known that a journalist will disclose the source of his information such sources will dry up.
> 3. If disclosure is made, those journalists will imperil their own position.
> 4. The reluctance to disclose is based on the ethics of the journalist's profession.
>
> The Press has not accepted, as have doctors and bankers, that their scruples may be overruled by the direction of the court.

The first and fourth justifications echoed long-standing arguments about honour, duty and ethics, given by the medical profession. The second and third mirrored the medical position in debates about VD and abortion and pointed to the negative consequences of forced disclosure. However, where potential medical martyrs had capitulated when faced with imprisonment, journalists were willing to go further in defence of their position. When their appeal was thrown out, Mulholland and Foster were held in contempt of court and sentenced to six months in prison.

In 1922, the PSC of the BMA had suggested that medical martyrdom could work as a strategy to change the law, provided local and national support could be drummed up for the cause. Naturally, as journalists, Mulholland and Fraser's imprisonment gained press attention. The Press Council and sections of the National Union of Journalists expressed concern, both at how the journalists had been treated by the court and at the implications of such judicial demands

(*The Times*, 7 May 1963, 12). If the courts required journalists to choose between revealing the identity of their sources and going to prison for contempt, there would likely be either growing numbers of journalists in prison or a decline in the number of willing informants as sources of information. The press sought to apply some pressure on government for the release of the journalists (*The Times*, 8 May 1963, 8), though some felt that the National Union of Journalists had not done enough to make the case, and thereby win greater public support for it. Certainly, there was evidence to suggest that the public was not enamoured by the journalists' cause. An editorial in *The Times* (18 March 1963, 11), noted that much of the correspondence it had received in connection with the imprisonment of Mulholland and Foster had demonstrated hostility to the press position. Mirroring the concerns raised by Members of Parliament in the debates over privacy, the editor noted that the case had:

> Broken the dam to a long pent-up, ever rising, flood of resentment against the practices of some newspapers. Intrusion, triviality, distortion, muck-raking, the inversion of values – the list of offences is long. They are real offences. The newspapers were warned years ago that if they went on the way they were going they would end by alienating those very sections of society upon whose good will the freedom and the working conventions of the press depend. This has now happened.

While acknowledging shortcomings in past practice, the editorial proceeded to argue in favour of the ongoing importance of good journalism in a free and democratic society – including the role of newspapers in holding the executive and courts to account. Mulholland (six months) and Fraser (three months) served out their sentences in low security prisons, where conditions were described as 'paradise' (*The Times*, 2 April 1963, 16). Although they had not succeeded in securing judicial recognition of a privilege for journalists, they had demonstrated the strength of their convictions by going to prison rather than disclosing the names of confidential sources. Section 10 of the Contempt of Court Act 1981 states:

> No court may require a person to disclose, nor is any person guilty of contempt of court for refusing to disclose, the source of information contained in a publication for which he is responsible, unless it be established to the satisfaction of the court that disclosure is necessary in the interests of justice or national security or for the prevention of disorder or crime.

Given that, at the time of the trial, the information being sought from Mulholland and Fraser related to a suspected Russian spy at the Ministry of Defence, it is unlikely that this legislation would have significantly altered the outcome of their appeal. Nonetheless, the importance of confidential sources to the workings of a free press in a democratic society has frequently been acknowledged in recent decades. Together with the balance to be struck between personal privacy, public interest and freedom of speech, this issue has been considered since, most recently in the Leveson Inquiry into the Culture, Practices and Ethics of the Press. As examples highlighted during the inquiry, and elsewhere, demonstrate, the issue of press intrusion into private medical matters has continued to provoke concern (*Kaye v Robertson and Another* [1991] F.S.R. 62; Leveson 2012, (2), 473, 482, 539, 564–572).

D v National Society for the Prevention of Cruelty to Children (NSPCC)

Journalists were not the only group to have an acknowledged need to protect sources of information, the identity of police informants was also protected. While, as detailed in Chapter 8, over the course of the twentieth century the courts generally increased their demands for disclosure of information in the interests of justice, *D v NSPCC* ([1978] A.C. 171) stands out as a counterpoint. The case revolved around whether the identity of the source of information given to the NSPCC could be disclosed in court. However, the significance of the case went beyond the anonymity of informants, to broader consideration of the grounds for claiming privilege and the need to balance competing public interests in the manner indicated by *Conway v Rimmer* [1968].[5]

The case stemmed from information given to the NSPCC about the treatment of a 14-month-old girl. The informant alleged that the girl had bruises on her head and stomach, was 'curiously immobile for her age' and appeared to receive no stimulation at home. An NSPCC inspector called round to the girl's house on the evening of 13 December 1973 and made inquiries with the mother. Upset at the allegation, the mother woke the child in order that the inspector could confirm that there were no signs of bruising. She also called the family's doctor to the house and asked him to examine the child. The doctor confirmed that the child was in good health, and had been seen by himself, or the partner at his practice, three times since July with no indication of mistreatment or other problems. In a subsequent affidavit the doctor confirmed these findings and indicated that the baby was 'well cared for by a loving mother' (*D v NSPCC*, 222). Evidently, there was no evidence to confirm the allegations made to the NSPCC, but the inspector 'gave the impression both to the mother and the doctor that he thought the allegations were true, though not proved' (*D v NSPCC*, 187). The impact of the allegation on the mother was significant. When her husband returned home and learnt of the allegation he demanded to know the name of the informant, but the inspector would not disclose it. Recognising that the mother was distraught, the doctor gave her a tranquilliser. She remained in a state of shock for several days, potentially suicidal. A consultant psychiatrist, who subsequently saw her, indicated that she was in a 'definitely depressive state'.

---

5 See Chapter 8.

As a result of the couple's ordeal, their lawyers sought to discover the source of the allegations against them. The NSPCC refused to disclose the name of the informant. An application to get the name in advance of legal proceedings, for damages against the NSPCC, was rejected by Master Jacob in mid-June 1974. The following day, the couple's solicitors issued a claim for damages against the NSPCC, citing negligence on the part of the inspector for failing to make proper inquiries about the informant or checking that the complaint had not been made maliciously, and for improper investigation when visiting the couple's home. The claim indicated that the identity of the informant was not known to the couple. They therefore required discovery of the necessary documents to assess whether legal proceedings against the informant were justified and, if so, to enable them. The NSPCC indicated that the identity of the informant could not be revealed as it had been disclosed to them in confidence. On 11 December 1974, Master Jacob ordered disclosure; but this ruling was overturned on appeal by Judge Croom-Johnson, in June 1975. The mother subsequently appealed to the House of Lords to require disclosure.

The case is of interest as it highlighted the evolving nature of the debate over disclosure by the mid-1970s. Much of the argument in the case focused on the issue of privilege, and a brief outline of the evolution of privilege was given, including reference to the Duchess of Kingston's case. However, the legal status of the NSPCC made the focus on privilege problematic. The NSPCC had been established by Royal Charter and was empowered through statute law to investigate allegations of child abuse and, where necessary, to bring legal actions against wrongdoers. However, it was not an arm of government or an official public service, and therefore could not claim Crown privilege. As Lord Denning emphasised, the real issue was not whether the NSPCC could claim privilege in the legal sense, but whether the court should compel the NSPCC to break their duty of confidence to the informant and force disclosure of the latter's name.

In order to do this, the court had to balance competing public interests in the manner suggested by the House of Lords in *Conway v Rimmer* [1968]. On the one hand, the work of the NSPCC reflected the public interest in protecting children and bringing their abusers before the legal justice system. This depended upon information provided by informants on the understanding that it would remain confidential. Indeed, adverts highlighting the fact that informants would be protected by confidentiality were used to encourage people to report information to the NSPCC. On the other hand, there was the public interest in disclosure of information to facilitate the justice system. It seemed likely that the mother in this case had been the subject of a malicious complaint, with severe implications for her emotional and mental health. To deny her the name of the informant would severely restrict, if not entirely inhibit, any legal remedy against her accuser. While the importance of confidentiality was generally recognised by the courts, it was not, in itself, considered sufficient grounds for privilege.

It is therefore highly significant that the House of Lords rejected the appeal, thereby protecting the documents from disclosure. In effect this indicated judicial willingness to recognise that the protection of confidential communications extended beyond those public bodies covered by Crown privilege and could outweigh the public interest in the disclosure of information to the courts typically required to facilitate justice. The parallels between the NSPCC argument and the interwar case for recognising medical privilege for VD doctors are striking. Both were quasi-public services – if anything the VD clinics had the stronger claim in this regard[6] – and advertised their work using a prominent guarantee of confidentiality. Both alleged that the efficiency and effectiveness of their service would be adversely affected if the courts chose to override the guarantee of confidentiality and demand disclosure. But whereas the interwar debates had been fought over legal concepts of privilege, in the post-*Conway v Rimmer* years, the judiciary could instead consider the broader balance of public interests. Moreover, such interests were not fixed but 'must alter by restriction or extension as social conditions and social legislation develop' (Lord Hailsham, *D v NSPCC*, 60). This appeared to hold out new hope that fresh consideration might be given to the issue of medical privilege. An impression further bolstered, by Lord Edmund-Davies' expression of support for changing the law to recognise medical privilege (*D v NSPCC*, 75).

VD Regulations

As Chapter 2 discussed, one of the earliest recognised exceptions to medical confidentiality in the modern period was the common law denial of medical privilege. Attempts to challenge this, especially in the 1920s and 1930s, focused on the issue of VD. The principles formulated by the Royal Commission on VD, encapsulated in the 1916 VD regulations, emphasised that there should be open access to free treatment, provided without coercion and carrying a guarantee of confidentiality. According to Evans (2001) these principles typified the approach to VD throughout the twentieth century, despite intense pressure for change during times of war. In 1942, Regulation 33B of the Defence (General) Regulations stated that any person named as a contact by two or more VD patients was required to attend a clinic for diagnosis and treatment. However, as Evans points out, the regulation was imposed in exceptional circumstances and represented a temporary shift in an otherwise consistent policy approach. Regulation 33B was allowed to lapse in 1947.

As detailed in Chapters 4–7, VD had been the central issue in many of the debates over confidentiality in the interwar years. It is therefore surprising that it provoked so little debate in the decades following the Second World War. Evans (2001, 240) points out that the incorporation of VD treatment schemes into the NHS structure was unlikely to pose significant problems. Since 1916 VD clinics had been 'a largely centrally funded service with national guidelines and monitoring,

6 For further detail, see the following section on VD Regulations.

employing salaried specialists', meaning that it was in effect 'an embryonic National Health Service'. In 1947, the Medical Society for the Study of Venereal Disease held a discussion on the future of the VD treatment services in the NHS (Harrison 1947, 145–54). Many of the participants pointed to the success of the approach in Britain compared to more coercive schemes abroad, and particularly to a fall in incidence of VD during the period 1921–40. This was attributed to 'expert diagnosis and treatment in specialist centres, set up conveniently for that purpose. Moreover, the published promise of strict professional and civic confidence emphasised indirectly, yet properly and happily, that the treatment centre was for treatment and not inquisition and telling on others' (Harrison 1947, 152). Ongoing success was therefore seen to be dependent on maintaining 'its ideals and principles, chief of which had been professional freedom in adequate treatment centres, under strict confidence'.

As noted in Chapter 8, the case of *C v C* [1946] had mirrored many of the issues of *Garner v Garner* [1920], with a doctor reluctant to provide confidential information about VD diagnosis and treatment in preparation of a divorce case, despite the patients' consent to disclosure. However, in contrast to *Garner*, *C v C* was not a precursor to a prolonged wrangle over the confidentiality of VD treatment or the need for medical privilege. There was some controversy the following year, when the 1916 VD regulations, revoked by the 1946 NHS Act, were not immediately replaced. The Minister for Health, Aneurin Bevan, was asked why 'the statutory protection of secrecy had been withdrawn from persons attending VD clinics under the new National Health Services Act' (*BMJ* 24 July 1948, 230). Bevan replied that while the old regulations had been revoked as a result of responsibility being transferred to regional hospital boards, VD treatment would continue to be 'as confidential as it always had been'.

This reassurance was not sufficient for some. Further concerns were expressed that while the new scheme included many of the original guiding principles for VD treatment, for example that treatment would be voluntary and free of charge, 'the important and necessary requirement of confidence on which all British VD treatment has been built, and on which all public propaganda is based, is deliberately left out' (*BMJ* 7 August 1948, 314). The writer asserted that such confidentiality had been a feature of VD treatment 'by custom and by statute' for the previous 30 years. This is striking as evidence of the fact that many were still labouring under the false belief that VD treatment was protected by a statutory obligation of confidentiality. As detailed in Chapter 4, the 1916 regulations had not been directly incorporated into statute law, a point repeatedly emphasised in the courtroom showdowns and policy debates of the interwar years.

Exercising his powers under section 12 of the NHS Act, Bevan subsequently addressed these concerns by creating a Statutory Instrument providing a new set of VD regulations in 1948. This stated:

> Every Regional Hospital Board and every Board of Governors of a teaching hospital shall take all necessary steps to secure that any information obtained by

> officers of the Board with respect to persons examined or treated for venereal disease in a hospital for the administration of which the Board is responsible shall be treated as confidential.

While conveying a clear sense of the importance of confidentiality to VD treatment the new regulations were unlikely to exempt such information from disclosure in all circumstances, including legal proceedings. However, in an echo of discussions in the 1920s, it was suggested that, until the new regulations had been subjected to a judicial decision, the point was 'not beyond doubt' (Speller 1971, 335).

In 1967, W.K. Bernfeld published an award winning article examining the issue of professional secrecy with special regard to VD.[7] It highlighted that doctors increasingly faced dual loyalty pressures in which they had to weigh the confidence of the patient against the interests of the community. Statute law relating to registration of births and deaths, public health or notification of infectious diseases, presented challenges and expert opinion often differed on the best course of action to take. Bernfeld's article perpetuated the myth that the 1916 VD regulations had incorporated professional secrecy into statute law. He also cited a number of precedents from both the UK and foreign jurisdictions, including the *Duchess of Kingston* [1776], *Garner v Garner* [1920] and *C v C* [1946]. Noting that the common law compelled doctors to disclose in court, Bernfeld also drew attention to the recent joint medico-legal report by the BMA, the General Council of the Bar and the Law Society, which suggested the absence of medical privilege could tend to defeat the ends of justice, and could be a barrier to frank disclosure by patients (BMA 1965).

While the primary aim of his article was to detail the position on confidentiality in relation to VD, his analysis of foreign cases suggested that a qualified privilege appeared feasible. However, the article's conclusion drew attention to the fact that: 'the problems of medical secrecy are complicated, and there is no unanimity about them. They have received scant attention in textbooks, and ignorance of them is not confined to medical men.' Quoting the biblical book of Ecclesiastes, Bernfeld pointed to the fundamental importance of each doctor knowing the correct time to speak or remain silent.

Despite intense debate, even confrontation on the issue in the past, Bernfeld's BMA-endorsed article was evidence that a great deal of ignorance and uncertainty remained. His belief that the 1916 VD regulations had incorporated confidentiality into statute law, combined with his final emphasis on each doctor's intuition being the key to resolving disclosure dilemmas, suggests that the courtroom battles and high-level discussions of the interwar years had not translated into meaningful lessons for the next generation of doctors. Bernfeld continued to publish on the issue via letters to medical journals (*BMJ* 17 April 1971, 170; *BMJ* 10 July 1971, 109; *BMJ* 21 July 1973, 174) and in an article in *The Cambrian Law Review*

7 An earlier version of the article had been awarded second place in the C.H. Milburn Prize by the BMA (*BMJ* supplement 6 May 1967, 63).

(Bernfeld 1972) that added further detail and examples to his 1967 piece, including a clarification that the confidentiality of information relating to VD had only been incorporated into a Statutory Instrument in 1948.

In 1968, new VD regulations were issued. The only change from the 1948 version was the extension of the final sentence by the addition of the words: 'except for the purpose of communicating to a medical practitioner, or to a person employed under the direction of a medical practitioner in connection with the treatment of persons suffering from such a disease or the prevention of the spread thereof, and for the purpose of such treatment or prevention.' (Speller 1971, 615) This addendum stemmed from the fact that many of the contact tracers used by clinicians to check the spread of infection were local authority employees. The 1948 regulations only applied to NHS staff, and some physicians were concerned that passing information to contact tracers could be viewed as a breach of the regulations. Confidentiality continued to be stressed in the 1974 National Health Service (Venereal Disease) Regulations, which, following reorganisation of the NHS structure, transferred the responsibility for the security of VD patients' information to health authorities. While still using the term venereal diseases in the title, the terms referred to 'sexually transmitted diseases'.

> Every Regional Health Authority and every Area Health Authority shall take all necessary steps to secure that any information capable of identifying an individual obtained by officers of the Authority with respect to persons examined or treated for any sexually transmitted disease shall not be disclosed except –
>
> (a) For the purpose of communicating that information to a medical practitioner or to a person employed under the direction of a medical practitioner in connection with the treatment of persons suffering from such a disease or the prevention of the spread thereof, and
>
> (b) For the purpose of such treatment or prevention.
>
> (1974 Statutory Instrument 29)

In short, although the terminology changed from VD to Sexually Transmitted Disease (STD) or Infection (STI), the extended category continued to be given special consideration in debates over confidentiality. The 1974 regulations, combined with NHS and Primary Care Trust directions on STDs from 2000, underpin current BMA guidance which states 'some health information is so sensitive that it is subject to additional legal restrictions on disclosure to other health professionals, for example, information capable of identifying an individual examined or treated for any sexually transmitted infection' (BMA 2012, 188). As a result, only health professionals directly involved in the patient's treatment for a sexually transmitted disease should have access to patient-identifiable information.

Hunter v Mann

VD was not alone as a long-standing issue that continued to attract special interest in relation to medical confidentiality in the latter half of the twentieth century. A doctor's obligation to report patients connected to a crime was also an ongoing topic of debate. As noted in Chapter 3, confusion over doctors' obligations to notify cases of criminal abortion had triggered a medico-legal consultation at the RCP in 1896. For a time at least, this appeared to have clarified the doctor's duty to medically treat, but in no other way assist, a patient suspected of being involved in a crime. The legal opinions had indicated that there was no absolute obligation on the doctor to notify the police. However, by 1914, judicial opinion was firmly against such discretion and medical and legal views polarised into confrontation. Subsequent cases suggested that the medical profession continued to exercise discretion, balancing notification of patients connected to crimes against the professional duty of confidentiality and the need to minimise barriers to individuals seeking appropriate medical attention.

In *Hunter v Mann* ([1974] 1 Q.B. 767) a doctor was charged and convicted of failure to provide information that would lead to the identification of drivers alleged to have committed offences under Section 168 of the Road Traffic Act 1972. Having treated two individuals who had been involved in a road accident, the doctor advised them to contact the police. They did not, but the doctor was subsequently approached by the police seeking information. The doctor refused, insisting that he could not disclose patient information without consent. Two factors are particularly noteworthy about the case. Firstly, though his appeal to the Divisional Court was unsuccessful, the doctor sustained his refusal to disclose the names of the patients and accepted the monetary fine imposed by the court. Not quite the martyrdom of imprisonment, but nonetheless an indication that some doctors were willing to stand by their conviction that confidentiality was a principle worth defending in practice. Secondly, both Boreham J. and Lord Widgery C.J. explicitly noted that the court's demand for disclosure was consistent with the rules set out by the BMA (*Hunter v Mann* [1974] 1 QB 774–775).

The point is highly significant, as the BMA had always been a staunch defender of the boundaries of medical confidentiality against perceived legal encroachment and, as noted earlier, had recently co-authored a report that renewed calls for recognition of medical privilege. A second report from the same joint committee representing the legal and medical professions in 1981 did not repeat the explicit assertion that the absence of medical privilege might tend to defeat the ends of justice. However, it did quote relevant paragraphs from the BMA Handbook of Medical Ethics, including:

> When asked by a Court to disclose information without the patient's consent, the doctor should refuse on the grounds of professional confidence and say why he feels that disclosure should not be enforced. The Court would be expected to take the doctor's statement into consideration, but if in spite of this he is ordered

> to answer the questions, the decision whether to comply or not must be for his own conscience. A decision to refuse, while illegal, is not necessarily unethical. (BMA 1981a, 14; see also BMA 1981b, 13–14 and BMA 1988, 14)

This advice was almost identical to that issued by both the Ministry of Health and the BMA in the early interwar years, even down to the veiled suggestion that going to prison might be the right thing to do from a moral, if not a legal, perspective – the spectral remnant of hopes for a medical martyr.

BMA Handbook, Critiques and Crossroads

On the face of it, the advice which the BMA Handbook offered on the issue of privilege in the late 1970s seemed largely, somewhat stubbornly, unchanged by the events of the interwar years and beyond. While the attempt 'to move a little from the safe waters of prescriptive ethics to the storms of contemporary medical dilemmas' was generally welcomed, a review in the *Journal of Medical Ethics* (1979, 5, 103–4) felt that the Handbook was 'neither a fully developed discussion of the highly complex issues now arising in medical ethics, nor is it (as its title might suggest) a simple compendium of guidance to practitioners on matters about which there is no disagreement within the profession'.

As detailed earlier,[8] the BMA had been proactive in defending against legal encroachment into the confidentiality of the doctor–patient relationship during the early decades of the twentieth century, but this had changed by the 1980s. The BMA Handbook of Medical Ethics identified three types of professional relationship between doctors and members of the public: the traditional therapeutic patient–doctor relationship; medical examinations where a doctor acted on behalf of a third party (for instance, occupational or insurance assessment); and instances where the medical examination was for research purposes. The traditional therapeutic relationship was still the most common form of medical work and confidentiality continued to be stressed as essential to the trust that lay at the core of the therapeutic relationship. However, in general 'the nature of professional confidence varies according to the form of consultation or examination' (BMA 1981b, 12).

The handbook listed five exceptions to the general rule of confidentiality: (1) where the patient consented to disclosure; (2) where, for medical reasons, it was undesirable to seek patient consent; (3) where the doctor had an overriding duty to society; (4) where identifiable information was required for medical research approved by an appropriate authority; and (5) where the information was sought as part of due legal process. As already noted, the importance of gaining patient consent to disclosure had been recognised for a long time, and cases such as *Garner* [1920] and *C v C* [1946] had clarified that such consent was sufficient

8 See Chapters 3 and 5.

to override the obligation of confidentiality even in cases of VD. Contemporary critiques noted that the other exceptions were sufficiently broad as to render 'the principle of confidentiality almost meaningless' (Thompson 1979, 58; McLean and Maher 1983, 174). Such analyses merit closer examination, as they highlight some of the conflicts, confusion and tensions at the core of debates over medical confidentiality at the time. In essence, they postulated that, while there was undoubtedly a functional role for confidentiality in promoting the communication necessary for efficient medical practice, it increasingly appeared to have little more than rhetorical value as a moral principle.

> What, one might ask, remains of a patient's right to privacy if a doctor's discretion is so large? If it were not in the doctor's own interest to maintain relationships of confidentiality, one wonders if the reaffirmation of the patient's right to privacy would amount to more than pious rhetoric. (Thompson 1979, 58)

Thompson queried why, if confidentiality was as strong a principle as was asserted by the BMA, more doctors did not go to prison rather than divulge professional secrets; and whether the privilege given to lawyers to withhold confidential information should be extended to doctors. McLean and Maher also noted that doctors had no privilege to refuse to disclose confidential patient information in court, and that statute law demanded disclosures by obliging doctors to notify certain diseases or provide information to the police. They concluded that recognition of such broad exceptions to the general rule of confidentiality undermined its validity as a meaningful moral principle.

Thompson's questions about the absence of medical privilege or medical martyrs, and McLean and Maher's emphasis on the implications of this for the principle of medical confidentiality, highlight the importance of historical analysis. As detailed in previous chapters, while emphasis was often placed on the fact that judges would balance the pros and cons of demanding disclosure of confidential medical information, the records suggest that this was little more than rhetoric intended to ease medical discontent at being forced to breach professional secrecy. Historical analysis highlights the overwhelming evidence that, with few exceptions, medical confidentiality was subjugated to legal interest in disclosure, even when highly sensitive information, such as treatment for VD in *Needham v Needham* [1921] or psychiatric evidence in *Nuttall v Nuttall and Twyman* [1964], was sought in civil divorce actions. While both the Ministry of Health and the BMA had mounted a defence of medical confidentiality in the early 1920s, no medical witness had been willing to demonstrate the force and extent of professional faith in the principle by putting the confrontational rhetoric into practice and going to prison as a medical martyr.

McLean and Maher argued that it was possible to adopt two different perspectives on the moral role of confidentiality in the patient–doctor relationship. The 'patient perspective' stemmed from the patient's right to privacy. The 'doctor's perspective' placed emphasis on the professional autonomy of the doctor. Both perspectives were reflected in debates over the boundaries of confidentiality, though in the absence of a right to privacy – not explicitly recognised until the Human Rights Act 1998, though partially encapsulated in a collage of other legal remedies prior to that – it was the doctor's perspective that tended to dominate. Again, this is interesting to consider further.

During attempts to gain some form of medical privilege, it was often pointed out that legal privilege was the client's, not the lawyer's, and any medical equivalent would be the patient's, not the doctor's, privilege. Naturally, this had prejudiced the argument against the recognition of medical privilege. Firstly, while citizens had a recognised right to access confidential legal advice, in the absence of an established right to privacy the case had to be made that a patient's confidences merited protection to the point that information was excluded from court. As noted below, patients typically sought medical advice in order to obtain a diagnosis. Therefore, it might be argued that, in the absence of medical privilege, they were implicitly consenting to subsequent use of such medical information in court. However, a specialist text on confidentiality prepared for the Medical Protection Society (Palmer 1988) indicated that 'despite a widely held belief to the contrary, confidential medical information is not privileged from disclosure'. This suggests that, despite the numerous debates of previous decades, there remained a widespread misunderstanding that medical privilege existed. It is therefore likely that patients were unaware that their information could be disclosed in court. Even if they were aware, they faced a dilemma if they suspected they had a disease, such as VD or mental health problems, which might be used against them in legal proceedings. They could neither get confirmation of the diagnosis and treatment, nor reassurance that the problem was something else, without taking the risk of producing self-incriminating medical evidence. As *The Lancet* had put it, 'anything you say will be taken down and used in evidence against you' (23 July 1927, 178). Absent expert knowledge, patients were forced to make an uninformed choice to expose themselves to possible legal repercussions or, fearful of this, place the health and welfare of themselves and others at continued risk.

Secondly, the analogy often drawn between professional relationships involving doctors, lawyers and clerics was imperfect. Certainly, in each case the relationship involved laypersons seeking guidance and expert opinion on matters which were acknowledged as requiring a basis of confidentiality to encourage frank disclosure and discussion. However, to a greater degree than in the other professional relationships, a doctor received information through more than spoken and written communication with the patient. At the time of the Duchess of Kingston's trial in the eighteenth century, a patient's description of their case history was the dominant factor in the diagnostic encounter. However, over the course of the nineteenth and twentieth centuries, the doctor's knowledge of the medical status of a patient was increasingly obtained through expert observation, physical examination and scientific clinical and laboratory tests (Reiser 1978; Le Fanu 2000). This shift from 'biographical' to 'techno-scientific' medicine (Pickstone 2000) tipped the scales of power in the medical relationship. The authority of lay clients in a private medical market diminished as diagnostic techniques based on modern scientific medical knowledge became standardised and medicine operated within a context of centralised public funding. Doctors gradually came to assume the dominant role in the medical relationship and, as a result of their knowledge, training and expertise, they often knew more about patients' health than patients themselves were aware. This shifting balance of authority and power in the medical relationship was no doubt a factor in some of the confusion over medical privilege. The insistence that medical privilege would be the right of patients, not doctors, was based on the model of legal privilege. However, in contrast to lawyers with their clients, in an era of paternalistic medicine, doctors often knew more than their patients about the patient's health.

Demanding such information under common or statute law therefore undermined both the privacy of the patient and the professional autonomy of the doctor. In the case of the controversy over the confidentiality of VD treatment, it appeared to prioritise the efficiency of the civil divorce courts over the combined importance of the privacy of patients; professional medical autonomy; the findings of a Royal Commission Report; the authority of public health policy and regulations endorsed by government; and the potential negative repercussions on the health and welfare of large numbers of the population.

However, legal privilege was not justified on the balance of principles but on the practical needs of an effective system of justice. The law prioritised the disclosure of confidential medical information whenever it would assist the legal process. As McLean and Maher argue, 'where the law does confer the privilege its true basis is not confidentiality as such but rather the value placed by the law on litigation' (1983, 181). This viewpoint corresponds to, and is considerably bolstered by, the analysis in earlier chapters. However, as *D v NSPCC* illustrated, the public interest in protecting confidential relationships carried far greater weight in judicial consideration of demands for disclosure in the years following *Conway v Rimmer* [1968]. A claim to medical privilege on grounds equivalent to the position of VD doctors in the early interwar years, argued along lines similar to the NSPCC defence in 1978, would have had a greater chance of success than all previous attempts. Yet, as highlighted in *Hunter v Mann* [1974] and in medico-legal texts at the time, the breadth of acknowledged exceptions to the principle in the BMA Handbook counted against this possibility. If the principle of medical confidentiality was perceived as increasingly hollow, it would contribute little weight when the court came to balance competing public interests.

Of course, in contrast to an organisation like the NSPCC, medicine fulfilled an increasingly broad variety of roles, connected to various public and private policies and agendas. The debate over medical confidentiality was not simply a balancing of competing principles, nor solely a prioritising of practical considerations. Recognising that modern healthcare in the UK involved changing patterns of inter-professional and para-professional relationships, which impacted on traditional understandings of confidentiality, Thompson suggested that the roots of the issue went far deeper.

> Whether we go along with this and accept the fact that in a Welfare State with a National Health Service there is an inevitable need for the dilution of confidentiality, in the interests of efficient patient care, systematic medical research, effective public health programmes and more rational health service planning; or whether we opt for a system which reinforces patient's rights and physician autonomy, say by giving patients their medical records, or reinforcing medical privilege in relation to confidential information, involves not just the moral issue of patients' rights versus public interest, but, more fundamentally, choices about what kind of society we wish to live in. It may well be too, that what is at issue in the present debate about confidentiality concerns the very nature of medicine as a profession: Is medicine to remain a consulting profession based on confidentiality, patient trust and medical autonomy and responsibility?; or is the doctor to become a paid functionary in an impersonal institution where industrial action is compatible with offering medical services to the public? (Thompson 1979, 61–2)

In effect, Thompson argued that the debate over the boundaries of medical confidentiality stood at a crossroads. The tendency to share patient information for a growing variety of uses and purposes could be accepted, or the importance of patient privacy might be reasserted – potentially revisiting the debate over medical privilege. However, the question was not just about patient rights, but about what role medicine was to play in society.

Over the course of two centuries, medicine had developed a new scientific knowledge base, advanced technological tools to assist diagnosis and a more effective arsenal of surgical and pharmaceutical therapies than ever before. Medicine's utility to the state certainly led to growing medical influence on public policy and, over time, produced new roles and greater job security for doctors. However, at the same time, information was 'becoming a mass product' (Vuori 1977, 176). The rise in medical authority was accompanied by increased interest in, and demands for, the information obtained in medical encounters. The new status of medicine as a significant force in society was mirrored by a corresponding growth in recognised exceptions to medical confidentiality – a moral principle traditionally regarded as a cornerstone of medical practice, but described as little more than increasingly hollow rhetoric by critiques of the 1980s. In the face of such significant changes, medicine was at the centre of a debate not just about aspects of law, or administration, or technological innovation, but about fundamental values.

> The issue of privacy is one of a conflict of values: the value of a greater understanding of society and of more intelligent methods of formulating policy and the value of allowing an individual to keep information about himself and his life private and unknown to others. (Vuori 1977, 174)

Confidentiality and Privacy

If, by the early 1980s, the debate over the boundaries of medical confidentiality stood at a crossroads, it has travelled two roads since, reflecting the binary nature of modern medicine as both science and art. The benefits of greater information sharing and electronic data storage have been embraced in order to facilitate administration, service efficiency, public health and the research that forms the modern scientific basis of medicine. This has directly entailed, and been influenced by, the development of new legislation focused on privacy, including the Data Protection Act 1998[9] and the Human Rights Act 1998. Legislative developments in this area reflect recent concerns about individuals' right to privacy; their right to know what personal data is kept about them, the uses to which it is put, and their right to view it (BMA 2001). The recommendations and principles within the Caldicott Committee Report (1997), and the subsequent implementation of Caldicott Guardians, also recognised the need for specific, named individuals to have responsibility for safeguarding patient-identifiable information within institutions where records might be used and shared across individuals, teams and departments.

In terms of research, threats to privacy have been reduced by using anonymous information wherever possible. Where identifiable information is necessary, specific patient consent is usually required in addition to ethical approval from an appropriate expert body, such as the Privacy Advisory Committee in Scotland.[10] In addition to the statutory recognition of individuals' right to privacy under Article 8 of the Human Rights Act, the rise of bioethics in response to concerns about unethical medical practice and research has placed renewed emphasis on the importance of patient autonomy. As highlighted by contemporary critiques of paternalistic, authoritarian medical practice and research (Kennedy 1981, Illich 1975), scientific medicine is a powerful force in modern society. Recognition that at times this posed a threat to, and had negative implications for, patients and research subjects was an important factor in the rise of bioethics with its emphasis on patient consent and autonomy (Boyd 2009; Beauchamp and Childress 2001). While legislation and ethical regulation have developed in response to concerns about personal privacy, research points to ongoing issues, particularly when interagency cooperation and data sharing are involved (6 et. al. 2010; 2007; 2005a; 2005b).

While medicine undoubtedly developed modern credentials as an applied science, it has also sought to maintain human values at its core. As Thompson put it, 'science is concerned with abstract and impersonal relationships of facts and propositions. Medicine, insofar as it is a human science is concerned with

9 Although it should be noted that much of the momentum for Data Protection in the 1980s came from the implications, for businesses, of international concerns about the lack of legislation in Britain (Raab and Mason 2005; Price 1984).

10 http://www.nhsnss.org/pages/corporate/privacy_advisory_committee.php.

the degrees of truthfulness possible in different kinds of personal relationships' (Thompson 1979, 63). While current professional guidance points practitioners to the relevant legislation on privacy and rights, and highlights recognised exceptions to medical confidentiality – patient consent, information required by law, and 'where it is justified in the public interest' – it also continues to stress the continued importance of confidentiality to the effective working of the basic unit of medical practice, and its role in building trust in the professional–patient relationship (GMC 2009; BMA 2012; O'Brien and Chantler 2003).

Epilogue

This book sets out a new, more detailed, history of medical confidentiality in Britain. The analysis has sought to lay the foundations of a better understanding of how the boundaries of confidentiality have evolved, examining the theoretical, practical and coincidental factors, that have shaped this evolution. The findings add detail and nuance to previous understandings. For example, detailed examination of the interwar years goes some way to answering Thompson's question about why more doctors did not go to prison rather than breach confidentiality (Thompson 1979). In the case of John Elliot, the Ministry of Health's medical martyr, he was afraid of its impact on his family and medical practice at a time when the BMA was undecided over whether its resources could be used to support such martyrs.

In some cases the analysis raises questions about the fundamental basis, and continued validity, of established interpretations. For example, the Duchess of Kingston's case underpins the common law denial of medical privilege and has been cited as authoritative precedent for the past two-and-a-half centuries. Yet, as Chapter 2 concludes, it is far from a wholly secure foundation. A more accurate understanding of the basis of the law's denial of medical privilege, and of the numerous attempts to change it since, is a significant addition to the established works that are often cited in textbooks on medical law and ethics (for cxample McHale 1993; Gurry 1984).

The lack of attention to detail at times skewed the analysis within influential contributions at key points of debate. For example, Davies' selective editing of Lord Chancellor Brougham's statement in *Greenough v Gaskell* [1833], quoted unchanged by Birkenhead in his published essay (Smith 1922), sought to manufacture a greater continuity of judicial opinion against medical privilege than actually existed. But such misinterpretations of precedent are not confined to those that have been altered to suit a desired argument. *Garner v Garner* [1920] has often been cited as evidence that the courts have authority to override medical confidentiality even when the doctor's obligation is backed by statute (Bernfeld 1967; Catterall 1980; McHale, 1993; Michalowski 2003). The absence of detailed historical analysis has allowed such myths to perpetuate into the twenty-first century. For example, the influential textbook: *Mason and McCall Smith's Law and Medical Ethics* continues to cite *Garner* [1920] as evidence that a court can override a doctor's plea of privilege 'even when there is a statutory obligation of secrecy' (Mason and Laurie 2006 and 2011). As detailed in Chapter 4, the 1916 VD regulations were not incorporated into statute law and the patient in *Garner* had given full consent to the disclosure, which, as acknowledged by the Ministry of Health at the time, was sufficient to override the restriction imposed by the regulations.

As noted at many points in the preceding chapters, there is a spectrum of medical relationships and a broad variety of issues in which the boundaries of confidentiality are discussed. Consequently, there has not been space to consider a number of pertinent issues, for example: the debates over confidentiality in relation to HIV/AIDS ; genetics/genomics; psychiatry; use of patient information after death; doctors' obligations to disclose information to parents or guardians when treating their children. Together with a detailed analysis of the evolution, implementation and interpretation of policy, guidance and legislation on the medical use of personal data for medical research and other purposes, these topics form the basis of ongoing research. Further attention must also be given to the international picture, both in terms of comparing the evolution of confidentiality in other jurisdictions and in assessing the influence of international law and codes of ethics on developments in Britain. Innovations in transportation and information technology have facilitated internationally mobile patients and healthcare professionals as well as the globalisation of health research and information/ data sharing. As a consequence, law, regulation, guidance and policy on medical confidentiality and privacy are increasingly considered, if not formulated, in international, cross-jurisdictional terms.

Undoubtedly the socio-legal, political and cultural contexts have influenced how the boundaries of medical confidentiality have been defined and redefined over the past two-and-a-half centuries. The debate over confidentiality has developed to reflect the changing balance between the art and science of medicine and the roles it plays in society. As medicine continues to evolve, both defining and being defined by its socio-legal context, so debates over the boundaries of confidentiality continue to arise. More detailed historical analysis has the capacity not only to help elaborate the developments of the past, but also to influence and shape those of the future.

Bibliography

6, P., Raab, C., Bellamy, C. 2005a. Joined-Up Government and Privacy in the United Kingdom: Managing Tensions Between Data Protection and Social Policy. Part I. *Public Administration*, 83 (1), 111–33.

6, P., Raab, C., Bellamy, C. 2005b. Joined-Up Government and Privacy in the United Kingdom: Managing Tensions Between Data Protection and Social Policy. Part II. *Public Administration*, 83 (2), 393–415.

6, P., Bellamy, C., Raab, C., Warren, A., Heeney, C. 2007. Institutional Shaping of Interagency Working: Managing Tensions Between Collaborative Working and Client Confidentialty. *Journal of Public Administration Research and Theory*, 17, 405–34.

6, P., Bellamy, C., Raab, C. 2010. Information-Sharing Dilemmas in Public Services: Using Frameworks from Risk Management. *Policy & Politics*, 38(3), 465–81.

Amos, A. 1829. *An Introductory Lecture Upon the Study of English Law*. London: Thomas Davison.

Amundsen, D.A. 2001. 'History' in J. Sugarman and D.P. Sulmasy (eds.) *Methods in Medical Ethics*. Washington: Georgetown University Press, 126–45.

The Annual Register, or a view of the history, politics, and literature for the year 1776. 1788. London.

Appleyard, J., Maden, J.G. 1979. Multidisciplinary Teams. *British Medical Journal*, 17 November 1979, 1,305–7.

Baker, R. 1995. Introduction. *The Codification of Medical Morality*. Volume 2, edited by R. Baker. Dordrecht: Kluwer.

Baker, R. 2009. The Discourses of Practitioners in Nineteenth and Twentieth Century Britain and the United States. *The Cambridge World History of Medical Ethics*, edited by L. McCullough and R. Baker. Cambridge: Cambridge University Press, 446–64.

Baker, R., McCullough, L. 2009. What is the History of Medical Ethics? *The Cambridge World History of Medical Ethics*, edited by L. McCullough and R. Baker. Cambridge: Cambridge University Press, 3–15.

Bartrip, P.W.J. 1990. *Mirror of Medicine. A History of the British Medical Journal*. Oxford: Oxford University Press and the British Medical Journal.

Bartrip, P.W.J. 1996. *Themselves Writ Large. The British Medical Association 1832–1966*. London: BMJ Publishing Group.

Bathurst, C. 1776. *The trial of Elizabeth Duchess Dowager of Kingston for bigamy*. London.

Beauchamp, T.L., Childress, J.F. 2001. *Principles of Biomedical Ethics*. 5th edition. Oxford: Oxford University Press.

Bernfeld, W.K. 1967. Medical Professional Secrecy with Special Reference to Venereal Diseases, *British Journal of Venereal Diseases*, (43), 53–9.

Bernfeld, W.K. 1972. Medical Secrecy. *The Cambrian Law Review*, 15, 11–26.

Best, W.M. 1849. *A Treatise on the Principles of Evidence and Practice as to Proofs in Courts of Common Law; with Elementary Rules for Conducting the Examination and Cross-Examination of Witnesses*. Philadelphia: T. and J.W. Johnson.

Birch, A.H. 1993. *The British System of Government* 9th edition. London: Routledge.

Birkenhead, Second Earl of 1959. *The Life of F.E. Smith. First Earl of Birkenhead.* London: Eyre & Spottiswoode.

Boyd, P. 2003. The Requirements of the Data Protection Act 1998 for the Processing of Medical Data. *Journal of Medical Ethics*, 29, 34–5.

British Medical Association 1926. *Handbook for Recently Qualified Medical Practitioners*. London: British Medical Association.

British Medical Association 1965. *Medical Evidence in Courts of Law. The Report of a Joint Committee of the General Council of the Bar of England and Wales, The Law Society and the British Medical Association*. London: British Medical Association.

British Medical Association 1981a. *Medical Evidence. The Report of a Joint Committee of the British Medical Association, The Senate of the Inns of the Court and the Bar and the Law Society*. London: British Medical Association.

British Medical Association 1981b. *The Handbook of Medical Ethics*. London: Medical Ethics.

British Medical Association 2001. *The Medical Profession and Human Rights. Handbook for a Changing Agenda*. London: Zed Books.

British Medical Association 2012. *Medical Ethics Today: The BMA's Handbook of Ethics and Law*. Third Edition. London: Blackwell Publishing.

British Medical Association Ethics Department. 2013. *Everyday Medical Ethics and Law*. London: BMJ Books and Wiley-Blackwell.

BMJ (4th and 18th April 1896).

BMJ (11 March 1899).

Brookes, B. 1988. *Abortion in England 1900–1967*. London: Croom Helm.

Brown, B.C. 1927. *Elizabeth Chudleigh, Duchess of Kingston*. London.

Burke, J.B. 1849. *Anecdotes of the Aristocracy*. London.

Burnett, J. 1811. *A Treatise on Various Branches of the Criminal Law of Scotland.* Edinburgh.

Burns, C. 1995. Reciprocity in the Development of Anglo-American Medical Ethics, 1765–1865, in *The Codification of Medical Morality*. Volume 2, edited by R.Baker. Dordrecht: Kluwer.

Caldicott Committee 1997. *Report on the Review of Patient-Identifiable Information*. London: Department of Health.

Carey, P. 2000. *Data Protection in the UK*. London: Blackstone Press Ltd.

Catterall, R.D. 1980. Confidentiality in the National Health Service and in the Service for Sexually Transmitted Diseases. *British Journal of Venereal Diseases*, 56(4), 263–6.

Clarke, L. 1990. *Confidentiality and the Law*. London: Lloyd's of London Press Ltd.

Clegg, H.A. 1957. Professional Ethics, in *Medical Ethics*, edited by M.Davidson. London: Lloyd-Luke Ltd., 31–46.

Cohen, J.M., Cohen, M.J. 1960. *The Penguin Dictionary of Quotations*. Harmondsworth: Penguin Books.

Cooter, R., Harrison, M. and Sturdy, S. 1998. *War, Medicine and Modernity*. Sutton: Stroud.

Crookshank, F.G. 1922. *Professional Secrecy*, London: Bailliere, Tindall & Cox.

Crookshank, F.G. 1926. 'Medico-Legal Problems in Relation to Venereal Disease', *British Journal of Venereal Diseases*, 2, 36–50.

Crowther, M.A. 1995. Forensic Medicine and Medical Ethics in Nineteenth-Century Britain, in *The Codification of Medical Morality*. Volume 2, edited by R. Baker. Dordrecht Kluwer, 173–90.

Crowther, M.A. 1998. Introduction. *Medicine and the Law: Proceedings of the 19th International Symposium on Comparative History of Medicine – East and West*. Tokyo.

Davidson, R. 2000. *Dangerous Liaisons. A Social History of Venereal Disease in Twentieth-Century Scotland,* Amsterdam: Rodopi.

Davidson, R. 2001. 'The Price of the Permissive Society' The Epidemiology and Control of VD and STDs in late-Twentieth-Century Scotland. *Sex, Sin and Suffering: Venereal Disease and European Society Since 1870* edited by R. Davidson and L. Hall. London: Routledge.

Davis, G., Elliot, R. 2011. Public Information, Private Lives: Dr James Craufurd Dunlop and the Collection of Vital Statistics in Scotland, 1904–1930, in *Medicine, Law and Public Policy in Scotland c.1850–1990,* edited by M. Freeman, E. Gordon and K. Maglen. Dundee: Dundee University Press, 105–24.

Dickson, W.G. 1855. *A Treatise on the Law of Evidence in Scotland.* Volume 2. Edinburgh.

Dix, D.K. and Todd, A.H. 1961. *Medical Evidence in Personal Injury Cases. The Medico-Legal Aspects of an Action for Damages Arising out of a Personal Injury*. London: H.K. Lewis & Co. Ltd.

Dworkin, G. 1979. Access to Medical Records. Discovery, Confidentiality and Privacy. *The Modern Law Review*, 42(1), 88–91.

Elwood, M. 1960. *The Bigamous Duchess. A Romantic Biography of Elizabeth Chudleigh, Duchess of Kingston*. New York: Bobbs-Merrill Co.

Evans, D. 1992. Tackling the Hideous Scourge: The Creation of Venereal Disease Treatment Centres in Early Twentieth-Century Britain, *Social History of Medicine*, 5(3), 413–33.

Evans, D. 2001. Sexually Transmitted Disease Policy in the English National Health Service, 1948–2000. Continuity and Social Change. *Sex, Sin and Suffering: Venereal Disease and European Society Since 1870* edited by R. Davidson and L. Hall. London: Routledge.

Farmer, L. 2003. Notable Trials and the Criminal Law in Scotland and England, 1750–1950, in *Droit et societé en France et en Grande-Bretagne (12–20 siècles). Fonctions, usages et représentations*, edited by P.H. Chassaigne and J.P. Genet. Paris.

Ferguson, A.H. 2006. The Lasting Legacy of a Bigamous Duchess: The Benchmark Precedent for Medical Confidentiality. *Social History of Medicine*, 19(1), 37–54.

Ferguson, A.H. 2009. Speaking Out About Staying Silent: An Historical Examination of Medico-Legal Debates Over the Boundaries of Medical Confidentiality, in *Lawyers' Medicine. The Legislature, The Courts and Medical Practice, 1760–2000*, edited by I. Goold and C. Kelly. Oxford: Hart Publishing, 99–124.

Ferguson, A.H. 2011. Exploring the Myth of a Scottish Privilege. A Comparison of the Early Development of the Law on Medical Confidentiality in Scotland and England, in *Medicine, Law and Public Policy in Scotland c.1850–1990*, edited by M. Freeman, E. Gordon and K. Maglen. Dundee: Dundee University Press, 125–40.

Ferguson, A.H. 2013. Medical Confidentiality in the Military, in *Military Medical Ethics for the 21st Century*, edited by M. Gross and D. Carrick. Farnham: Ashgate, 209–24.

Fissel, M.E. 1993. Innocent and Honourable Bribes: Medical Manners in Eighteenth Century Britain, in *The codification of medical morality*, edited by R. Baker, R. Porter and D. Porter. Dordrecht: Kluwer, 19–45.

Foote, S. 1778. *A trip to Calais; a comedy in three acts*. London.

Frevert, U. 1995. *Men of Honour. A Social and Cultural History of the Duel*. Cambridge.

General Medical Council 2009. *Confidentiality*. London. ISBN: 978–0–901458–38–4.

Gentleman's Magazine, The 1776. *The Gentleman's Magazine and Historical Chronicle*. Vol. 46.

Gentleman's Magazine, The 1809. *A Selection of Curious Articles from the Gentleman's Magazine. In Three Volumes.* Vol. 3. London: Longman, Hurst, Rees and Orme.

Gervat, C. 2003. *Elizabeth. The Scandalous life of the Duchess of Kingston*. London.

Glaister, J. 1886. Medico-legal risks encountered by medical practitioners in the practice of their profession, *Glasgow Medical Journal*, September.

Glaister, J. 1910. *A Textbook of Medical Jurisprudence and Toxicology*, 2nd edition. Edinburgh.

Glaister, J. 1938. *Glaister's Medical Jurisprudence and Toxicology*, 6th edition. Edinburgh: E and S Livingstone Ltd.

Gordon, I., Turner, R., Price, T.W. 1953. *Medical Jurisprudence*. Edinburgh: E and S Livingstone Ltd.

Gregory, J. 1772. *Lecture on the Duties and Qualifications of a Physician*. London.

Gurry, F. 1984. *Breach of Confidence*. Oxford: Clarendon.

Haakonssen, L. 1997. *Medicine and Morals in the Enlightenment: John Gregory, Thomas Percival and Benjamin Rush*. Amsterdam: Rodopi.

Hall, L.A. 2001. Venereal Diseases and Society in Britain, From the Contagious Diseases Acts to the National Service. *Sex, Sin and Suffering: Venereal Disease and European Society Since 1870* edited by R. Davidson and L. Hall. London: Routledge.

Halsbury, Earl of 1931. *Halsbury's Laws of England*, 2nd edition. London: William Clowes and Sons Ltd.

Hargrave, F. 1781. *A Complete Collection of State Trials*. Volume 11. London.

Harrison, L.W. 1947. 'The Control of Venereal Diseases Under the National Health Service', *British Journal of Venereal Diseases*, 23(4), 145–54.

Hibbert, C. 1998. *George III. A Personal History*. London.

Higgs, E. 2004. *The Information State in England*. Basingstoke: Palgrave Macmillan.

Hole, R. 1996. *Selected Writings of Hannah More*. London.

Howell, T.B. 1816. *A complete collection of State Trials and proceedings for high treason and other crimes and misdemeanours from the earliest period to 1783*. London: T.C. Hansard.

Hume, D. 1819. *Commentaries on the Law of Scotland, Respecting Crimes*. Volume 2. Edinburgh.

Huxley, A. 1994. *Brave New World*. London: Flamingo.

Illich, I. 1975. *Medical Nemesis: the Expropriation of Health*. London: Calder and Boyars.

Interdepartmental Committee on Insurance Medical Records. 1920. London: His Majesty's Stationery Office.

Jenkinson, J. 2002. *Scotland's Health 1919–1948*. Bern.

Jewson, N.D. 1974. Medical Knowledge and the Patronage System in 18th Century England. *Sociology*, 13.

Jones, G. 1986. *Social Hygiene in Twentieth Century Britain*. London: Croom Helm.

'Professional Confidences of Medical Men' in *Justice of the Peace* (21 April 1900, 245–6).

Kennedy, I. 1981. *The Unmasking of Medicine*. London: Allen and Unwin.

Kennedy, I. and Grubb, A. 1994. *Medical Law: text with materials*. London: Buttreworths., 639.

Kenny, D.J. 1982. Confidentiality: the Confusion Continues. *Journal of Medical Ethics*, 8, 9–11.

Kent, A. 2003. Consent and Confidentiality in Genetics: Whose Information is it Anyway? *Journal of Medical Ethics*, 29, 16–18.

Kiernan, V.G. 1988. *The Duel in European History. Honour and the Reign of the Aristocracy*. Oxford.

Kitchin, D.H. 1936. *Legal Problems in Medical Practice*. London: Edward Arnold and Co.

Kitchin, D.H. 1941. *Law for the Medical Practitioner*. London: Eyre and Spottiswoode.

Lachman, P.J. 2003. Consent and Confidentiality – Where are the Limits? An Introduction. *Journal of Medical Ethics*, 29, 2–3.

Law Reform Committee. 1967. *Sixteenth Report (Privilege in Civil Proceedings)*. London: HMSO. Cmnd 3472.

Lawrence, C. 1994. *Medicine in the Making of Modern Britain, 1700–1920*. London: Routledge.

Lee Osborn, J. 1915. *Lainston and Elizabeth Chudleigh*. Winchester.

Le Fanu, J. 2000. *The Rise and Fall of Modern Medicine*. London: Abacus.

Leslie, D. 1974. *The Incredible Duchess: the Life and Times of Elizabeth Chudleigh*. London.

Lesser, H., Pickup, Z. 1990. Law, Ethics and Confidentiality. *Journal of Law and Society*, 17(1), 17–28.

Leveson, L.J. 2012. *An Inquiry into the Culture, Practices and Ethics of the Press. Report. 4 Volumes*. London: HMSO.

Lyall, R. 1826. *The Medical Evidence Relative to the Duration of Human Pregnancy, As Given in the Gardner Peerage Cause, Before the Committee for Privileges of the House of Lords in 1825–6: With introductory remarks and notes*. London: Burgess and Hill.

McCullough, L.B. 1998. *John Gregory and the Invention of Professional Medical Ethics and the Profession of Medicine*. Dordrecht: Kluwer.

McCullough, L.B. 2009. 'The Discourses of Practitioners in Eighteenth Century Britain.' *The Cambridge World History of Medical Ethics*, edited by L. McCullough and R. Baker. Cambridge: Cambridge University Press, 403–13.

McHale, J.V. 1993. *Medical Confidentiality and Legal Privilege*. London: Routledge.

McHale, J.V., Fox, M. And Murphy, J. 1997. *Health Care Law: Text, Cases and Materials*. London: Sweet & Maxwell.

McLaren, A. 1993. 'Privileged Communications: Medical Confidentiality in Late Victorian Britain.' *Medical History* 37 (2), 129–47.

McLean, S.A.M., Maher, G. 1983. *Medicine, Morals and the Law*. Aldershot: Gower.

Maehle, A-H. 2003. Protecting Patient Privacy or Serving Public Interests? Challenges to Medical Confidentiality in Imperial Germany. *Social History of Medicine*, 16, 383–401.

Maehle, A-H. and Pranghofer, S. 2010. 'Medical confidentiality in the late nineteenth and early twentieth centuries: an Anglo-German comparison', *Medizinhistorisches Journal*, 45, 189–221.

Manchester, A.H. 1980. *A Modern Legal History of England and Wales 1750–1950*. London.

Martin, E.A. 2002. *A Dictionary of Law*. Oxford.

Mason, J.K., Laurie, G.T. 2006. *Mason and McCall Smith's Law and Medical Ethics*, 7th edition. Oxford: Oxford University Press.

Mason, J.K., Laurie, G.T. 2011. *Mason and McCall Smith's Law and Medical Ethics*, 8th edition. Oxford: Oxford University Press.

Melville, L. 1927 (and 1996 reprint). *Notable British Trial Series*. Edinburgh and London: William Hodge & Co.

Mendelson, D. 2012. The Duchess of Kingston's Case, the Ruling of Lord Mansfield and the Duty of Medical Confidentiality in Court. *International Journal of Law and Psychiatry*, 35, 480–89.

Michalowski, S. 2003. *Medical Confidentiality and Crime*. Aldershot: Ashgate.

Mooney, G. 1999. Public health versus private practice: the contested development of compulsory infectious disease notification in late nineteenth century Britain, *Bulletin of the History of Medicine*, 73, 241.

Morgan, D. 2001. *Issues in Medical Law and Ethics*. London: Cavendish Publishing.

Morgan, K., Morgan J. 1980. *Portrait of a Progressive. The Political Career of Christopher, Viscount Addison*. Oxford University Press.

Morrice, A.A.G. 1999. *Honour and Interests*: *Medical Ethics in Britain and the Work of the British Medical Association's Central Ethical Committee, 1902–1939*, University of London, M.D. Thesis.

Morrice, A.A.G. 2002a. Should the doctor tell?: medical secrecy in early twentieth-century Britain, in *Medicine, Health and the Public Sphere in Britain, 1600–2000*, edited by S. Sturdy. London, 60–82.

Morrice, A.A.G. 2002b. Honour and Interests: Medical Ethics and the British Medical Association, in *Historical and Philosophical Perspectives on Biomedical Ethics*, edited by A-H Maehle and J. Geyer-Kordesch. Aldershot, 11–35.

Newman, G. 1920. *Annual Report of the Chief Medical Officer 1919–1920*. London: His Majesty's Stationery Office.

Nokes, G.D. 1950. Professional Privilege. *The Law Quarterly Review*, vol. 66, 88–103, London: Stevens and Sons Ltd.

O'Brien, J., Chantler, C. 2003. Confidentiality and the Duties of Care. *Journal of Medical Ethics*, 29, 36–40.

Oldham, J. 1992. *The Mansfield Manuscripts and the Growth of English Law in the Eighteenth Century*. Vol.1. London.

Orwell, G. 1989. *Nineteen Eighty-Four*. London: Penguin.

Palmer, R.N. 1988. *Consent, Confidentiality and Disclosure of Medical Records*. London: The Medical Protection Society.

Paris, J.A., Fonblanque, J.S.M. 1823. *Medical Jurisprudence*. London: W. Phillips.
Pearce, G.H. 1979. *The Medical Report and Medical Testimony*. London: George Allen & Unwin.
Pearce, P., Parsloe, P., Francis, H., Macara, A., Watson, D. 1988. *Personal Data Protection in Health and Social Services*. London: Croom Helm.
Pelham, C. 1845. *The Chronicles of Crime; or, the Newgate Calendar*. Volume 1. London.
Pellegrino, E.D. 2003. The Moral Foundations of the Patient–Physician Relationship: The Essence of Medical Ethics. *Military Medical Ethics* (The Borden Institute, 2003), 3–21. Accessed online: http://www.bordeninstitute.army.mil/published_volumes/ethicsVol1/ethicsVol1.html.
Percival, T. 1803. *Medical Ethics; or a Code of Institutes and Precepts, Adapted to the Professional Conduct of Physicians and Surgeons*. Manchester.
Phillips, R. 1988. *Putting Assunder. A History of Divorce in Western Society*. Cambridge: Cambridge University Press.
Phipson, S.L. 1921. *Manual of the Law of Evidence for the use of students*. 3rd edition. London: Sweet and Maxwell Ltd.
Phipson, S.L. 1942. *The Law of Evidence*. London: Sweet and Maxwell Ltd.
Pickstone, J.V. 2000. *Ways of Knowing. A New History of Science, Technology and Medicine*. Manchester: Manchester University Press.
Polson, C.J. 1955. *The Essentials of Forensic Medicine*. London: English Universities Press.
Porter, R. 1985a. William Hunter: a Surgeon and a Gentleman, in *William Hunter and the Eighteenth Century Medical World*, edited by W. F. Bynum and R. Porter. Cambridge.
Porter, R. 1985b. Lay Medical Knowledge in the Eighteenth Century: the Evidence of the Gentleman's Magazine. *Medical History*, 29, 138–68.
Porter, R. 1997. *The Greatest Benefit to Mankind*. London: Fontana Press.
Price, D. 1984. The Emergence of a UK Data Protection Law. *Yearbook of Law, Computers and Technology*, 1, 131–5.
Raab, C.D. and Mason, D. 2005. Researching the Origins of UK Data Protection. *Information, Communication and Society*. 8(2), 235–7.
Reiser, S.J. 1978. *Medicine and the Reign of Technology*. Cambridge: Cambridge University Press.
Rentoul, E., Smith, H. 1973. *Glaister's Medical Jurisprudence and Toxicology* 13th edition. Edinburgh: Churchill Livingstone.
Rowland, P. 1975. *Lloyd George*. London: Barrie & Jenkins.
Royal Commission on Venereal Diseases. 1916. *Final Report of the Commissioners* London: His Majesty's Stationery Office.
Ryan, M. 1831. *A Manual of Medical Jurisprudence, Compiled from the Best Medical and Legal Works*. London: Renshaw and Rush.
Saundby, R. 1907. *Medical Ethics: A Guide to Professional Conduct*, 2nd edition. London: Charles Griffin & Co.

Savage, G. 1990. The willful communication of a loathsome disease: marital conflict and venereal disease in Victorian England, *Victorian Studies*, 35.

Searle, G. 1976. *Eugenics and politics in Britain, 1900–1914*. Leyden: Noordhoff.

Simpson, K. 1962. *A Doctor's Guide to Court. A Handbook on Medical Evidence*. London: Butterworths.

Smith, F.E. 1922. Should a Doctor Tell? in *Points of View*. London, 33–76.

Smith, J.G. 1825. *An Analysis of Medical Evidence: Comprising Directions for Practitioners, in View of Becoming Witnesses in Courts of Justice and an Appendix of Professional Testimony*. London.

Smith, R.G. 1993. The Development of Ethical Guidance for Medical Practitioners by the General Medical Council, *Medical History*, 37, 56–67.

Speller, S.R. 1948. *The National Health Service Act, 1946 Annotated Together with Various Orders and Regulations Made Thereunder*. London: H.K. Lewis & Co.

Speller, S.R. 1971. *Law Relating to Hospitals and Kindred Institutions*. London: H.K. Lewis & Co.

Speller, S.R. 1973. *Law of Doctor and Patient*. London: H.K. Lewis & Co.

Stair Memorial Encyclopedia. Online edition.

Sturdy, S. 2002. Alternative publics: the development of government policy on personal health care, 1905–11. *Medicine, Health and the Public Sphere in Britain, 1600–2000*. London: Routledge, 241–59.

Sugarman, J. and Sulmasy, D.P. 2001. *Methods in Medical Ethics*. Washington: Georgetown University Press.

Sugarman, J. and Sulmasy, D.P. 2012. *Methods in Medical Ethics, Second Edition*. Washington: Georgetown University Press.

Tait, G. 1834. *A Treatise on the Law of Evidence in Scotland*. Edinburgh.

Tapper, C. 1968. Review of: Law Reform Committee: Sixteenth Report on Privilege in Civil Proceedings, in *The Modern Law Review*, 31:2 (March), 198–202.

Todd Thomson, A. 1831. *Lecture, Introductory to the Course of Medical Jurisprudence, Delivered in the University of London on Friday January 7th 1831*. London.

Thompson, I.E. 1979. The Nature of Confidentiality. *Journal of Medical Ethics*, 5, 57–64. *Journal of Medical Ethics* (1979, 5, 103–4).

Traill, T.S. 1840. *Outlines of a course of lectures on medical jurisprudence*. Edinburgh: A. and C. Black.

Vuori, H. 1977. Privacy, Confidentiality and Automated Health Information Systems. *Journal of Medical Ethics*, 3, 174–8.

Waddington, I. 1975. The Development of Medical Ethics – A Sociological Analysis, in *Medical History*, 19(1), 36–51.

Waddington, I. 1977. General Practitioners and Consultants in Early Nineteenth-Century England: The Sociology of an Intra-Professional Conflict, in *Health Care and Popular Medicine in Nineteenth Century England*, edited by J. Woodward and D. Richards. London: Croom Helm, 164–88.

Waddington, I. 1984. *The Medical Profession in the Industrial Revolution*. Dublin: Gill and Macmillan.

Waddington, I. 1990. The Movement Towards the Professionalisation of Medicine. *British Medical Journal*, 690.

Wellman, C. 1999. *The Proliferation of Rights*. Oxford: Westview Press.

Worboys, M. 2004. 'Unsexing Gonorrhoea: Bacteriologists, Gynaecologists, and Suffragists in Britain, 1860–1920', *Social History of Medicine*, 17, 41–60.

Wilkinson, A.B. 1986. *The Scottish Law of Evidence*. London & Edinburgh.

Wishart, L. 1998. NHS Records: Past, Present and Future. *Health Libraries Review*, 15, 279–88.

Wort, A.W.E. 1926. 'Medico-Legal Problems in Relation to Venereal Disease', *British Journal of Venereal Diseases*, 2, 51–8.

Zamiatan, E. 1960. 'We', in *An Anthology of Russian Literature in the Soviet Period from Gorki to Paternak*, edited by B.G. Guerney. New York: Random House.

Index